248 SMO
Smoley,
Inner

INNER CHRISTIANITY

A Guide to the Esoteric Tradition

Richard Smoley

PARK CITY LIBRARY
DISCARD
Park City, Utah 84060
Phone: (435) 615-5600

SHAMBHALA
Boston & London
2002

Shambhala Publications, Inc.
Horticultural Hall
300 Massachusetts Avenue
Boston, MA 02115
www.shambhala.com

© 2002 by Richard Smoley
All rights reserved. No part of this book may be reproduced in
any form or by any means, electronic or mechanical, including pho-
tocopying, recording, or by any information storage and retrieval
system, without permission in writing from the publisher.

9 8 7 6 5 4 3 2 1

First Edition
Printed in the United States of America

♾ This edition is printed on acid-free paper that meets the
American National Standards Institute z39.48 Standard.
Distributed in the United States by Random House, Inc.,
and in Canada by Random House of Canada Ltd

Grateful acknowledgment is made to the following:

Lindisfarne Books, for permission to quote excerpts from Daniel Andreev, *The Rose of the
World*, translated by Jordan Roberts. Translation copyright © 1990, 1997 Daniel Andreev
Charity Foundation. Praxis Institute Press, for permission to quote excerpts from *Gnosis:
Study and Commentaries on the Esoteric Tradition of Eastern Orthodoxy* by Boris Mouravieff,
translated by S. E. Wissa and Maneck d'Oncieu, edited by Robin Amis. Red Wheel/Weiser
Inc., for permission to quote excerpts from *St. John of the Cross: Alchemist of the Soul*, edited and
translated by Antonio T. de Nicolás, published by Samuel Weiser Inc., 1996; and from *Sefer
Yetzirah: The Book of Creation in Theory and Practice*, by Aryeh Kaplan, published by Samuel
Weiser Inc., 1990. Robert Powell, for permission to reprint excerpts from *Meditations on the
Tarot*, published by Amity House, 1985; reprinted by Jeremy P. Tarcher, 2002. Translation
copyright © 1985, 2002 by Robert A. Powell. Portions from *A Course in Miracles* copyright
1975, 1992, 1996 used by permission of the Foundation for *A Course in Miracles*, Inc., 41397
Buecking Drive, Temecula, CA 92590. All rights reserved. *A Course in Miracles* is a registered
trademark of the Foundation for *A Course in Miracles*. Image from Thomas Bromley, *Der Weg
zum Sabbath der Ruhe* (1778) reproduced courtesy of Bibliotheca Philosophica Hermetica,
Amsterdam. Image of Russian icon crucifix courtesy of St. Isaac of Syria Skete, Boscobel,
Wisconsin, www.skete.com.

Library of Congress Cataloging-in-Publication Data
Smoley, Richard, 1956–
Inner Christianity: a guide to the esoteric tradition / by Richard Smoley.
p. cm.
Includes bibligraphical references and index.
ISBN 1-57062-810-6 (pbk.)
1. Mysticism. 2. Theosophy. 1. Title.
BV5083 .S66 2002
248—DC21
2002004717

What you are looking for is what is looking.

—FRANCIS OF ASSISI

CONTENTS

ACKNOWLEDGMENTS

O F THE MANY PEOPLE to whom thanks are due for this book, the foremost by far are Katie Boyle, my agent, who was a great help and support to me in developing this project, and Joel Segel, my editor at Shambhala, whose investment of a tremendous amount of insight, dedication, and hard work made this a far better book than it could otherwise have been.

Of the countless others who have given me invaluable advice and guidance about this project, I would particularly like to thank Robin Amis, Christopher Bamford, the Reverend Cynthia Bourgeault, John Carey, Glyn Davies, Alice O. Howell, Warren Kenton, Jay Kinney, Jacob Needleman, the Reverend Laris A. Salins, Vlad Shilinis, John Shirley, and Arthur Versluis. I owe them all a great deal. And finally, my warmest gratitude to Megan, whose love and affection gave me much comfort throughout the writing of this book.

Sandisfield, Massachusetts
December 2001

INNER
CHRISTIANITY

INTRODUCTION

I F ONE SINGLE THEME HAS DOMINATED the history of the past century, it is loss of faith. The implacable course of events has cast doubt upon progress, civilization, political and economic systems, even the essential decency of human nature. Christianity has not been spared. Starting in the nineteenth century, science began to show that the earth had been born not six thousand years in the past, as the Bible seemed to suggest, but billions of years ago. Even the Gospels themselves no longer seemed like Gospel truth, as historical and critical methods revealed that much in the life of Christ was not historical fact but myths and legends that attached themselves to him after his time.

These developments have drawn forth a complex array of reactions from clergy and laity alike. Some have actively rejected this knowledge, taking refuge in traditionalism and fundamentalism. Others have tried to integrate the new perspectives into their religious life, only to be left with a vague and unsatisfying liberal faith. Still others are disaffected from religion in general or simply bewildered.

Whatever course we choose, one thing becomes obvious: it is now next to impossible to take faith unreflectively. We no longer live in a conceptual world framed by the comforting certainties of church doctrine and the literal truth of the Bible. And yet, as disorienting and disillusioning as the process of modern inquiry has been, it has not destroyed the religious search but has invigorated it. Rather than contenting themselves with secondhand truths, people have begun to ask how they themselves can know the presence of the divine.

This impulse has fed the explosion of New Age religions, alternative spiritualities, and traditions brought over from the East that we have seen in recent decades. Many of these religions, both new and newly imported, stress enlightenment as a goal. They say that our ordinary state of consciousness is not the highest one of which we are capable, but a low-grade, delusory state. Spiritual disciplines such as meditation can free us from this oblivion and restore us to our full birthright as human beings.

On a parallel course, the perennial interest in Christian origins has led scholars to reexamine many ancient texts and to unearth new ones: the Dead Sea Scrolls and the Nag Hammadi Library are the most famous examples. Some of these works suggest that early Christians not only reached insights similar to those of the Eastern religions but also had a sophisticated understanding of human consciousness in their own right. Many were concerned with what they called *gnosis*, a word that means "knowledge" in Greek. This is knowledge of a very specific kind—direct, intuitive knowing that surpasses ordinary reason and confers spiritual liberation. Gnosis strongly resembles enlightenment as portrayed in Hinduism and Buddhism.

Although interest in these ancient teachings is considerable, many people assume the teachings were lost long ago, the victims of official suppression and popular neglect. But in fact careful investigation shows that these truths have always been kept alive in the Christian tradition and indeed have fed the life of Western civilization like a great underground stream that only rarely rises to the surface. There have always been teachers and groups that have managed to reach these states of higher consciousness and have passed their knowledge on to the present.

Knowledge that liberates consciousness is often described as *esoteric*. The word "esoteric" is somewhat forbidding, usually connoting something obscure, exotic, and irrelevant to daily life—in short, something "far out." But etymologically the word means exactly the opposite: it comes from the Greek *esotero*, which means "further in." You have to go "further in" yourself to understand what this knowledge is about. In this book I will use the terms "inner Christianity" and "esoteric Christianity" interchangeably.[1]

Esotericism teaches that this world within us is as rich and diverse as the outer world and consists of many different levels of being. Furthermore, these levels exist in a more or less objective way: those familiar with them can discuss them intelligibly with each other and will find that their experiences are essentially similar, much as everyone will say a ball is round. Although these levels stand between us and God, they do so not as obstacles but as way stations. Christ said, "In my Father's house are many mansions" (John 14:2).[2] The Greek word here translated as "mansions" literally means "way stations."

Some thinkers differentiate the *esoteric* from the *mystical*, a distinction that can be useful as long as one is not too rigid about it.[3] Esotericism is characterized by an interest in these different levels of consciousness and being. Mysticism is not quite so concerned with these intermediate states; it focuses on reaching God in the most direct and immediate way. The mystic wants to reach his destination as quickly as possible; the esotericist wants to learn something about the landscape on the way. Moreover, mysticism tends more toward passivity: a quiet "waiting upon God" rather than active investigation.

Both the mystical and the esoteric paths are generously represented in the Christian tradition. Examples of the former include the fourteenth-century English text known as *The Cloud of Unknowing*, which emphasizes coming to God in the stillness of the heart; the Quietism of seventeenth-century Spain; and Quaker spirituality, with its focus on the still experience of the Inner Light. This book, on the other hand, is chiefly about the esoteric strain: it attempts to discuss some of these different levels between God and the physical realm and to show how you might experience them for yourself.

These brief points suggest what esoteric Christianity offers to the individual: a way of self-knowledge—a way, perhaps, to the ultimate knowledge of Self. It also offers a resolution of the age-old dilemma of faith. As even the most casual reader of the New Testament can see, faith originally meant conviction or certainty: "Thy faith has made thee whole" (Luke 17:19). But over the centuries the term has been watered down into connoting a blind trust in secondhand dogma despite one's own better judgment. For the esoteric Christian, faith is indeed vital, but it is not blind trust; rather, it is "the evidence of things not seen" (Heb. 11:1). Faith in this sense is the conviction, deeply felt and unshaken by whatever the world may say, that something real and vital lies beyond the surface of appearances. In this sense, faith too is a way station. It is the gateway to knowledge.

To Christianity collectively, esotericism offers an outlook that can revitalize the tradition and cut through difficulties that now seem almost insurmountable. One example is biblical interpretation, which now focuses almost exclusively on the literal truth of Scripture. Fundamentalists hold to scriptural inerrancy: the Old and New Testaments are literally true. Moderns, on the other hand, claim that while the Bible is *meant* to be literally true, it is a collection of legends and myths that often have little to do with what really happened.

In their pure form, both views are dead ends. Fundamentalism requires us to take Genesis literally, believe that people used to live hundreds of years, and accept various odd but miraculous interventions of God in history. The liberal perspective makes no such requirements, but in writing off so much of the central sacred texts of the tradition, it tends to weaken and even invalidate the Christian message. The endless debate about the "historical Jesus" versus the "Christ of faith," which has been going on for over two centuries without a satisfactory resolution, is the most obvious example of this impasse.

Esotericism differs from conventional views in holding that the Bible has always been meant to be read on several different levels, of which the literal is only one and in fact the lowest. The third-century Church Father Origen writes:

> Very many mistakes have been made because the right method of examining the holy texts has not been discovered by the greater number of readers . . . because it is their habit to follow the bare letter. . . .
>
> Scripture interweaves the imaginary with the historical, sometimes introducing what is utterly impossible, sometimes what is possible but never occurred. . . . [The Word] has done the same with the Gospels and the writings of the Apostles; for not even they are purely historical, incidents which never occurred being interwoven in the "corporeal" sense. . . .
>
> And who is so silly as to imagine that God, like a husbandman, planted a garden in Eden eastward, and put in it a tree of life, which could be seen and felt. . . . And if God is also said to walk in the garden in the evening, and Adam to hide himself under a tree, I do not suppose that any one will doubt that these passages, by means of seeming history, though the incidents never occurred, figuratively reveal certain mysteries.[4]

As we will see, these "certain mysteries" have to do with the furthest reaches of human consciousness and potential. Viewed from this perspective, the story of the Fall is not an antiquated folktale but a vivid and accurate account of the human predicament, and the story of Christ is not only an account of a historical man but also a figurative representation of the path that each of us must follow to attain liberation. As Christopher Walton, a nineteenth-century English esotericist, put it, "all that is said and declared, and recorded in the gospel, is only a plain record of that which is said and done, and doing in yourself."[5]

Esoteric spirituality thus differs from *exoteric* (or outer) religion, which is the form of the faith that is known to the public at large. Esoteric Christianity has long been secret and to some degree inaccessible, but this is not out of a hard-hearted elitism. It is partly because for centuries the mainstream churches looked askance at anyone who did not see divine truth as they did and shunned or hunted down such people. But even in our more open-minded era, esoteric work still requires the effort and sincerity to look within. This is not always pleasant or easy, and the forces of exterior life generally pull one away from it. "Many are called, but few are chosen," said Christ (Matt. 22:14). Ultimately this "choosing" is a process of self-selection.

Outer Christianity also focuses on salvation in the afterlife. You ask for help from Christ in purging your sins and taking away the threat of damnation. Inner Christianity does not deny that there is an afterlife that will be shaped by our actions in the present, but it is less concerned with obtaining salvation in the future than with attaining illumination now. This difference can be seen in examining the word used in New Testament Greek usually translated as "repentance," which is *metanoia*. Usually this is seen as a change in life direction: making amends for wrongs and asking for God's help now and at the hour of our death. But *metanoia* literally means something like a "change of mind," even, perhaps, a change in attention. In ordinary life, attention is directed outward, toward the world of sensations, thoughts, and feelings. With a certain shift in attention, the mind is directed within, toward the center of being, beyond all thoughts and representations, where God meets the individual self. Such "repentance" may indeed involve a change in one's way of life, but from an esoteric point of view, such changes are likely to develop organically out of an increase in consciousness. As you see and understand more of the inner worlds, love, kindness, and compassion become more spontaneous and natural.

How does inner Christianity relate to Christianity as we commonly understand it? Is it a denomination of its own, a movement within a particular church, or an attempt at reforming the church as it now exists?

The relation between esotericism and exoteric religion is a subtle one. It can best be understood by looking at diagram 1-1, which can be traced to the Abba Dorotheus, a Greek Orthodox elder of the seventh century.[6]

External life, known in the Christian tradition as "the world," is the circumference of the circle. External or exoteric religion can be placed here as well. In the Bible, this is symbolized by the story of the Tower of Babel, the level of the "confusion of tongues," where everyone speaks a different language. And so in the world there are legions of religions, each carping at the others, each insisting that it alone is true and right and that all the rest are false. But the further you go toward the center, toward God, the closer the two paths are. In the inner circle, the esoteric level, two different teachings (at points A and B) are not so far apart. Esotericists of different faiths may feel more affinity for one another than they do for members of their own religions who see things only from the exterior.

This helps account for the discomfort esotericists have aroused among religious leaders. Esoteric spirituality does not necessarily challenge ecclesiastical authority but does not necessarily validate it either.

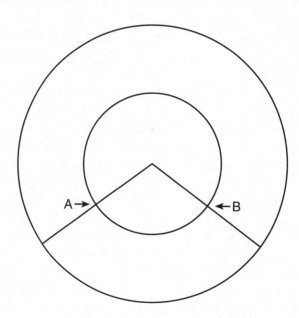

DIAGRAM 1-1 *The circle of the inner and the outer faith. Exoteric religion is represented by the outer circle, esotericism by the inner. Those on the outside are comparatively far apart. The further one progresses toward the center—which represents both God and the center of one's own being—the closer one finds oneself to others who are on the same path.*

Those pursuing a path of inner Christianity can be found in all denominations, and outside of them as well. This is not because dogmas and doctrines are of no interest to the esotericist, but because no single doctrine ever completely or satisfactorily expresses spiritual truth. Language that was powerful and compelling in one era becomes misleading in another (today, for example, no one quite seems to know even what traditional terms like "soul" and "spirit" really mean). Esotericists have the responsibility of trying to see inner reality as well as they can and expressing it according to the needs and understanding of the time.

This leads to the purpose of the present book. I came to write it as an outgrowth of a previous work, entitled *Hidden Wisdom: A Guide to the Western Inner Traditions*, which I wrote in collaboration with Jay Kinney when we were the editors of *Gnosis*, a now-defunct journal of Western esotericism. *Hidden Wisdom* covered many topics from Sufism and Freemasonry to shamanism and ritual magic, and for most of these it was easy enough both to explain their central teachings and to recommend books that could serve as intelligent introductions. But when it came to the chapter on esoteric Christianity, the situation was quite different. While there are a number of extremely powerful works written about this tradition (which I will refer to in the course of this book), they are all dense and demanding; they also tend to overcomplicate the subject to a certain degree. I found that people to whom I had recommended these texts tended to find them archaic, impenetrable, or off-putting.

This book is an attempt to create something more accessible. Much of it is gleaned from classic texts, both obscure and well known; I have given references for these when possible. Others have been taken from the oral tradition; still other ideas are my own and I must take responsibility for them. To discuss a tradition like this is inevitably to reformulate and reinterpret it. There is no "pure" teaching apart from the individuals who work with it, no book or authority that can be looked at as a final arbiter; as we have seen, even Scripture itself can be a slippery slope. This fact puts a responsibility on the reader: more than most forms of discourse, esoteric thought calls upon you to assimilate it, not on the basis of citations and credentials, but by its resonance with your own being.

The Gospel alludes to this issue when it says of Christ "that the people were astonished at his doctrine, for he taught them as one having authority, and not as the scribes" (Matt. 7:28–29). The "scribes" are the spiritual pettifoggers of all eras, who insist on quibbling over chapter and verse. Christ was able to take them on, as many passages in the

Gospels show, but his authority did not come from erudition or skill in debate. Rather, it came from a knowledge that went deeper than the letter of the law. This is what "astonished" the people. At the same time, there had to be some deeper knowing in the people themselves that could recognize this authority, that could hear in it the ring of truth. It is this intuitive knowing (which all of us possess, whether or not we pay any heed to it) that a reader must bring to bear on any spiritual text; otherwise it merely becomes a matter of hearsay and second-hand information.

This book is also an attempt to meet the needs of the tradition as I see it at present. The esotericist often finds himself in the position of a fat man riding on a small airplane: he may be asked to shift position in order to put the vehicle more on balance. In current Christian discourse, I see an enormous interest in the devotional side of the tradition, in prayer, contemplation, and mysticism. Indeed, Christianity has always laid great emphasis on the heart, the emotional life of the soul as it is lived in communion with God.

No one could deny that this dimension is necessary on the spiritual path, but it is not sufficient. For the spirit to develop in a harmonious and integrated fashion, the pole of love must be counterbalanced by the pole of knowledge. It is this aspect that I see as most lacking in Christianity today. While there is no scarcity of theology and biblical scholarship—which has tremendous value in its place—almost all of it is at the outer rim of Dorotheus's circle, grappling with the details of the literal level and with truth in its most superficial form. Knowledge of the inner levels of experience has been for the most part forgotten. It is primarily this need that this book is meant to fill.

Of course, the polarity between love and knowledge is not a rivalry. These two opposites are like the sexes; they are differentiated to create not strife but dynamism. Left to its own, devotion becomes sentimental and even fanatical, while knowledge becomes dry and pedantic. When the two are connected and integrated, knowledge—which after all arises from a love of truth—begins to feed and delight the heart, which in its turn warms and stimulates the energy for further exploration. A seventeenth-century Englishman named John Pordage expressed this truth by saying that the essence of the esoteric Christian path could be symbolized by the image of an eye in a flaming heart.[7] I hope this book will point toward such an integration.

I should make one final point for those who are justifiably suspicious about much writing that styles itself Christian. This book is not an attempt, explicit or implicit, to sell Christianity, nor is it meant to bring straying believers back into the fold. It is meant to suggest that the universal truths of esoteric knowledge are expressed just as much in Christianity as in other traditions; and for many in our culture, these truths will be most clearly and comprehensibly stated in Christian terms. In the current mood of spiritual inquiry and freedom, it may be time to open up the gates of this knowledge for a wider audience.

PART ONE

History

1

Threads of a Hidden Teaching

N O   O N E   H A S   E V E R   W R I T T E N a definitive history of inner Christianity; perhaps no one can. Unlike outer history, its principal deeds lie not in wars or battles or political upheavals, but in the souls of seekers, far from the noise of the world. Even so, it would be wrong to say that this tradition is cut off completely from the life of great events. Time and again it has made its presence felt in Western civilization, sometimes taking center stage, more often standing in the background. Before examining the teachings of inner Christianity, it would be helpful to trace some of its strands from the earliest times to the present, focusing on those likely to have the most interest and meaning today.

THE SECRET GOSPEL

In 1958 Morton Smith made the kind of discovery every scholar dreams of. While researching manuscripts at Mar Saba, a great Eastern Orthodox monastery near Jerusalem, he was perusing an otherwise unremarkable volume. In it he found copied by hand "a letter of the most holy Clement, author of the *Stromateis*," written to one Theodore.

Smith gaped incredulously at the text before him. "The most holy Clement" was Clement of Alexandria (c. 150–c. 215), one of the earliest and greatest of the Church Fathers; no letters of his were known to have survived. Smith was even more amazed by what Clement's letter said: that in addition to the familiar Gospel of Mark, there was another, secret Gospel, which Mark had written in Alexandria "for the use of those being perfected" and which would "lead the hearers into the innermost sanctuary of that truth hidden by the seven [veils]."

Clement's letter quotes a passage from this Gospel, which tells of the resurrection of a "young man" not unlike Lazarus. Six days after being raised from the dead, the young man comes to Jesus, "wearing a linen cloth over his naked [body]." Jesus spends the whole night with him, teaching him "the mystery of the kingdom of God."[1] What this "mystery" was we do not know. The text breaks off in mid-page.

After devoting several years of research to this letter, Smith, by then a professor at Columbia University, came to conclude that it had indeed originally been written by Clement (although the Mar Saba copy had been made in the eighteenth century). Even more astonishingly, he discovered that the passage about the initiation of the young man fit perfectly into the standard text of Mark, after what in the standard version is chapter 10, verse 32. Smith suggested that the passage that Clement set down was not a later addition but part of the actual Gospel that was withheld from the general public and reserved for those who had received the inner knowledge of the Christian mysteries. He determined that this passage is describing an initiation into these mysteries, indicated by the fact that the young man is wearing only a linen cloth—the traditional garment for this rite. Smith also concluded that there was further knowledge not written even in the secret Gospel but imparted by word of mouth to those deemed worthy.

That the Christian faith may originally have been closer to an occult lodge or a secret society than to a religion should not come as a complete surprise. Secrecy is a major theme in the Gospels: Jesus teaches in parables, refusing to explain them except to his disciples; he heals people and insists that they keep quiet about it; even the great passage in the third chapter of John, in which Nicodemus comes to Jesus by night, may be an account of an initiation like the one in Mark's secret Gospel.

The evidence for Christianity as an initiatic faith founded upon secret knowledge is not limited to hints in the canonical Gospels or to Clement's tantalizing fragment. Another startling piece of evidence for this view lies in an enigmatic work called the *Gospel of Thomas*. Fragments of this Gospel in the original Greek were found in the nineteenth century, but the complete text was only discovered in a Coptic translation as part of a cache of scriptures found in Nag Hammadi, Egypt, in 1945.

Thomas is extremely short and simple. It consists of 114 *logia* of Jesus—sayings, usually aphorisms or parables—connected with the minutest amount of narrative. The very simplicity of *Thomas* suggests that it may be extremely ancient; it may even be older, and closer to Christ himself, than the canonical Gospels. Structurally it resembles Q (from the German *Quelle*, or "source"), a similar collection of sayings, now lost, that most scholars believe served as a primary source for Matthew and Luke.[2]

Equally remarkable is the portrait that *Thomas* paints. Here Jesus does not preach the end of the world; he performs no miracles; he does not claim to rescue people from their sins or to be the Messiah long awaited by the Jews. The Jesus of *Thomas* enigmatically mentions a secret knowledge that confers spiritual liberation; as he says in the opening verse, "Whoever finds the interpretation of these sayings shall not experience death."[3] Like Clement's fragment of Mark, *Thomas* even hints at an initiation. At one point Jesus takes Thomas aside to impart secret teachings to him. When he returns, the other Apostles ask him what Jesus said. Thomas replies, "If I tell you one of the things which he told me, you will pick up stones and throw them at me; a fire will come out of the stones and burn you up" (*Thomas*, 13).

The earliest Christians we know of who were concerned with this inner knowledge, or gnosis, were called the Gnostics: Thomas's Gospel is usually regarded as a Gnostic text. The conventional view is that Gnosticism was a heresy that grew up in the second century. The writings of Church Fathers such as Irenaeus, Tertullian, and Clement himself depict it as such. But if *Thomas* is as old as it seems, it suggests that Gnosticism in some form is not a deviation from Christ's teaching but may hark back to Christ himself.

More and more, scholars are coming to believe that from the outset the Apostles understood Christ's message in different, even contradictory, ways. Almost immediately these divergences produced several "faith communities," each clustered around a particular Apostle and having its own slant on Christianity. They included the church in Jerusalem, led by James, the brother of Jesus, which continued to observe the Jewish Law; Paul's churches, which did not feel obliged to follow the Law; the Johannine community associated with John; and the Christianity of Thomas, centered in Syria.[4] Even in New Testament times there were disputes among these groups, as we can see from Acts and Galatians. The Johannine and Thomas communities tended the most toward what was later called Gnosticism, but even Paul's teaching was sometimes understood in this light: Valentinus, one of the greatest of the Gnostics, traced his teachings back to Paul.[5] As the Gnostics liked to stress, Paul said, "We speak the wisdom of God in a mystery, even the hidden wisdom, which God ordained before the world to our glory" (1 Cor. 2:6).[6]

For the Gnostics, what was most important was not deliverance from sin; it was awakening the "hidden wisdom" to which Paul alluded. And the deliverance it promised was not from eternal damnation but from what esoteric Christians have always called the "world"—the congeries of forces in life to which human consciousness is subject.

This intrinsic hostility to the world, which is one of the earmarks of the ancient Gnostic tradition, evokes a deeply felt truth in the human soul. We know the world is not as it was meant to be; we know there is something better, and each of us instinctively aspires to it. We also sense that something stands between us and this happiness. In the twentieth century this came to be identified with various types of social control, not only totalitarianism but the subtler and more pervasive forms of mass manipulation and deceit. This is one reason Gnosticism has come into intellectual fashion in recent decades. But to regard the ancient Gnostics as mere forebears of today's hermeneutics of suspicion does them little justice. The Gnostic dread of the world cut much deeper.

Its central theme can be detected obliquely in Mark's secret Gospel, which speaks of the "truth hidden by the seven [veils]." The number seven here is not just a piece of mystical obfuscation but refers to an ancient esoteric view of the universe. The earth was seen as the center; surrounding it were the spheres of the seven planets as they were then known: the moon, Mercury, Venus, the sun, Mars, Jupiter, and Saturn. Esoteric philosophers believed that the spirit, as it took incarnation, passed through the spheres of each of these planets in turn, each of which in turn imbued it with its own negative characteristics—Venus with lust, Mars with anger, Jupiter with gluttony, and so on. (These can also be correlated with the Seven Deadly Sins of later Christianity.) By the time the soul reached earth, it was fettered by the very qualities that determined its nature.

For the Gnostics, the bondage of the world consisted not of external political and social control, or even the natural limits of physicality, but the nature of the mind as it has been molded by the planets. These influences were personified as the *archons*, the rulers of the seven planetary spheres, who were not servants of the true, good God but inimical celestial gatekeepers. To be liberated was to vanquish their dominion, not in the outside world, but in oneself. The Epistle to the Ephesians alludes to this idea: "For we wrestle not against flesh and blood, but against principalities, against powers, against the rulers of the darkness of this world, against spiritual wickedness in high places" (Eph. 6:12).

Although expressed in mythic terms, the Gnostic view was extremely sophisticated. It recognized one of the most essential truths of spiritual life: that the things in ourselves with which we most identify—the personality with its likes and dislikes, loves and hatreds—are not ourselves in the deepest sense but encrustations that fetter and impede the true essence of the self. Only spiritual illumination can free this self.

The Gnostics did not invent this teaching; in different forms, it can be found in many different texts and traditions: the Zoroastrian teachings of ancient Persia, Jewish mystical treatises, the Hermetic texts of late Egypt, and even the works of philosophers such as Plato. Although many scholars have exerted themselves to determine the source of these teachings, it is probably safest to assume that, then as today, human interaction enabled many currents and ideas to flow and counterflow, influencing and being influenced in their turn. This is particularly likely if, as I have suggested, esotericism tends to be less rigid about sectarian differences than external religion is.

Yet in the end Gnosticism failed. It reached its peak in the second and third centuries and fell into decline afterward, vanishing more or less completely by the fifth century. One reason for its disappearance certainly lies in its insistence on inner knowledge and experience, which was sure to limit its audience. Inner illumination has never had mass appeal.

Gnosticism may also have perished because it tended to be individualistic, idiosyncratic, and diffuse. Each Gnostic teacher had his own system and his own intricate and arcane picture of the universe. These tendencies did not allow the Gnostics to form a cohesive polity such as orthodox Christianity, which, with its tight but flexible network of bishops, was developing in the second and third centuries.

Moreover, the Gnostic emphasis on inner illumination aroused some discomfort in this nascent ecclesiastical establishment. As the scholar Elaine Pagels has pointed out, "Gnostic teaching . . . was potentially subversive of this order: it claimed to offer every initiate direct access to God of which the priests and bishops themselves might be ignorant."[7] This was bound to be irritating to the priests and bishops. Consequently, they launched into a vigorous campaign against Gnosticism. Once they achieved secular power, as they did when Christianity became the state religion of the Roman Empire in the fourth century, they were in a position to come down on the Gnostics and other heterodox Christian sects with the might of the state.

But politics secular and sacred do not fully explain the failure of Gnosticism. Perhaps the ultimate reason for its extinction was that it simply became too gloomy. A certain suspicion, if not loathing, toward the world had been implicit in it from the start: "Whoever has come to understand the world has found (only) a corpse, and whoever has found a corpse is superior to the world," we read in *Thomas* (56). The Gnostics believed that the world is irremediably evil, created not by the true, good God but by a second-rate deity known as the Demiurge (from a Greek word meaning "craftsman"). Gnosis is a way of fleeing from this jerry-built universe; Jesus was a messenger sent by the true God to help us escape. In the end this implacable hostility to ordinary reality simply became too depressing, "too hostile to the world," in the words of the scholar Kurt Rudolph.[8]

CLEMENT AND ORIGEN

If Christianity rejected Gnosticism, it did not reject gnosis. Clement opposed the Gnostics; in fact, his letter mentioning the secret Gospel of Mark is chiefly devoted to combating a libertine Gnostic sect known as the Carpocratians. But the central theme of Clement's chief work, the *Stromateis* (meaning "Patchwork" or "Miscellanies"), was to show that the orthodox Christian faith was perfectly consistent with true gnosis. Clement goes so far as to characterize the true Gnostic as the summit of Christian virtue; gnosis, the knowledge of God, is an end worthy in itself, even the supreme end. He writes, "Could we, then, suppose any one proposing to the Gnostic whether he would choose the knowledge of God or salvation; and if these, which are entirely identical, were separable, he would without the least hesitation choose the knowledge of God."[9] Clement's influence probably prevented a decisive split between the esoteric and exoteric faces of the church in his day, ensuring that it would continue to provide a hospitable dwelling for gnosis—at least for a time.

An equally important influence on early esoteric Christianity was Clement's pupil Origen (185–253 A.D.). Origen is an embarrassing figure for those who claim that there has been a single consistent doctrine handed down from Christ and the Apostles, for Origen's teachings were considered orthodox in their own time and only condemned by the church some two hundred years after his death. Before then his formidable learning and prolific output (he wrote about a thousand books, only a few of which have survived), along with his personal piety and devotion, had led him to be described as "the greatest teacher of the Church after the Apostles."[10]

Yet Origen taught a number of ideas that differ from mainstream Christian doctrine as it has come down to us. He argued for the preexistence of souls before earthly life, for reincarnation, and for a final *apocatastasis* or restoration of all things at the end of time that at least theoretically includes the redemption of the Devil himself. The fact that he could expound these views within the church of his era suggests that they are compatible with the essence of Christ's message. It also leads one to think that later pronouncements of orthodoxy may have closed off some ways of understanding that could be helpful today.

Origen also speaks of different levels of existence, both visible and invisible. His is essentially a hierarchical system. At the top is God the Father, followed by the Son and the Holy Spirit (Origen's views on the Trinity were not entirely consistent with later formulations—one reason he was eventually condemned). Below this divine level is that of the "rational natures" who exist on a purely spiritual level. Some of these are good, some evil; in short, they are angels and devils. Then follows what Origen calls "those spirits who are judged fit by God to replenish the human race"—the souls of humans.[11] Finally there is the physical realm we know.

This system says there are four basic levels of existence—the *divine*, the *spiritual*, the level of the soul or *psyche*, and the *physical* realm. This doctrine can be found in other Western esoteric systems, notably the Kabbalah, which speaks of four worlds that correspond exactly to these levels, as well as in Gnosticism, which developed hierarchies of creation that were far more complex than this. The fundamental difference between Gnostic systems and Origen's was that the Gnostics viewed the celestial intermediaries entirely in negative terms, as demonic and tyrannical.

This cosmic scheme parallels the inner anatomy of human beings. Each of us is a microcosm, a reproduction of the universe in miniature. In the hidden teachings of Christianity there are three levels to the human makeup: the spirit (in Greek, the *pneuma* or "breath"), the soul (*psyche* in Greek), and the physical body. This tripartite structure is central to esoteric Christianity. It existed before Origen and goes back at least to Paul (see, for example, in his reference to the "spiritual body" of resurrection, 1 Cor. 15:44). One thing about this schema that may seem peculiar is that it distinguishes between the spirit and the soul—a demarcation that has often been ignored by Christian thinkers (in fact an ecumenical council of the ninth century explicitly stated there was no difference between the spirit and the soul, contrary to the Bible itself). While this distinction may seem quite abstract, it is not. The Greek word for the soul is *psyche*—literally, the psyche, the nexus of thoughts, emotions, and desires that occupy most of our inner lives. The spirit, or *pneuma*, is consciousness in a purer form, as we shall see in the next chapter.

Origen goes on to say that these three tiers are paralleled by three different levels of meaning in Scripture. He writes:

> One must therefore portray the meaning of the sacred writings in a threefold way upon one's own soul, so that the simple man may be edified by what we may call the flesh of the scripture, this name being given to the obvious interpretation; while the man who has made some progress may be edified by its soul, as it were; and the man who is perfect and like those mentioned by the apostle: "We speak wisdom among the perfect; yet a wisdom not of this world, nor of the rulers of this world, which are coming to nought; but we speak God's wisdom in a mystery, even the wisdom that hath been hidden, which God foreordained before the worlds unto our glory"—this man may be edified by the spiritual law, which has "a shadow of the good things to come." For just as man consists of a body, soul, and spirit, so in the same way does the scripture.[12]

Although many of Origen's ideas were to be rejected by normative Christianity, his concept of different levels of meaning in Scripture was not. In a modified version it formed the core of biblical exegesis throughout the Middle Ages.[13] Even for us today it serves as a reminder that the Bible has more dimensions than the purely literal and that they apply to inner growth.

THE WORK OF MONASTICISM

Another strand of the Gnostic tradition left its mark on mainstream Christianity: the need for the liberation of the spirit from its bondage to the world.[14] This liberation was sought by a group of men and women who retreated from the world into the deserts of Egypt starting in the third century. They came to be known as the Desert Fathers and Mothers, and they were the first monks and nuns in Christianity. Initially they enacted their quest in solitude and were called *anchorites*, or hermits. The most famous was named Anthony, who was the subject of a famous biography written by the Church Father Athanasius the Great. According to Athanasius, Anthony, in his quest for union with God, was assailed by negative thoughts and passions that took the form of demons—a story that has inspired many great works of art, including Hieronymus Bosch's *Temptation of Saint Anthony* and a novel of the same name by Flaubert.

Despite their reclusive ways, the Desert Fathers began to attract disciples, and communities started to form around them. The first organized monastic community was founded by a man named Pachomius in 324 and soon came to number nine thousand. It was followed by others all over the eastern Mediterranean, some of which continue to this day.

The Desert Fathers used a number of methods to bring themselves closer to God in the silence of their cells. One was a prayerful reading of Scripture, especially the Psalms. They tried to chant the entire Psalter aloud each day, or, failing that, at least over the course of a week. Another was the practice of "unceasing prayer," an attempt to follow Paul's exhortation to "pray without ceasing" (1 Thess. 5:17). In later centuries, this would evolve into the Prayer of Jesus, also known as the Prayer of the Heart, which involved repeating a one-line prayer—"Jesus Christ, Son of God, have mercy on me, a sinner" is the most common version—until it took root in the unconscious mind and became synchronized with the beating of the heart; hence its name. The Jesus Prayer has made its chief home in Eastern Orthodoxy, where it has been practiced more or less continuously since the earliest centuries. Over the past generation it has found new adherents in the West and is now practiced by Americans from many different denominations.

In these early centuries of Christianity, monasticism was also arising in the West, leading to the establishment of large communities in settings as far-flung as North Africa and Ireland. The Desert Fathers and their successors made their presence felt through figures like John Cassian, whose *Conferences* records his experiences with the ascetics of the Eastern Roman Empire and would infuse much of their thought and practice into Western Christianity. But the most seminal figure was Benedict of Nursia (480–547), who established the great monastery at Monte Cassino in Italy and formulated *The Rule of Saint Benedict*, a guide to monastic life that the Benedictine Order still follows today.

Although the *Rule* deals with details as apparently trivial as sleeping arrangements, rest periods, and the qualifications of the monastery cellarer, much of it is devoted to the Divine Office, a series of seven services that are interspersed throughout the monks' day in accordance with the verse from the Psalm: "Seven times a day do I praise thee because of thy righteous judgments" (Ps. 119:164). This points to the central goal of monasticism: to arrange one's life so that one is never far from remembrance of God. The monks are required to occupy themselves with manual labor, but only in a strictly circumscribed period. Much of the rest of the day is devoted both to collective services and to private devotions, including reading sacred texts. *Lectio divina*, or "divine reading," a contemplative reading of Scripture, has always been a central practice among the Benedictines.

One thing that seems to be absent from the monastic writings is any kind of preoccupation with society at large. Monasticism took its form in late antiquity, when the Western Roman Empire was crumbling and barbarian invasions were hitting in wave after wave. A modern person might ask, Where was the Christian concern of these monks for the sorrows and ravages they saw around them? Did they retreat into their cloisters simply to avoid a difficult situation?

No doubt some did, and from the modern point of view social concern may seem low on the monks' list of priorities. But a broader perspective suggests that the monasteries performed an extremely vital function. They served as repositories of learning and civilization in an age when these seemed almost certain to perish entirely. As little as we sometimes think we have left of classical civilization, we would have much less still if the monks had not preserved what they did. They also cleared land for agriculture and provided sound management of that land, creating the economic basis for European civilization. "In a sense they determined the whole future history of Europe," writes historian Paul Johnson; "they were the foundation of its world primacy."[15]

This raises a major issue in esoteric work: the relation between the individual's quest for God and the needs of a society as a whole. Monasticism's key role in forging the modern West suggests that there is no conflict between inner development and contributing to the larger good of humanity; in fact, an individual can develop fully only if he or she takes part in a larger work of this kind. The nature and purpose of such a work may not be immediately apparent: the monks' central role in building Western civilization became clear only centuries later. And despite ebbs and flows in their fortunes in the years since, monasteries continue to serve as repositories for spiritual knowledge. In recent years a number of monastic practices, such as chanting of the Psalms and the Prayer of the Heart, have been making their way back into the public domain.

THE MEDIEVAL VISION

Occasionally one encounters people who feel a powerful nostalgia for the Middle Ages. In material terms this is baffling: who would want to forsake the comforts of modernity for the squalor, disease, and cruelty of that time? But in another sense this longing is easy to understand. More than any other era before or since in Western civilization, the Middle Ages were founded upon a profound spiritual vision that integrated the highest levels of being with the lowest.

We see this expressed most powerfully in the Gothic cathedrals, which take stone, that most solid and unforgiving of substances, and make it seem to surge upward and touch the vaults of heaven. The creators of these great edifices were informed by a sense of sacred harmony that they consciously expressed in the geometric harmonies of their buildings; in the words of the nineteenth-century esotericist Franz Josef Molitor, "Christian architecture, particularly of the Middle Ages, derived from a theosophic element which was part Pythagorean and part kabbalistic."[16] The inner logic of the cathedrals' designs suggest why they retained such artistic consistency even though they often took a century or more to complete. It also explains the effect these buildings have on the state of mind of those who enter into them; even people without any religious sensibility frequently experience a sense of exaltation and sublimity.

The most powerful literary portrait of the medieval vision appears in the *Divine Comedy* of Dante Alighieri (1265–1321), which tells of the poet's spiritual journey through the depths of hell, up the Mount of Purgatory, and into the celestial spheres, culminating in a vision of the divine love of the Trinity, *l'amor che muove il sole e l'altre stelle*—"the love that moves the sun and the other stars."

Dante's poem is, of course, to be read on a number of levels. In the words of the twentieth-century French esotericist René Guénon, the *Divine Comedy* presents an allegory "that simultaneously veils and unveils the successive phases through which the consciousness of the initiate passes in order to reach immortality."[17] These include the various levels of hell, which in terms of modern depth psychology portray a confrontation with the shadow—the dark, repressed sides of the psyche that need to be recognized and transcended. In Dante's *Inferno*, these are represented by hell's circles, each of which is devoted to one of the vices, such as sloth, gluttony, anger, and pride. The release of these vices is represented in the *Purgatorio*, while the *Paradiso* describes the ascent through the celestial spheres, each of which is governed by one of the seven classical planets, and beyond them, the realms of the fixed stars, the "prime mover," and the "empyrean," or fiery dimension.[18]

We have already encountered Dante's celestial vision in the system of the Gnostics, but here it has been transformed. The rulers of the planetary spheres are no longer evil cosmic gatekeepers, the personification of "spiritual wickedness in high places," but stewards of the celestial dimensions. Those who are redeemed ascend to the level that is best suited for them. The cosmic prison of Gnosticism has been transformed into a terrace of paradises.

Dante almost certainly did not know of the Gnostics' teachings directly. By his time they had long been discredited and forgotten. How, then, did he come upon this knowledge? He was a member—and possibly a leader—of an esoteric secret society known as the Fedeli d'Amore, the "Faithful Ones of Love," which transmitted this knowledge from esoteric Islam (again reminding us of the constant cross-fertilization of esoteric culture).[19] On the other hand, the portrait of an earth surrounded by the rings of the planetary spheres reflects the Ptolemaic vision of a geocentric universe, which was still prevalent in the science of Dante's time. Today, on an exterior level, this system is nothing more than a fossil in the cabinet of scientific history. Yet in an inner sense it still retains tremendous power and value. For although Dante's odyssey is portrayed as a journey in space—into the center of the earth, up the Mount of Purgatory, and into the celestial spheres—it is really about a journey to the center of one's own being, where one is ultimately greeted by God.

THE TRIUMPH OF RATIONALISM

Like all things in this world, the towering edifice of medieval civilization held as much darkness as light. The attempt to encompass all the universe in a sweeping Christian vision, so sublimely articulated in Dante's poem, came to be embodied in what the historian Paul Johnson has called "the total society" of a Catholic civilization to which everyone belonged perforce. As Johnson describes it, "Membership of the society, and acceptance of its rules, was ensured by baptism, which was compulsory and irrevocable. . . . Those who, in effect, renounced their baptism by infidelity or heresy were killed. For the remainder, there was total agreement and total commitment. The points on which men argued were slender, compared to the huge areas of complete acquiescence which embraced almost every aspect of their lives."[20]

It is no coincidence that at this time esoteric Christianity increasingly began to be buried and hidden. This was in part due a change in intellectual climate. In the thirteenth century the philosophy of Thomas Aquinas, later known as Thomism, came to be the dominant form of theology in Catholicism (and remains so more or less down to the present). In this system reason is the highest form of human knowledge and constitutes the truest way of knowing God. Consequently, direct spiritual experience becomes suspect; it cannot be trusted in its own right but must submit to the touchstone of reason, and reason must in turn accord with the theology of the church. Catholicism in that era thus became prone to a philosophical rigidity that was the internal correlate to the ideal of the "total society" and fostered bigotry and persecution.

This is precisely what occurred in the High Middle Ages. At this time we see the rise of the Inquisition, which was created in 1231 by Pope Gregory IX to deal with certain heretical sects that were then burgeoning, notably the Cathars (from the Greek *katharos*, or "pure"), a radically dualistic sect, centered in the south of France, that may represent a continuation of the Gnostic tradition. Like the Gnostics, the Cathars hated and despised the world. They believed that the universe is a confused mixture of two warring principles, the light and the dark. The world we know is a creation of the dark force. Salvation consists of purifying the spark of light, or consciousness, in oneself and escaping from the world. The Cathars performed a secret rite known as the Consolamentum, similar to baptism, that they believed would confer this blessing.

Disturbed by this competition, the Catholic Church instigated a ruthless persecution of the sect. Marauding troops wiped out whole villages of believers, often without stopping to inquire whether their victims were Cathars or Catholics. In 1244 the last Cathar stronghold at Montségur fell to the invaders. Disdainful of the evil world to the last, 205 Cathars marched singing into the bonfires that were prepared for them.

Nor did the increasingly paranoid church limit its attacks to enemies on the outside. In 1307, some sixty years after the Cathars were crushed, Pope Clement V ordered the suppression of the Knights Templar, a military monastic order founded in 1118 to protect Christian pilgrims to the

Holy Land. This treacherous attack, carried out on an order that had fought with such conspicuous valor in the Crusades, was grounded on charges that the Templars conducted secret rites involving blasphemy, heresy, and sodomy.

It is impossible now to tell if these claims had any truth in them; in true medieval fashion, they were extracted from Templars under torture. Most historians agree that the order was persecuted chiefly because the king of France coveted the Templars' considerable wealth and coerced the pope into helping him get it. On the other hand, like the Cathars, the Templars did hold secret initiatic rites (although we do not really know what they were). Whatever the fiscal motives for their suppression, it was also partly inspired by the church's persistent fear of secret societies that might command a deeper allegiance than that owed to the church itself. Catholicism has long been hostile to the notion of any spiritual power or illumination apart from what is conferred by its own rites. The official view is that the sacraments are both necessary and sufficient for salvation; any talk of higher truths or initiatic knowledge, however circumspect or deferential to Catholic doctrine, is considered subversive. The church tends to regard the esoteric inner circle not as a deeper dimension of the external church but as an inimical fifth column.

The fate of Meister Eckhart (c. 1260–c. 1329) is a case in point. Eckhart was a Dominican monk who expounded a radical idea for his time: the essential unity of God with humankind. This concept has always been extremely problematical in outer Christianity, which argues for the ultimate personhood of both God and human beings—a personhood that is usually seen as an unbridgeable gulf dividing the two. But for Eckhart, "the Father ceaselessly begets his Son and, what is more, he begets me as his Son—the self-same Son!"[21]

Ideas like these led to a condemnation of twenty-eight of Eckhart's propositions by a papal bull. Although he escaped excommunication (probably by a timely death), he was always faced with the conflict between his own inner knowledge and the pressures of external authority. After his death the pope decreed that Eckhart had been deceived by "the father of lies" into "sowing thorns and thistles among the faithful." His writings fell into eclipse and for hundreds of years were preserved only by groups such as the Friends of God, a fourteenth-century esoteric society, and later by Quakers and Anabaptists. Only in the last century have Catholic scholars rehabilitated his memory somewhat in the eyes of their own faith.[22]

In the Eastern Orthodox Church, the struggle between external and internal authority rarely reached the same pitch. In the first place, its metropolitans and patriarchs never enjoyed the centralized power possessed by the papacy. In the second place, the Eastern Orthodox nations, including the Byzantine Empire and Russia, were fighting a centuries-long struggle against Mongol and Turkish invaders, which reduced both the inclination and the capacity of the church to root out enemies within. Finally, Eastern Orthodoxy has always been more sympathetic to esotericism than has its Western counterpart. This is in part because the monks played a far more important role in formulating Orthodox theology and so kept some awareness of gnosis alive; in the West, by contrast, theology came to be the province of the universities, which were immersed in rational Thomism.

During the fourteenth century Eastern Orthodoxy saw a climactic debate about the nature of knowledge within its ranks. The ancient tradition, supported by a monk named Gregory Palamas, held that gnosis transcends reason and is thus the highest form of knowledge. Palamas fell into a long and bitter debate with an opponent named Barlaam of Calabria, who advanced the view, then becoming prevalent in the Western universities, that rational knowledge was supreme.

The outcome in Orthodoxy was the opposite of that in the West: Palamas won the debate, and since then, in Orthodoxy reason has always had to take second place to higher, spiritual perception. This moment in religious history, for the most part forgotten today, has helped shape the two halves of Europe far more than is generally acknowledged. It has also meant that esoteric knowledge has more of a home in Eastern Orthodoxy than it has had in Catholicism. To this day the Orthodox monasteries at Mount Athos in Greece are said to contain a tradition of spiritual practice that has been handed down unbroken from the Desert Fathers. Some of it is described in the *Philokalia*, a compilation of inner teachings recorded between the fourth and fifteenth centuries.[23]

THE BRETHREN OF THE COMMON LIFE

Even in the West, esoteric knowledge did not completely vanish. But in most instances it was transmitted in small groups outside the ecclesiastical framework. One example is a lay order known as the Brethren of the Common Life.[24]

Although their origins are somewhat obscure, the founder of the Brethren is generally thought to have been a Dutchman named Geert Groote (1340–84). The son of a wealthy burgher who died in the Black

Plague, Groote was educated in canon law in Paris and was preparing for a conventional career in the church. One day he was accosted in a crowd by an unknown Friend of God who told him, "Why are you standing here, intent on empty things? You ought to be another man." The shock of this encounter impelled him to turn his back on his plans and become an itinerant preacher in the Netherlands.[25]

Groote's activity lasted only four years until he too died of the plague, but in this time he started a seminal movement to foster a devout life in ordinary men and women. Those who were inspired by him decided to band together and live communally, hence their name. These people were not monks and nuns in the ordinary sense. They did not take monastic vows but continued to live as laity. Moreover, unlike the monks of this period, who frequently lived either off the incomes of their large estates or by aggressive fund-raising, the Brothers and Sisters supported themselves by their own labor. Many worked copying devotional manuscripts by hand (the printing press would not be invented till the next century). The movement soon spread over the Netherlands and Germany, reaching its heyday in the early fifteenth century.

Strong evidence suggests that the Brethren of the Common Life were an esoteric school. Their surviving texts—of which there are many—suggest a lively and profound interest in the different levels of the "inner man." As the scholar John van Engen observes, "In this exploration of the inner man, there was a good deal of psychology. . . . They recognized, as both schoolmen and monks . . . had earlier, the need to understand the makeup of the soul, and they set out systematically to exploit that knowledge in behalf of training and disciplining their inner selves."[26] To read of their exercises for "remembering Christ" in daily life is fascinating and bears strong resemblances to the mindfulness practices of esoteric schools today, as we shall see in chapter 8.

The role of the Brethren in late medieval Christianity is a matter of dispute. Some scholars regard them as precursors of the Reformation, others as firm upholders of the Catholic faith. Both views have sound reasons to back them up. Certainly the Brethren's roots in Catholicism were strong. The movement they led came to be known as the *devotio moderna*, or "modern devotion," not because they claimed to be innovators, but because they wanted to revive the interior spirituality of the Desert Fathers. They did not see themselves as schismatics and never came into doctrinal conflict with the church. In fact, one of the most popular Catholic devotional titles of all time, the anonymous *Imitation of*

Christ, was probably the work of a Brother named Thomas à Kempis. When the Reformation actually came in 1517, the *devotio moderna* had long since passed its peak, but the few remaining fragments of the movement maintained their allegiance to Rome.

On the other hand, in some respects the *devotio moderna* did foreshadow the Reformation. While Brothers and Sisters listened respectfully to sermons at mass, they would also go back to their collective residences and listen to a collation—a kind of informal sermon—delivered by a senior member of the community, suggesting that spiritual knowledge was not to be received exclusively at the hands of the clergy. They also wrote and distributed devotional texts in the vernacular, including translations of Scripture into Dutch and German. While this seems innocuous today, at the time it was potentially inflammatory. The Catholic Church regarded Jerome's Latin Vulgate as its official version of Scripture, and translations of the Bible into the spoken languages were not encouraged, because it was not felt that ordinary believers could approach the scriptures without falling into error. Other such translations in that period came from John Wyclif in England and the followers of Jan Hus in Bohemia, both of whom the church condemned as heretics.

The Brethren of the Common Life never suffered the same fate, because unlike Wyclif and the Hussites they had no doctrinal differences with Rome. Yet in their attempt to pursue a spiritual path outside the normal church structure, they pointed to the inadequacy of the increasingly corrupt and commercialized hierarchy for guiding souls. In taking responsibility for their own interior lives, they did help pave the way for the Reformation.

HERMETICISM AND KABBALAH

The Brethren of the Common Life flourished in nations that were backwaters in the Europe of the time. Another esoteric movement—or rather, two interconnected movements—sprang up much closer to the centers of power and indeed helped feed and inspire the Italian Renaissance.

The first was inaugurated by the rediscovery of the *Corpus Hermeticum*, a series of esoteric writings attributed to a legendary divine being called Hermes Trismegistus ("Thrice-Greatest Hermes"). Like many Greek texts, it was brought to Italy after Constantinople fell to the Turks in 1453.

The *Corpus Hermeticum* immediately drew a great deal of attention, for Renaissance scholars believed Hermes Trismegistus had been a contemporary of Moses, and they thought these texts contained the occult wisdom of ancient Egypt. (Although scholars since then have shown that these texts only go back to the early centuries of the Christian era, these texts probably contain more of the wisdom of the Egyptians than they have been given credit for.)[27] Around 1492 Cosimo de' Medici, the great Florentine patron of the arts, asked the scholar Marsilio Ficino to interrupt his translations of Plato into Latin and translate the Hermetic writings first. Ficino complied, and for the next century and a half his translations revived the tradition of Hermeticism, which permeated all aspects of Renaissance culture and which continues to exercise an influence down to the present.

The Hermeticists see the planets as influencing all areas of human and natural life: each planet has plants, minerals, and geometrical symbols associated with it. Individuals afflicted by adverse astrological aspects are supposed to use remedies based on the appropriate planets. Ficino, who believed himself predisposed to melancholy because of the placement of the baleful planet Saturn in his astrological chart, sought to assuage his condition by surrounding himself with plants and stones associated with the benign planets Venus and the sun.

To someone today, the writings of the Renaissance Hermeticists may seem outmoded and bizarre. Yet it may not be wise to dismiss them too hastily, for what we seem to be lacking in the present era is precisely this sense of connection to the larger cosmos. We might look up at the stars at night and feel the conflicted impression that these bodies are both unimaginably remote and intimately bound up with our souls. The esoteric worldview suggests that there is a deep truth behind this intuition of a hierarchical cosmos that is reflected in our own makeup. This worldview seems to have been in danger of being lost in the late medieval era as well, as the church came to prefer rationalistic Thomism to an esoteric perspective. The Hermetic impulse tried to push the balance in the other direction.

A parallel movement involved the introduction of the Kabbalah, the esoteric tradition of Judaism, into Christianity. The relationship between these two streams has always been a complex one. Kabbalists themselves have traditionally held that this teaching was embedded in Judaism from the outset. But modern scholars tend to see it as the result of a number of influences converging upon Judaism in the centuries immediately before and after Christ. Gershom Scholem, the greatest modern scholar of the Kabbalah, saw its origins in the influence of Gnosticism upon Judaism in that period.[28]

The truth about the Kabbalah's origins is probably a combination of these two perspectives. If, as I have suggested, esotericists tend to feel closer to one another than do their more externally oriented coreligionists, naturally these teachings would interpenetrate far more than we customarily imagine. Thus there would have been links between Kabbalists and Christian esotericists all along—and even between them and their counterparts in the pagan world. On the other hand, the Jewish tradition is undeniably older, and Christianity owes a great deal to it. Origen's levels of meaning in Scripture, for example, were adopted by Jewish exegetes in the medieval era,[29] but Origen's own ideas were inspired by Philo of Alexandria, a Jewish philosopher who lived around the time of Christ and explicated the Torah in an allegorical fashion.

In the fifteenth century, the Kabbalah was overtly introduced to the Christian tradition, and it has remained a part of esoteric Christianity ever since. The first man to discuss it openly was a pupil of Ficino's named Giovanni Pico della Mirandola (1463–94). Working with a Jewish convert to Christianity named Flavius Mithridates, who translated a number of Kabbalistic texts into Latin at breakneck speed, the precocious Pico—then only twenty-three—emerged in 1486 with nine hundred theses for public debate, many of them Kabbalistically inspired.[30]

Pico introduced a number of Kabbalistic ideas to the educated Christian public. Among these was the belief that on Mount Sinai Moses received, in addition to the written Law and the standard oral law, later codified in the Mishnah, a secret oral law that he handed down only to adepts. Pico said that Christ himself did the same: "He preached to the masses in parables and separately to the few disciples to whom it was given to understand the mysteries of the kingdom of heaven plainly without figures of speech." Pico also quoted the sixth-century theologian known as Dionysius the Areopagite, who said that "it was a prescribed and holy custom in the church not to communicate the most secret dogma in writing, but only by voice and to those who had been properly initiated."[31]

This secret doctrine, Pico said, was the Kabbalah, but it was not the property of the Jews alone. Indeed, he believed that Moses, who was "learned in all the wisdom of the Egyptians" (Acts 7:22), had received it in Egypt, and that Greek sages such as Pythagoras and Plato had taken it from the same source. In short, this esoteric wisdom is the common heritage of the West, forming an unseen current that links Judeo-Christian civilization with the great cultures of the remote past.

Perhaps the most influential teaching of the Kabbalah is its system of ten *sefirot* or "principles," which are said to provide a framework for understanding not only the nature of God (insofar as he is knowable to us) but also the workings of the universe itself. The basic Kabbalistic diagram, the well-known Tree of Life, describes the interrelation of these *sefirot*.[32] Each *sefirah* (this is the singular; *sefirot* is the plural) is associated with one of the Hebrew names of God as well as with universal principles such as wisdom, understanding, expansion, and limitation. They are also correlated with planets, colors, angels, metals, and other things. The great Renaissance magus Cornelius Agrippa went so far as to connect them with the gods of Greece and Rome. Some Kabbalists have said that all humanity was originally monotheistic and that polytheism only arose when people began worshiping the *sefirot* as individual deities.

THE BROTHERS OF THE ROSY CROSS

The mixture of Kabbalah and Hermeticism in the early modern era was a rich and heady one. It inspired the great mages of the Renaissance—adepts in the arts and sciences and also in the mysteries of magic and invocation. Their names still have a ring of awe: Cornelius Agrippa, Paracelsus, John Dee, Giordano Bruno. To these must be added the legendary figure of Doctor Faustus, who supposedly sold his soul to the Devil for power and occult knowledge. His damnation, as described in Marlowe's tragedy, pointed toward the popular fears of these enigmatic figures. Most of them fell afoul of sacred and secular rulers at one point or another: John Dee, the great magus of the court of Queen Elizabeth, once had his house set afire by a sorcery-fearing mob, and Bruno, a lapsed Dominican monk, was burned at the stake in Rome in 1600.

The quest for inner knowledge is rarely a popular one. It is too far afield of common interests and arouses the suspicion of those who fear and hate anything beyond their own horizons. Consequently, esotericists tend to work either in isolation or in small enclaves—lodges or secret societies—that conceal themselves from the world's eyes except when their work requires them to step onto the public stage.

One of the most striking examples of a more public face for esotericism can be found in a mysterious seventeenth-century movement known as Rosicrucianism. The Rosicrucians, or Brothers of the Rosy Cross, were another in the series of esoteric orders that we have already glimpsed in the Templars, the Fedeli d'Amore, and the Brethren of the Common Life. But whereas these earlier orders tended to conceal their true nature, the Rosicrucians proclaimed their existence in two anonymous tracts published in Germany around 1615 and entitled the *Fama fraternitatis* ("The Rumor of the Brotherhood") and the *Confessio fraternitatis* ("The Confession of the Brotherhood"). Their goal was "sincerely to profess Christ, condemn the Pope, addict ourselves to the true Philosophy, lead a Christian life, and daily call, entreat, and invite many more into our Fraternity."[33]

The Rosicrucians were devoutly Christian and steadfastly Protestant. Although the symbol of the Rosy Cross has many meanings, one of these points to Lutheranism, since Martin Luther's own personal emblem bore a rose, a cross, and a heart. But the Brothers of the Rosy Cross were not merely interested in sectarian causes. Their goal was that "man might . . . understand his own nobleness and worth, and why he is called Microcosmus, and how far his knowledge extendeth into Nature."[34]

Here we find the modern era in nutshell. Unlike medieval Christianity, which often stressed the wretchedness and baseness of humanity, the Rosicrucians emphasized the "nobleness and worth" of the human race. And instead of "esteeming Popery, Galen, and Aristotle," as the *Fama* puts it, the Brothers encouraged a direct exploration of the secrets of nature. They helped set the stage for two of the main trends of the modern era: human rights and experimental science.

And yet the Rosicrucians remained extremely elusive. While the manifestos call all men of goodwill to join, many who tried to respond never found them; among these seekers was the French philosopher René Descartes. Hence they came to be nicknamed "the Invisibles." In any event, the Rosicrucian movement was soon submerged in the Thirty Years' War that erupted in Europe in 1619, and little more was heard of it—at least for the time being.

But the Rosicrucians were not finished. In the nearly four hundred years since the manifestos, a number of esoteric societies, large and small, have traced their origins to this secret brotherhood. The largest and best-known is the Ancient and Mystical Order of Rosae Crucis (AMORC), based in San Jose, California, and famous for its magazine ads and correspondence courses, but there are many others as well.

Even these organizations do not represent the whole of the Rosicrucian legacy, for an intricate web of evidence connects this movement with the rise of Freemasonry (known also as Masonry).[35] While Freemasonry was an old esoteric order that thrived in Scotland from late medieval times (possibly representing a continuation of the Templar legacy), in the seventeenth century it was brought to England, where it was associated with the rise of the scientific revolution.[36] Elias Ashmole, one of the founders of the Royal Society in London, which to this day remains one of the world's most prestigious scientific bodies, also happens to be the first Englishman known to have been initiated as a Freemason. In the eighteenth century Masons played key roles in the American and French revolutions, while Giuseppe Garibaldi, one of the leaders in the unification of Italy in the nineteenth century, was Grand Master of Italy's Masonic lodge. Thus the Rosicrucian program of human dignity and scientific inquiry bore fruit in the Western civilization that we know today.

SAINT-MARTIN AND MARTINISM

Rosicrucianism and Freemasonry are chiefly Protestant in inspiration. (Popular belief to the contrary, Freemasonry is not anti-Catholic in doctrine or ritual, but its secrecy led to its condemnation by Pope Clement XII in 1738, a position that the Catholic Church has never reversed.)[37] Many of the other esoteric luminaries of the seventeenth and eighteenth centuries were Protestant as well. Jacob Boehme, a seventeenth-century German shoemaker who wrote a number of profound works on esoteric Christianity, was a Lutheran, as was Emanuel Swedenborg, the great Swedish polymath whose clairvoyant powers inspired him to write voluminous descriptions of his journeys to the spirit world.

It is true that exoteric Protestants have been hard on esoteric Christians: Boehme was hounded by the pastor of his town for teaching heresy, and Swedenborg had to publish his books in London because the Lutheran state church would not allow them to appear in Sweden. But generally the diffuseness and greater toleration of the Protestant tradition has given more leeway to those who do not always fall in step.

This is not to say that the Catholic Church totally repudiated esotericism, although it is probably fair to say that since the High Middle Ages this particular form of spiritual endeavor has been in the background there. Among those who remain in the folds of the church, there is often a tremendous reluctance to theorize about or even speak of spiritual experience. We only need look at the works of Teresa of Avila (1515–82), one of the greatest esoteric Christians in the Catholic tradition, to see this. Teresa's understanding of inner states has been rivaled by few, yet her writing is suffused by protestations of ignorance and inadequacy that seem at times forced. She writes, for example, "These interior matters are so obscure to the mind that anyone with as little learning as I will be sure to have to say many superfluous and irrelevant things in order to say a single one that is to the point. . . . Before I get to [interior matters] I shall have to explain many things that are well known—it is bound to be so when a person is as stupid as I."[38] While humility is a natural response to the *mysterium tremendum* that is the divine, such fulsome caution may also be motivated partly by fear of straying too far into theologically dangerous terrain.

There have been esoteric orders within Catholicism, but the church's longstanding suspicion of secret societies has not provided a favorable habitat for them. One example is a French society known as La Fraternité du Paraclet ("The Brotherhood of the Paraclete"), which can be traced back to the fifteenth century and which in 1668 was subsumed by another society called L'Estoile Internelle ("The Internal Star"). Both of these were connected with the Holy Grail and with devotion to the Sacred Heart of Jesus. Membership was highly selective: L'Estoile Internelle could have only twelve members at one time. Demanding strict fidelity to the church and the king of France, these orders became nearly extinct during the French Revolution. Later attempts to revive them, in the words of a seeker named Marcel Clavelle, "each time came up against the scruples, which were moreover unjustified, of the Catholics . . . who were afraid to engage in a path that seemed susceptible of disapproval by the ecclesiastical authorities." An esotericist named Louis Charbonneau-Lassay attempted to bring La Fraternité du Paraclet to life again in the early twentieth century, and it appears to have survived in some form until 1951, when it was "put to sleep."[39]

Nonetheless, esotericism has persisted among Catholics, as we can see with a movement that arose in eighteenth-century France called Martinism in homage to its founding figures, Martinez de Pasqually (1727–73) and Louis-Claude de Saint-Martin (1743–1803). In 1768 Pasqually initiated Saint-Martin into an esoteric order known as the Temple des Élus Cohens ("Temple of Elect Priests"). The Élus Cohens specialized in magical invocation, which was ultimately intended to put the initiate in contact with "the Vision of the Repairer, Jesus Christ."[40]

Dissatisfied with their excessively magical emphasis, Saint-Martin eventually drifted away from the Élus Cohens. He sought to bring the teachings of their tradition more in line with what he called "Christian mysticism," thus introducing a more devotional aspect into the esotericism of his time. He established his own line of teaching in Paris in 1793, which continued privately through one-to-one initiation for a hundred years. In 1890 Gérard Encausse (who wrote under the pen name "Papus"), along with other initiates in Saint-Martin's line, established the Martinist Order in Paris and attracted a number of influential members; Tsar Nicholas II is said to have been master of a Martinist lodge in Russia.[41] After Papus's death in 1916, the order began to splinter. Today a number of different organizations operate in several nations, including France, Canada, the Netherlands, and the United States; some individuals also follow the Martinist path independently.

MAGIC, RITUAL, AND TAROT

One highly influential Christian esotericist who remained a devout and practicing Catholic was Alphonse Louis Constant (1810–75), best known by his pen name of Éliphas Lévi. Lévi, the son of a poor shoemaker, was educated at the seminary of Saint-Sulpice near Paris but eventually left, partly because of the hypocrisy he saw there, partly because he did not feel himself able to live up to the vow of chastity. (He later had a brief marriage to a woman who deserted him.) He turned first to radical politics and eventually to esotericism, but never broke with the Catholic Church.

Lévi wrote a number of books; the best-known are *Dogme et rituel de la haute magie* ("Dogma and Ritual of High Magic") and *Histoire de la magie* ("History of Magic"). As their names suggest, these works occupy themselves with ritual magic, an important part of the inner Christian tradition. Although many esotericists since Lévi's time have sniggered at his naïve enthusiasms, his inconsistencies, and his purple prose, he has influenced them more than they may care to admit, particularly in his explications of magic and the Tarot.

For Lévi, ritual magic is not an attempt to conjure up demons and force them to do one's bidding, nor does it try to win love or riches by means of bizarre spells or amulets. Rather, it is a religious act of high merit, using esoteric knowledge to attain perfection. This is done through the imagination guided by the will. "The Great Work," he writes, "is, before all things, the creation of man by himself, that is to say, the full and entire conquest of his faculties and his future; it is especially the perfect emancipation of his will."[42]

Magic in this sense is supremely important for many Christian esotericists. It is the other side of the ascent through the subtle realms, for here the magician is attempting to make the energy of these realms descend and manifest on earth. He or she becomes the living link between heaven and earth—a process that requires rigorous training. In the Catholic Church, the priest performs the sacraments *ex opere operato*—from the act itself. This means that even if he is bored or distracted while saying mass, the bread is still transformed into the Host as long as the rite is carried out correctly. In magic it is not so; supreme concentration is necessary. A distracted mind renders the operation useless or even harmful.

Lévi's most famous contribution to esoteric thought and practice has to do with the Tarot. The Tarot is a deck of seventy-eight cards similar to ordinary playing cards, its greatest difference being that it has a set of twenty-two additional cards bearing such names as the Fool, the High Priestess, and the Devil. The Tarot originated (probably in fourteenth-century Milan) as a trick-taking game somewhat like whist or bridge, in which the twenty-two extra cards served as a set of permanent trumps. But for Lévi, the Tarot is the key to all mysteries: "An imprisoned person with no other book than the Tarot, if he knew how to use it, could in a few years acquire universal knowledge."[43] He connected its trumps, the "Major Arcana," to the letters of the Hebrew alphabet and the paths of the Kabbalistic Tree, providing the starting point for practically all modern esoteric study of the Tarot, in which the cards are used for contemplation as well as for more mundane purposes such as fortune-telling.

Many others have found inspiration in these enigmatic images. One of the greatest works of Christian esotericism of the twentieth century, written by a Russian émigré named Valentin Tomberg (1900–73), is called *Meditations on the Tarot*.[44] It consists of long, discursive, though profound discussions of the Major Arcana. For Tomberg too, who was born a Lutheran but converted to Catholicism in midlife, the Tarot is the ultimate key to the Christian mysteries—including those of the church.

The English-speaking world owes much of its knowledge of both the Tarot and ritual magic to an esoteric society known as the Hermetic Order of the Golden Dawn. The Golden Dawn, as it is usually called for short, was founded in London in 1888 by three senior Freemasons with

Rosicrucian links.[45] It probably never had more than a couple of hundred members, and it splintered into several factions in 1900. But its influence on the spiritual destiny of Britain and even the United States would be hard to overestimate.

The Golden Dawn's curriculum ranged far beyond the boundaries of what is customarily called Christianity. Golden Dawn initiates made one of the first translations of the *Sefer Yetzirah* ("Book of Formation"), the earliest and most influential of all Kabbalistic texts, into English. The order's interests also included the British mysteries such as the Grail stories (believed to be a holdover from pagan Celtic traditions): two Golden Dawn members, the poet William Butler Yeats and his inamorata, the beautiful and charismatic Maud Gonne, wanted to revive the pre-Christian Celtic faith of the Irish.

Nonetheless, the Golden Dawn's numerous and elaborate initiations center on the mystery of the death and resurrection of Christ. They focus on making contact with the Holy Guardian Angel, which in the order's terms is one's own higher self or true will. To do this involves the sacrifice—the "crucifixion"—of the personal ego. Thus Christ's passion and resurrection is seen not as an event that happened once two thousand years ago but as a process that each individual must personally undergo in order to be transformed.[46]

Various heirs to the Golden Dawn legacy are using ritual magic in a Christian context today. Many of these trace their lineage back to Dion Fortune, the pen name of Violet Mary Firth (1890–1946), a Golden Dawn pupil who wrote many books on occult topics. Some of these present-day practitioners include Gareth Knight (the pen name of Basil Wilby) and his pupil Nicholas Whitehead, as well as the London-based Society of the Inner Light, founded by Dion Fortune herself.

MODERN FIGURES

The twentieth century saw a number of powerful esoteric thinkers and visionaries in the West, most of whom dealt with Christianity. One was René Guénon (1886–1951), a French metaphysician whose writings expound one major theme: a hidden esoteric doctrine that lies at the center of all the great world religions. Guénon's interests were far ranging; he began by exploring Freemasonry and Hindu teachings, and ended his life as a practicing Muslim in Cairo. In the 1920s and 1930s he turned his considerable erudition and power of thought to Christian symbolism, publishing a large number of articles on this subject in small French Catholic journals.[47] His masterpiece is probably *The Symbolism of the Cross*, which explicates the different levels of being using the model of a three-dimensional cross; we will explore it in more detail in chapter 3.

The Austrian esotericist Rudolf Steiner (1861–1925) had no direct connection with the Golden Dawn, although he too regarded himself as an heir to the Rosicrucian heritage. Steiner began as a conventional scholar—he spent several years editing Goethe's scientific writings—but his clairvoyant talents came to the fore when he was around forty, and he began to write and lecture on esoteric topics, founding an esoteric movement known as Anthroposophy ("wisdom of the human being"). He soon became a highly popular speaker and applied his spiritual knowledge to areas as diverse as architecture, physics, dance, agriculture, and education. His contributions remain highly influential today: his biodynamic method of farming has become popular in the organic movement, while the Waldorf schools, also based on Steiner's ideas, are a widespread and respected form of education across the United States and elsewhere.[48]

Steiner's ideas owe a great deal to those of H. P. Blavatsky, founder of the esoteric school known as Theosophy, and in fact for a while he was connected with the Theosophists, though he broke with them because he felt they did not pay enough heed to the centrality of the Christian mystery. For Steiner, Christ's passion and death on the cross—which he called "the Mystery of Golgotha"—is the pivotal moment in human history. Steiner's cosmology is extremely complex, and I cannot do justice to it here, but in essence he saw human and cosmic evolution as a process spanning many aeons, during which spirit incarnates into matter and then slowly evolves out of it again. Steiner believed that the Mystery of Golgotha, in which Christ's blood spilled onto the earth, was a key moment in this drama, not only redeeming humanity but spiritualizing the earth itself on a subtle level.

One of the more interesting esoteric Christian movements today was directly inspired by Steiner's teachings. Known as the Christian Community or the Movement for Religious Renewal, it was begun in 1922 by a number of people who sought Steiner's guidance in basing a religious practice on his teachings. The Community is centered on sacramental observance, principally on the Eucharist or, as it is called, the Act of Consecration of Man. The Movement is small (no figures are available, though estimates for worldwide membership range from fifteen thousand to twenty-five thousand), but it does address many modern concerns, including a need for congregational participation in ritual and equality for women: ever since its inception, the Movement has ordained women as priests.[49]

C. G. Jung (1875–1961), one of the greatest psychologists of the twentieth century, also had strong affinities with inner Christianity. Jung, though he was not connected with any church or tradition, devoted much attention to Christian symbols and ideas. One of his strangest and most powerful works is a short text called *Seven Sermons to the Dead*, written in 1916 at a time of great personal crisis. The speaker of these sermons is a Gnostic teacher named Basilides, and the doctrine it proclaims, in enigmatic language, is essentially a Gnostic myth of the loss and restoration of the primordial Pleroma or fullness.[50] In later works Jung continued to return to Christian themes: his *Answer to Job* deals with the evolution of the Old Testament God into the less wrathful deity of the New; and *Aion: Researches into the Phenomenology of the Self* investigates the symbol of the fish associated with Christ.

In esoteric thought, Jung stands out for his rigorously (and for some excessively) phenomenological approach. He is reluctant to state metaphysical truths; rather, he accepts the constraints of his profession and understands the symbols he examines simply as truths about the human psyche. Thus he is not interested in theological statements about Christ but simply sees him as a symbol of the Self, the supreme aspect of the psyche, which transcends and integrates all others.[51] If this has proved occasionally frustrating—the philosopher Martin Buber once accused Jung of trying to reduce God to psychic processes—Jung's psychology nonetheless has opened up whole new vistas on aspects of consciousness that were long obscured or ignored. Many esoteric Christians today, whether or not they consider themselves Jungians, are deeply indebted to this sage of the psyche.

Another figure who has been influenced by the esoteric Christian tradition and has influenced it in turn is G. I. Gurdjieff (1866?–1949). Born in the Caucasus, Gurdjieff early became fascinated with the unexplained mysteries of the universe and set out on a quest for knowledge that took him as far afield as Egypt and Central Asia. He appeared in Moscow in 1914 and began to take on pupils, the most famous of whom was the philosopher P. D. Ouspensky (1878–1947). Fleeing Russia with his pupils after the Revolution, Gurdjieff eventually made his way to Paris, where he taught the "Work," as his disciples continue to call it, until his death.

The sources of Gurdjieff's teaching are a matter of speculation and debate, and no really satisfying answer has emerged, but he hinted that he was teaching esoteric Christianity. At his Institute for the Harmonious Development of Man, a school he set up near Paris in the 1920s, he once told the pupils: "The aim of this Institute . . . can be expressed in few words: the Institute can help one to be able to be a Christian. Simple! That is all."[52]

The essence of Gurdjieff's philosophy has to do with "the sleep of man." Although we think we lead our lives in waking consciousness, he says, in fact we go around in a hypnotic stupor. The chief feature of this stupor is dissociation between the three principal parts of our being: the mind, emotions, and body. Only by long and assiduous work in unifying these "centers," as he calls them, can one truly fulfill the commandments of Christ. Otherwise it is impossible: a person is too much at the mercy of the conflicting centers pulling in opposite directions. "Let every one ask himself, simply and openly, whether he can love all men," Gurdjieff said. "If he has had a cup of coffee, he loves; if not, he does not love. How can that be called Christianity?"[53] For Gurdjieff, attaining higher consciousness is a prerequisite for being able to carry out the teachings of Christ.

Boris Mouravieff (1890–1966), another refugee from the Russian Revolution, insisted that Gurdjieff was presenting an incomplete and unauthorized version of esoteric Christianity. Mouravieff produced a three-volume work of his own as a corrective. Entitled *Gnosis: Study and Commentaries on the Esoteric Tradition of Eastern Orthodoxy*, it is a great though perplexing work. It resembles Gurdjieff's teaching on a number of points while differing considerably from it as well, for example, on the issue of human responsibility: Gurdjieff insisted that human beings in their state of sleep are not responsible for their actions, while Mouravieff espoused the more familiar Christian teaching that, however asleep we may be, we nonetheless remain responsible. In his last years Mouravieff taught in Geneva; after his death his students seem to have dispersed, although currently some are trying to revive his teachings.

While Mouravieff's presentation of inner Christianity remains invaluable, it is Gurdjieff who has been the more powerful and visible influence in the tradition at large. A number of those who trace their lineage to Gurdjieff and Ouspensky have explored esoteric Christianity, including the philosopher Jacob Needleman, whose book *Lost Christianity* correlates Christian ideas with Gurdjieff's, and Robin Amis, an Englishman whose book *A Different Christianity* describes his investigations into Orthodox traditions on Mount Athos (Amis is also the chief person responsible for reviving Mouravieff's thought in recent years). Other pupils of Ouspensky's have prepared translations of the *Philokalia*.[54] Maurice Nicoll, a British psychiatrist who studied with both Gurdjieff and Jung, produced an impressive esoteric approach to the Gospels in his books *The New Man* and *The Mark*.

THE NEW AGE

Gurdjieff, Jung, and Steiner are often seen as seminal figures of the New Age, a loosely defined movement that has left an indelible mark on the American spiritual landscape.[55] Other esoteric Christian influences have made themselves felt here as well, such as Rosicrucianism. The Rosicrucians of AMORC disseminated esoteric ideas throughout the world through books and correspondence courses. And one of the most famous and influential New Age communities is Findhorn, a collective based on the northern tip of Scotland, renowned for its phenomenal vegetables, allegedly produced by communicating with nature spirits. In his autobiography, Findhorn's founder, Peter Caddy, revealed that he had received much of his own guidance and inspiration from a Rosicrucian master whom he calls Dr. Sullivan.[56]

While there have been other major influences on the New Age (the prime ones being H. P. Blavatsky's Theosophy and Hinduism and Buddhism imported from Asia), it is undoubtedly true that the movement often has a strong esoteric Christian flavor. Even those with no allegiance to Christianity make frequent reference to the "Christ consciousness" or the "Christ within." But New Age teachings differ from the Christianity taught in the churches. Not only do they stress individual responsibility for one's beliefs, but they also tend to favor such doctrines as karma and reincarnation. They also lay great emphasis on personal evolution—a term borrowed from Darwin but in this case referring to the growth of the individual (and collective) soul over many lifetimes.

The Christology of the New Age is also at variance with the familiar notion of Jesus Christ as the incarnate Son of God, fully human and fully divine. For New Agers, "Christ consciousness" usually means a level of being and awareness that each of us will, indeed must, attain in the course of our evolution. Jesus Christ himself is often regarded as an *avatar*—a Hindu term meaning an embodiment of the divine. Many

New Agers would agree with Hindus (who sometimes honor Jesus as an avatar as well) in seeing Christ's coming not as a unique event but as one of many divine incarnations that have occurred over the aeons. Thus Pensatia, a New Age writer of the 1960s, speaks of "the Avatar Jesus, the Christed One."[57]

Possibly the most powerful connection between the New Age and esoteric Christianity lies in an enigmatic work known as *A Course in Miracles*. The *Course*, as its devotees call it, is one of the most curious phenomena of recent times. It is a channeled work, which means that the woman who wrote it down, a New York psychologist named Helen Schucman, did not claim to have originated it but believed it was transmitted telepathically to her—in this case, from an inner voice claiming to be that of Jesus Christ. Schucman, who personally always remained slightly skeptical about this work, shared it with several associates, who published it privately in 1975. Since then the *Course* has sold hundreds of thousands of copies (chiefly through word of mouth) and inspired countless study groups all over the world. Best-selling authors like Gerald Jampolsky and Marianne Williamson borrow liberally from it.[58]

The *Course* is a twelve-hundred-page work consisting of a text setting out its theory, a workbook containing 365 daily lessons as a "course in mind training," and a brief teacher's manual explaining some basic concepts in more detail. It teaches the "Atonement" between God the Father and the Son, the collective consciousness of humanity. Atonement is needed because at the beginning of time the Son managed to introduce a thought of separation into his relationship with God, and so retreated into the fragmentation of the body and the physical world. These are the product of separated mind, known as the "ego."

Some have remarked the resemblance between the *Course* and certain Gnostic teachings, particularly the notion that the world we know is the product of a lower and deluded form of the mind. In the *Course*'s teaching, God creates ceaselessly as a means of extending his love. His creations, including us as the collective Son of God, have the power to create in love as well but in our self-generated sense of fear and separation have instead made the world we see. We must escape from this deluded frame of mind. "My meaningless thoughts are showing me a meaningless world," says one of the lessons in the workbook. "I can escape from the world I see by giving up attack thoughts," says another.[59]

So far this sounds like the world hatred of the Gnostics. But here the *Course* departs from Gnosticism. If the world we see is ultimately a delusion, then nothing in it is real; God's true and loving creation cannot be harmed. Forgiveness is thus the only sane response to all events, however dark and evil they may appear: "Forgiveness is my function as the light of the world," the *Course* instructs the seeker to say.[60] Its ultimate message is uncompromising love and forgiveness despite all appearances. "There is one thought in particular that should be remembered throughout the day," it says. "It is a thought of pure joy; a thought of peace, a thought of limitless release because all things are freed within it."[61]

The eloquence and power of the *Course*'s teachings have provoked a great deal of comment. There has been much debate over whether it could really have been channeled by Jesus. Fundamentalists charge that its teachings do not always accord with Christ's words in the Gospels—but then the *Course* admits as much itself, arguing that the Apostles misunderstood and distorted Jesus' message. (Many modern scholars agree.) In the end, however, there is no way of proving or disproving claims about the work's unseen author. Like all teachings and scriptures, the *Course* must be taken on its own terms—not by way of credentials but by how it speaks to one's own being.

The fact remains that the *Course*, as thousands of people have found, is a powerful means of spiritual transformation. Although it is sometimes misrepresented as a compendium of feel-good nostrums, actually it teaches a rigorous form of mental discipline that, if scrupulously observed, would lead one to exclude all thoughts of hate and negativity. Anyone who carried out its teachings in full would be a saint.

CONTEMPORARY CHURCHES AND GROUPS

Today a number of churches and denominations (all extremely small, the largest probably claiming no more than five thousand members nationwide) claim to present esoteric Christianity. They include the Christian Community; several Swedenborgian denominations; and the Liberal Catholic Church, founded by a Theosophist named C. W. Leadbeater in the early twentieth century, which remains closely connected to Theosophy. There has also been a small-scale Gnostic revival, as some churches, chiefly in California, have sought to renew the Gnostic heritage for modern sensibilities: Stephan Hoeller's Ecclesia Gnostica Mysteriorum in Hollywood is a prime example. One curious case involves a small group known as the Holy Order of MANS, which began by teaching New Age

Christianity in the 1960s, but which converted en masse to an ultraconservative form of Eastern Orthodoxy after its leader's death in 1974, renaming itself Christ the Saviour Brotherhood.[62] There are many others, the vast majority consisting of no more than a congregation or two.

More mainstream forms of Christianity have also attempted to explore the inner heritage of their faith. There is a revival of the Prayer of the Heart in Western denominations as well as in Eastern Orthodoxy; Centering Prayer, a contemplative technique devised by contemporary Benedictine monks using *The Cloud of Unknowing* as a model; and the Taizé tradition, the creation of French monks who have devised a prayer service centered around an "icon cross"—a life-sized image of the crucified Jesus rendered in two-dimensional form in the manner of Orthodox icons. It is laid flat at the front of the chapel, and individuals come up and kneel before it or sometimes even lie on it as a way of releasing their personal burdens and identifying with the passion of Christ.

These are the most obvious instances of people working with esoteric Christianity today, but there are many others who avoid the public eye. Those who have managed to preserve the inner tradition through centuries of obscurity and suppression are a tiny minority, and we often know little about them either in the past or in the present. But it sometimes happens that a seeker comes upon these teachings in a form she can assimilate. The circumstances will inevitably be unique and almost certainly unexpected—a lecture, say, a book, a group, or an encounter with another person. Often the seeker hardly even realizes that something has been transmitted until later, perhaps much later. It does not matter. What *does* matter is that a certain indefinable yet very real impulse jumps the barriers of individual identity and causes something to grow inside the soul. In the language of Christ's parable, a seed has landed on good ground, and the tradition continues for another generation.

PART TWO

The Vision

2

The World and the Fall

A MAJOR THEME IN CHRISTIANITY has to do with that problematic entity known as the "world." The Desert Fathers went into seclusion to escape it; the Gnostics and Cathars reviled it; and even Christ himself speaks of the world in ambivalent or harsh terms: "He that hateth his life in this world shall keep it unto life eternal" (John 12:25). "Whoever has come to understand the world has found (only) a corpse, and whoever has found a corpse is superior to the world" (*Thomas*, 56).

The most familiar interpretation of the "world" has to do with the social order. Some early Christians no doubt equated it with imperial Rome, which treated them with such brutality. Later eras saw the world as the web of temptations that distracts the Christian from the straight and narrow path to salvation. So it is portrayed in John Bunyan's *Pilgrim's Progress*, whose hero is almost pulled from the road to heaven by Mr. Worldly Wiseman and persecuted by the riotous and wicked inhabitants of Vanity Fair. Some fundamentalists today see the world as the corrupt and immoral society of the United States. They have tried to withdraw from it into enclaves of their own making, educating children at home and avoiding intercourse with the community at large.[1]

It is easy enough to see the world this way. Most of us have found it unpleasant or hostile at times. And yet taken to its logical conclusion, this view leads both to paranoia and to a weird sanctimoniousness. Salvation becomes the property of an exclusive elect, and all those who fall outside the charmed circle are dismissed as lost, evil, or even subhuman, to be kept at arm's length lest they contaminate believers with their wickedness. Such an attitude ultimately fosters a hatred of one's fellow humans—perhaps the supreme violation of the Gospel's message.

THE WORLD AND "I"

A simple exercise may provide another avenue of approach to this notion of the world. It will probably come more easily to experienced meditators (indeed most meditative practice is, in one way or another, designed to cultivate this kind of consciousness), but even if you have no such experience, you should be able to realize the main point.

Sit comfortably, in a relaxed but alert position. Have your back as straight as possible; you can prop yourself up with pillows against the back of a chair if you like. Let your attention settle down and, to the best of your ability, allow the ordinary preoccupations of your day to subside.

Look around the room you are sitting in. It may or may not be familiar; that does not matter. Only be sure to cultivate a sense of the presence of yourself as you sit in your chair. This is where you are; around you, outside you, is the visible and sensible world.

Now close your eyes and bring your attention to your body. Be aware of your sensations—the breath, perhaps, or the beating of the heart, or the feelings in your back as it presses against the chair. If you pay attention, you can catch a glimpse of two things: an experience, a muscle sensation, say, and an "I" that is experiencing it.

Go deeper still, to the river of thoughts, images, and emotions that are probably coursing in front of your mind. You may try to stop the flow of this stream of consciousness, as it has sometimes been called. Probably you will fail. The thoughts and images, memories, ideas, speculations, and plans will most likely continue whether you want them to or not.

In this realm also you can observe two things: an "I" that is experiencing and something that is experienced. As you continue, even your most intimate feelings and desires will pass before you like images on a screen. If you can remain both relaxed and alert (admittedly a difficult balance), you may have a sense of something very quiet and small in you. It seems to have no power, no volition of its own, yet it is that in you which is constantly awake and experiences all that passes for your life. In the strictest sense, you cannot even observe it, for it is actually *that which observes*. If you look for it, you find that it continually recedes further and further, for there is no limit to this "I" that experiences. To use words attributed to Francis of Assisi, "What you are looking for is what is looking." You can follow this thread of consciousness back for as long as you like, but you may find this exercise to be of value even if you can do it for only a few seconds.

This is an extremely simple practice, but it goes to the heart of inner Christianity, for it introduces two of the primordial forces not only of an individual's makeup but also, it is taught, of the universe itself. These forces have been given many names in many traditions, but in esoteric Christianity the part that *is experienced*—whether inside ourselves or outside—is generally called the "world."

That which *experiences*, on the other hand, is known by many names: the "kingdom of heaven" or "kingdom of God," the "light," "Sophia" or "Wisdom," the "Word" or "Logos," and *nous* (a Greek word usually translated as "mind" but actually meaning something more like "consciousness"). All these terms reveal different aspects of this primordial Self, or experiencer, but for the most part this book will refer to this principle as the "I" or the "true 'I,'" pointing to the truth that this principle is not external to your consciousness but essential to it. Rudolf Steiner says, "Body and soul are the vehicles of the 'I'; it works in them. Just as the physical body has its center in the brain, the soul has its center in the 'I.'"[2] And Boris Mouravieff comments, "The consciousness of the real 'I' . . . [is] the only permanent point which exists within us, hidden behind our ever changing personality; always dragged along by the torrent of our thoughts, our feelings, our passions or sensations. . . . In modern life, contact with the real 'I' is rather exceptional."[3]

Understood in this way, these terms cast new light on many Gospel texts. When Christ says, "Be of good cheer; I have overcome the world" (John 16:33), he is giving a one-sentence summary of inner Christianity, for, as we shall see, the "I" does need to overcome the "world" to be freed. And when the Gospel says of the Logos, "The world knew him not" (John 1:10), this is because the world, strictly speaking, cannot know; it is what *is* known. "I am the light of the world" (John 8:12) points to the truth that the "I" that perceives is what makes it possible for the world to be seen at all; without a perceiver, an experiencer, it is nothingness.

In the text known as the "Hymn of the Pearl" in the Gnostic *Acts of Thomas*, the "I" is symbolized by a pearl guarded by a monster in the middle of the sea, which a young man has to go down to Egypt to rescue.

Egypt, the sea, and the monster are all symbols of the world that surrounds this pearl of consciousness but fails to devour or crush it.[4] In the words of John's Gospel, "the light shineth in the darkness, and the darkness comprehended it not" (John 1:5).

There is another set of names for this primordial duality. The "I," that which *experiences*, is known as *spirit*. The world, that which *is experienced*, is known as *matter*. Matter in this sense does not refer to physical substance alone; even a thought or emotion is "matter" in this sense. Spirit, on the other hand, is not a ghostly entity lurking somewhere in the sky. It is that which is alive and awake in us. This suggests why so many people have felt that they have sought the spirit and not found it: they do not realize that the spirit in them is literally what is doing the looking. As Christ said, "The kingdom of God cometh not with observation; Neither shall they say, Lo here! Or, lo there! for, behold, the kingdom of God is within you" (Luke 17:20-21).

If you did the exercise attentively, you may have been struck by the impression that many of the things that you thought were you are actually somehow exterior to you. This is the truth. Even conventional psychology teaches that many of our ideas and attitudes are not innate to us but are merely a matter of conditioning. Inner Christianity goes a step further and suggests that even what seems to be truly innate—the deepest instincts of the body itself—is also a part of the world that is experienced, and that the "I" can detach itself from these things. To be aware of this distinction is to begin to have inner freedom.

The "I" that is the kingdom of heaven is not the ordinary self; they are two separate things. This is one of the central teachings of esoteric Christianity. The ordinary self that goes throughout the day—which I will call the *ego*—is the you that you are most familiar with. It consists of your likes, dislikes, your social and familial role, your status in society, even your physical drives and desires. It is not the true "I"; it is an internalized picture of the world and the sum of our experiences in dealing with this world. Some texts call the ego "self-will." The fourteenth-century *Theologia Germanica* says, "The more man follows after and grows in self-will, the further he is from God and the true Good."[5] In most of us this "self-will" is much better developed than the "I" that is the kingdom of heaven.

Somewhat confusingly, certain texts speak of the *lower* self as the "I." Again in the *Theologia Germanica* we read: "The more of self and I, the more sin and wickedness, the less of self and I the less of sin. It has also been written: The more Mine and I, that is to say I-attachment and self-

ishness, recede, the more God's I, that is God himself, increases in me."[6]
But the context makes the distinction clear: here the "self and I" is the ego,
while "God's I" refers to the true "I." As Catherine of Genoa, a fifteenth-
century Catholic saint, puts it, "My Me is God."[7]

Thomas Merton, the celebrated twentieth-century Trappist monk,
elaborates on the difference between the two "I"s:

> There is an irreducible opposition between the deep transcen-
> dent self that awakens only in contemplation, and the superficial,
> external self which we commonly identify with the first person
> singular. We must remember that this superficial "I" is not our
> real self. It is our "individuality" and our "empirical self" but it is
> not truly the hidden and mysterious person in whom we subsist
> before the eyes of God. The "I" that works in the world, thinks
> about itself, observes its own reactions and talks about itself is not
> the true "I" that has been united to God in Christ. It is at best the
> vesture, the mask, the disguise of that mysterious and unknown
> "self" whom most of us never discover until we are dead.[8]

Despite the problems with this term, to speak of the higher self, the
primordial principle of consciousness, as the "I" in many ways remains the
best option. While other names cast powerful glints of meaning on this
concept, they run the risk of suggesting that this consciousness lies outside
of ourselves rather than at the center.

You may have tried to do the exercise above and felt you did not
have much success. You may have been disturbed by the phone or some
other annoyance, or you may have found you could not concentrate or
that you simply lost interest. This is perfectly common; probably everyone who has tried to meditate has had many such experiences. As a matter of practical advice, a good spiritual teacher would most likely tell you
not to become discouraged but to firmly and patiently return to the exercise, and to do this as often as distractions arise. Yet the very existence
of distractions, the very unwillingness you may feel in making any effort
toward consciousness, points up a truth to which spiritual traditions give
much weight.

In and of itself, of course, one mere exercise is of no great importance.
But the difficulties associated with it, if examined closely, turn out to be
those that pervade everyday life. Most people most of the time feel themselves to be at the mercy of the world. Frequently these preoccupations

take the form of bodily urgings: one can hardly feel at peace when cold, hungry, thirsty, or tired. Yet even if these needs are met, the mind often begins to twist itself around plans and worries about the future. It may start thinking about status, friendship, and hurt feelings and begin to tally up the intricate social balance sheet that takes up so much time and energy in human life. Or it may find itself worrying about politics, the state of the world, the fate of those far away.

If you pursue your inquiry far enough, you may decide that there is something in the mind that wants to occupy itself with these distractions, that is even fond of them or at any rate feels it cannot live without them. This may seem like a mildly interesting but perhaps ultimately trivial insight. In fact it is not; it is much more crucial than it may seem. To understand this issue more fully, it may be helpful to take another look at the legend of the Fall.

THE MEANING OF THE FALL

The problem of evil has ceaselessly preoccupied philosophers and theologians as well as ordinary people. Why are there such things as suffering and grief? Not surprisingly, the answers are manifold: evil exists so that we may have free will; it is a punishment for rebelling against the will of God; it is the necessary counterpart to good, and good would be meaningless without it; or it is an illusion, the result of a misperception. All these answers have some merit, no doubt, but after a while one goes away with the unsettling impression that they are little more than guesses or rationalizations.

The Christian view of the origins and nature of evil has always been based on the story of the Fall in Genesis. Despite its antiquity, it remains one of the most profound explanations of the human predicament—as is shown by the fact that it continues to live in the minds of people who no longer take it literally. And of course it makes no sense to take it literally. We have already seen Origen's comments that "these passages, by means of seeming history, though the incidents never occurred, figuratively reveal certain mysteries." Obviously God did not get mad at the human race because somebody ate a piece of fruit in Armenia six thousand years ago. But this need not blind us to other truths that are revealed in the Genesis account and indeed cannot be expressed any other way.

The story is familiar: the fruit of the "tree of the knowledge of good and evil" is forbidden to the primordial man and woman. God warns, "In the day that thou eatest thereof, thou shalt surely die." The serpent, who is "more subtil than any beast of the field," tells them the opposite: "Ye shall not surely die. . . . Your eyes shall be opened, and ye shall be as gods, knowing good and evil" (Gen. 2:17–3:5).

Who is telling the truth in this curious myth? Most people assume that God is right and the serpent is lying. But the serpent does not seem to be lying. For when the man and the woman eat of the fruit, their eyes are in fact opened. For the first time they know they are naked, and they cover themselves with fig leaves.

On a closer look it seems to be God who is the liar, since the punishment meted out to the disobedient couple is not death, but rather a painful and burdensome life. God tells the man, "In the sweat of thy face shalt thou eat thy bread," while to the woman he says, "In sorrow shalt thou bring forth thy children."

The ancient Gnostics were inspired by this strange tale to create their theology of two gods. One was the inferior deity called the Demiurge. He created the man and woman but was jealous of them and so forbade them to eat of the Tree of Knowledge. The serpent, in contrast, as the messenger of the true, good God far above, inspired the first pair to partake of the fruit that opened their eyes. The Demiurge, along with all his creation, is evil. The only hope for humanity is somehow to find an exit from this aberrant universe.

And yet in the end it seems misguided to regard the Creator God as wicked. A closer reading of the Genesis account suggests that the disobedient man and woman were not punished but given what they wanted. They wished to "know good and evil." Knowledge in its truest sense is not factual knowledge, knowledge "about" something; it is direct experience of it. The familiar biblical use of the word "to know" to refer to sexual intercourse points to this truth. The man and woman could not know good and evil without experiencing these things directly, so they were cast out of a garden of comfort and bliss and sent into a world where food comes only through hard work and where childbirth is painful and dangerous. They entered the world that we see around us.

The tradition often portrays the Fall as enslavement to sensual experience. The Orthodox sage Maximus the Confessor writes, "The tree of knowledge of good and evil would . . . be the body's power of sensation, which is clearly the seat of mindless impulses. Man received the Lord's commandment not to involve himself actively and experientially with these impulses, but he did not keep that commandment."[9]

The inevitable consequence was an inversion of human life as God had meant it to be. In the primordial state, the man and the woman had been placed in the garden to tend it and to keep it. In that condition the "I" functioned as it was meant to; nature and the world submit to it naturally. This is the inner meaning of those myths in which Adam exercises a benign rulership over the animal kingdom in the garden. The Bible says that God himself brought all living creatures to Adam "to see what he would call them" (Gen. 2:19).

Such is not our situation today. We are at perpetual variance with nature, sometimes seeming to gain the upper hand, sometimes falling victim to the predations of tooth and claw. Inner Christianity teaches that the Fall was a descent into the life we know, with its urgings and desires and distractions. In the primordial state, the true "I," the kingdom of heaven, was the rightful ruler of human life. In life as we know it in ourselves, the world is the boss; the "I" is small, attenuated, and often helpless. This is the fallen state. We experience it in almost every waking moment. It is the "death" of which God warned the primordial couple.

This cosmic descent or "death" is sometimes portrayed as ignorance or obliviousness. In the "Hymn of the Pearl," for example, the young hero, the scion of a royal house, becomes besotted with the Egyptians' food and drink and forgets his origins. At other times it is characterized as willful disobedience, as when the Prodigal Son decides to leave his father's house and dwell in a foreign country. His sensual indulgence leads to pain and remorse and he soon longs to return home (Luke 15:11–16). This, Christ seems to be saying, is our position in the world.

The Fall offers one example of how inner Christianity departs from a literalistic rendition of Genesis. The Garden of Eden was not a place on earth. The garden of delight ("Eden" means "delight") existed on another plane from the physical realm we know. This is the world of "forms," or what is sometimes called the imaginal realm. The primordial man and woman were made of subtler stuff than our physical bodies are now; this is the hidden meaning of the "dust of the earth" from which man was formed. Only after the Fall did humanity descend into physicality. But it is not the state we were meant for, and there is always some measure of discomfort and dissatisfaction with life here.[10]

Many people have some experience of what Genesis seems to mean by the "garden" or "Eden." You may recall a dream you may have had at some point in your life: you were in a realm in which everything was perfect and in which you felt completely at home—so much at home, in fact, that the idea of returning to your customary waking life depressed you somewhat. You may have spent the next day or so longing to return to such a dream—and you may also have had the odd sense that this was not a dream in the ordinary sense, for your consciousness was as lucid and alert as in what passes for waking life. This may have been a memory of the primordial state of humanity—and an expression of the desire to return to it. Many legends depict this state in the form of countries that are connected with, yet are somehow apart from, our physical world. Probably the most famous example is Shambhala, the mythical realm said by Tibetan Buddhists to exist somewhere in northern or central Asia and where enlightenment is easy to attain. Tales of the Elysian Fields in Greco-Roman myth; of Belovodye, an elusive, Brigadoon-like land in the Altai mountains of Asia; and of Lyonesse and Avalon in the Arthurian tales suggest a similar idea.

One level of the descent from the "garden" of the imaginal realm could be seen as a plunge into vegetative life. Remember that the man and woman sewed aprons for themselves out of fig leaves. This points to the teaching that there is a part of human nature that has much in common with plants: we are born, grow, reproduce, and die. A verse in Isaiah alludes to this fact: "All flesh is grass, and all the goodliness thereof is as the flower of the field" (Isa. 40:6).

Upon expelling the man and woman from the garden, the Lord also made for them "coats of skin." Artists usually portray these as animal skins, and in a sense they are right, because it is taught that we also have an animal nature: the aspect of ourselves that is concerned with dominance, status, and power—all of which we can observe in other species of social animals. In the end there is not much difference between the executive who wants to become head of the company and the stag who wants to be the lord of the herd, nor does it require great brilliance to see the essential similarity between a bar brawl and a dogfight. Thus the tradition is suggesting that the two "coverings" imposed upon the consciousness of the true "I" as it fell are the vegetable and animal levels of our own minds.

The symbols of the Tree of Life and the Tree of Knowledge of Good and Evil cast further light on our condition. The Tree of Life is a universal symbol. To some extent it arises from the natural affection people feel for trees, but there is also something else at play. The tree is the most visible and obvious image for the essential unity of all that is. It has a single trunk yet ramifies outward in countless branches and twigs and leaves: it is the living representation of the world, which for all its multiplicity has its one life in God. The Tree of the Knowledge of Good and Evil, on the other hand, is the opposite of the Tree of Life. It represents a sense of separation and polarity: we know good only by comparing it to evil. The awareness of an underlying unity has been lost: "eating of" this tree means being aware of the multiplicity while remaining oblivious to the one source from which it all arises. As the Bible says, when Adam and Eve eat of the Tree of Knowledge, they are no longer able to partake of the Tree of Life.

It may seem unjust that we today should be punished for some offense by a pair of people who lived a long time ago—if they ever lived at all. And it is true that the Bible portrays Adam and Eve as the common progenitors of the human race. Here too, though, there is another aspect to the story. In the esoteric traditions, Adam is not an ancestor but a prototype or a collectivity—one enormous being in whom each individual man and woman is but a single cell, for this esoteric Adam is androgynous. The Bible alludes to this idea in the verse "Male and female created he them; and blessed them; and called their name Adam, in the day when they were created" (Gen. 5:2).

The Martinist Papus sums up these ideas when he writes:

> To occultists, Adam does not represent an individual man, but rather the sum total of all men and women in their ulterior differentiation. This universal man filled the whole of the . . . interzodiacal space, over which he reigned as lord and ruler. . . .
>
> The imagination of Adam, . . . stirred by the rebel Angel, presented before the mind of universal man a line of reasoning which has almost invariably, and at all times, brought about every fall of man, both individual and universal. According to this line of argument: that which is seen immediately and materially is more powerful than that which is ideal, invisible and perceptible only to the spirit.

After the Fall, Papus adds, "each cell of Adam became an individual human being. . . . From that time forward man was to refine and purge away the lower principles he had added on to his nature by means of suffering, resignation in the face of trial, and the abandonment of his will into the hands of the Creator."[11] *A Course in Miracles* presents a similar idea in portraying the world of physicality as the consequence of the separation.

"Adam," in esoteric Christianity, also refers to this sense of fragmentation, loss, and bondage to the world. John Bunyan describes it with his customary vividness in the mouth of his character Faithful:

> When I came to the foot of the hill called Difficulty, I met with a very aged man, who asked me what I was and whither bound. I told him that I was a pilgrim going to the Celestial City. Then said the old man, Thou lookest like an honest fellow; wilt thou be content to dwell with me for the wages that I shall give thee? Then I asked him his name and where he dwelt. He said his name was Adam the First, and that he dwelt in the town of Deceit. I asked him then what was his work and what the wages that he would give. He told me that his work was many delights; and his wages that I should be his heir at last. . . .
>
> Then it came burning hot into my mind, whatever he said and however he flattered, when he got me home to his house, he would sell me for a slave. So I bid him forbear to talk, for I would not come near the door of his house. Then he reviled me and told me that he would send such a one after me that should make my way bitter to the soul. So I turned to go away from him; but just as I turned myself to go thence, I felt him take hold of my flesh and give me such a deadly twitch back that I thought he had pulled part of me after himself.[12]

Note that Adam is linked to the seeker through the "flesh"—the capacity to feel and sense. Thus the Fall is not so much a matter of inherited guilt or original sin but a decision that the human race has made as a whole to "know good and evil" through the experience of the senses. As the fourteenth-century English mystic Walter Hilton writes:

> Light up thy lantern and see in this image five windows by the which sin cometh into thy soul, as the prophet saith: *Mors ingreditur per fenestras nostras*. Death cometh in by our windows. These windows are our five wits [senses], by the which thy soul goeth out from himself and seeketh his delight and his feeding in earthly things.[13]

And it is undeniably true that anyone who is born as a human on this planet will come to know good and evil through the physical senses. Of course, individual allocations of happiness and woe vary wildly, often without apparent regard for justice or merit. No one can really say why.

We only know that, to some degree or another, each of us will have the occasion to taste both sorrow and joy. This, Genesis suggests, is the result of our own decision to be part of humanity and to share in its griefs and victories. This decision took place before our birth as individuals, perhaps even before the birth of time. As the Russian esotericist Nikolai Berdyaev writes, "The Fall . . . is anterior to the world, for it took place before time began and, in fact, produced time as we know it."[14]

Hence the Fall can be seen as an entrance into the dimension of time. This helps explain the meaning of the serpent in the Genesis account. Although the serpent is usually equated with the Devil as tempter and seducer, Genesis does not refer to the Devil at all. I will have occasion to talk more about the Devil in later chapters, but here let me simply point out that there is another, perhaps deeper, meaning for the serpent. It can be seen most clearly in an ancient symbol called the *ouroboros*, which means "tail-eater" and which depicts a circular snake swallowing its own tail.

The *ouroboros* is a symbol of time. Because it is circular, some may think it alludes to the idea that time proceeds in endlessly repeating cycles. This may be true to some degree, but the symbol refers more to the idea that time—or at any rate our experience of time—is a self-perpetuating ring that traps us in the realm of the Fall.

How does this work? Look at your experience in any given moment—even as you read these pages. You may have a sense of being tugged in many directions by the demands of things you have done or not done in the past or need to do in the future. Whether or not these demands are real and legitimate, they are pulling you away from your experience of the present moment. You may also notice something irritating or debilitating in these thoughts, as if they are sucking energy out of you. This is time as experienced in the fallen state.

On the other hand, you may recall occasions where you felt free and exhilarated. They may have occurred while you were gazing at some beautiful vista, while you were doing a task that absorbed you completely, or even in sexual climax. In these moments time fell away; the demands of past and future did not exist. You may remember these moments as the happiest of your life, for you were free from the tail-eating serpent known as time in whose clutches we come to know good and evil.

We may have a glimpse of the primordial experience of time from Emanuel Swedenborg's *Heaven and Hell*, where, on the basis of his own visions of unseen realms, he describes how the angels in heaven regard it:

Regardless of the fact that everything in heaven happens in sequence and progresses the way things do in the world, still angels have no idea or concept of time and space. This lack is so complete that they simply do not know what time and space are. . . .

The reason angels do not know what time is (although everything proceeds in sequence for them the ways things do in the world, so completely that there is no difference) is that there are no years and days in heaven, but changes of state. Wherever there are years and days, there are times. Where there are changes of state, there are only states.

Swedenborg goes on to say that even in the world we know, the experience of periods of time "is entirely relative to . . . states of affection. They seem short when people are involved in pleasant and happy affections, long when they are involved in unpleasant or disagreeable ones; in states of hope or expectation they seem of various lengths."[15]

The Genesis account has another curious detail. Once God discovers that the serpent has beguiled the woman, he says to it, "Thou are cursed above all cattle, and above every beast of the field; upon thy belly shalt thou go, and dust shalt thou eat all the days of thy life" (Gen. 3:14). This suggests that, in the fallen state, the circular serpent known as time has a horizontal dimension—and this is exactly how we experience it, as a linear sequence of moments. We do not usually think of time as the *ouroboros*, a self-perpetuating cycle out of which we can step if we know how.

Yet we can make this step. Despite our predicament, we as humans ultimately remain superior to the constraints of time. That is why God tells the woman, "I will put enmity between thee and the woman, between thy seed and her seed; it shall bruise thy head, and thou shalt bruise his heel" (Gen. 3:15). To "bruise the head" of the serpent is to step outside time in the kinds of moments I mentioned above. Even so, in the condition of the Fall, we always come back; this is how the serpent "bruises the heel" of the woman's seed.

Another aspect of this symbol can be seen in the fact that the serpent is a reptile. As is well known, humans possess a "reptilian brain," identified with the medulla oblongata, which governs the impulses and responses necessary for survival. While it would be absurd to suggest that this part of the brain is in itself the root of all evil, the symbol does point to the idea that in the fallen realm, life is not conscious but reflexive. A human being under the sway of the serpent's influence does not reason but reacts to desires and fears as swiftly and unthinkingly as a snake strikes at its prey. In the Christian tradition, these unthinking impulses are known as "passions." The sixth-century monk Isaac of Syria said, "Passions are like dogs, accustomed to lick the blood in a butcher's shop; when they are not given their usual meal they stand and bark."[16]

While an unconscious and reflexive way of life may be appropriate for snakes and dogs, it is less so for humans. When we react in a reptilian fashion—as we often do in daily life—we are allowing ourselves to fall subject to forces we were meant to govern. Humanity, it is taught, was created "to replenish the earth and subdue it" (Gen. 1:28). We were meant to serve as a kind of deputy of the divine in the manifest world and to rule over the realms of form rather than being ruled by them. When the true Self, the "I" that is the kingdom of heaven, is the master of our being, we are free from the stress and strife of the world. As the fifth-century mystic Isaiah the Solitary put it, "If your intellect is freed from all its enemies and attains its sabbath rest, it lives in another age, an age in which it contemplates things new and undecaying."[17] (Even for comparatively advanced practitioners, this "age" is likely to last for only a moment or two at a time.) But when we allow ourselves to be ruled by the passions, we fall prey to the world and all its disorder. Indeed, its disorder comes about because we ourselves are not doing the job we were made for.

The image of the serpent has many other dimensions. To use a term popularized by C. G. Jung, the serpent is an *archetype*: it points to a primordial energy in the human psyche that underlies all of its particular manifestations in symbol and myth. The esoteric Christian tradition offers at least two other interpretations of the serpent. One says that it represents *illusion*, the force that pulls the mind away from its own truth, ensnaring it in fantasy and desire.[18] Another says that the serpent has to do with *forethought*, which would accord with what I have already said about our experience of time. Forethought is our capacity to remember the past and anticipate the future—the source of many of our advances and many of our pains. In Greek myth the name of Prometheus, the Titan who stole fire from the gods and gave it to humanity, incurring the wrath of Zeus, also means "forethought," suggesting that this capacity endows us with technological prowess but can also alienate us from the deeper expanses of being.

None of these interpretations necessarily contradicts the others; rather, each adds further dimensions. Forethought, for example, as the ability to conceptualize a still-invisible future, can be seen as a function of

THE VISION

the imagination. If we were to try to understand the serpent as a universal archetype, we would have to look at it in the context of myths and cultures around the world—something that is clearly beyond the scope of this book. But such an examination would most likely show that the serpent is regarded as an ambiguous figure, sometimes beneficent, sometimes inimical. It endows us with great earthly power, but perhaps this comes at the cost of something greater whose loss we have almost forgotten.

If this force of the serpent pulls us away from our own inner center through our passions, does this mean that the body's desires—which seem to be the root of passion—are evil and must be stifled at all costs? This is a step that has often been taken in the Christian tradition, but it has generally proved to be a fruitless one. There is a subtle but profound difference between being internally free from passions and repressing them.

Christ's parable about the two servants, one "faithful and wise" and the other "evil" (Matt. 24:45–51), addresses this issue. Esoterically these servants refer to aspects of the human character. In the absence of the master (the "I," or true Self), the "faithful and wise servant" gives the household "meat in due season." That is to say, the conscious mind or ego, when it is in a well-ordered state, can prudently decide which urges to satisfy and which to deny. The "evil servant," on the other hand, "shall begin to smite his fellowservants, and to eat and drink with the drunken." Here one part of the psychological apparatus starts to take over and oppress the others. While this can lead to gluttony or drunkenness, it can also veer to the other extreme, creating a kind of internal monster, a superego whose indulgence lies in insane forms of self-recrimination and chastisement—internally "smiting his fellowservants." Even some of Christ's most ardent followers have not always heeded his warnings on this score. The "sabbath rest" of which Isaiah the Solitary speaks is not like the rule of a totalitarian state, where peace comes at the cost of terror and repression. Rather, it is the capacity to experience one's own feelings fully without being identified with them.

MYTH AND ACTUALITY

At this point some may ask where the scientific worldview fits into this perspective. Is it possible to give credence to the ideas that I have discussed here and continue to believe in such things as the Big Bang and Darwin's theory of evolution?

As we have seen, the Genesis account is not literally true. Rather, it is a *myth*—although exactly what that term means may not be entirely clear. Often it is taken to mean an old wives' tale, a made-up story to amuse or frighten the credulous. More recently, under the influence of Jung and his disciple Joseph Campbell, people have begun to see myths as having deep psychological import. By this view, although these tales may not be accurate pictures of reality, they say a great deal about the human psyche.

The Jungian view is helpful, but only up to a point. In the end it fails to satisfy the human urge to find out the truth behind things, to discover why the universe is as it is. As interesting as it may be to see psychological truths in the story of Eden, we may feel disappointed if it has not in some way told us how we got here.

An esoteric perspective sheds a different light on myths: it says they are telling us about dimensions other than our own. All spiritual traditions teach that there are many realms and gradations of existence, of which physical reality is only a narrow band. But human beings can experience these unseen realms as well; indeed, we have done so, not only in dreams and altered states, but also in the dimensions of existence that extend before birth and after death. Some spiritual texts refer to these as "chambers" or "palaces" or "heavens"; Eden is one, but only one, of them.

On the other hand, we do not experience these dimensions as a matter of course; except for rare individuals and those who have trained their minds through spiritual discipline, we encounter these states fleetingly and haphazardly. Furthermore, these dimensions do not always resemble our own in even the most basic elements. We have already seen how our experience of time is a result of the Fall, and, as Swedenborg suggests, time and space are different in higher realms. The philosopher Immanuel Kant held that such modalities as time, space, and causality are "categories" through which the human mind experiences the world; as we are now, we cannot know directly, but only through the lenses of fallen perception. In Paul's famous words, "For now we see through a glass, darkly; but then face to face; now I know in part; but then shall I know even as also I am known" (1 Cor. 13:12).

If this is so, then we can glimpse the dynamics of higher realms only figuratively, through symbols and stories. While these pictures are necessarily inaccurate, they are the closest we can come to the truth with our present means of understanding. This is the origin of myth and legend. It also explains why, despite the astonishing similarities among different systems of myth, there are also many discrepancies. The centrifugal force of "Babel," in which each person expresses things in his or her own words, has us in its clutches.

But there is also something profoundly beneficial in coming to grips with myths. From an esoteric perspective, learning is not so much a matter of assimilating factual information as opening up the mind so that it may experience higher truths for itself. With this kind of learning, one has a sense of remembering something that has been buried at the back of one's head. Plato alluded to this experience when he said that all learning is *anamnesis*—recollection.[19]

From an esoteric perspective, the Fall of humankind did happen, but it did not happen on any segment of history's timeline; rather, the Fall engendered time as we now experience it. Hence it neither confirms nor contradicts any scientific theories about human origins, which deal purely with the physical realm. Instead, the Fall took place in another dimension and in fact involved a collective decision made by humanity to leave that dimension. Our whole experience on this earth—its triumphs, disasters, wars, civilizations in ascent and decline, its philosophy and art, and its science as well—is a consequence and expression of the fallen state.

A gloomy picture, perhaps. Yet no one can deny that life is vexing and problematic. Unlike the animals and plants, which seem perfectly adapted to their niches in the order of life, we humans are outcasts and misfits, restless, at times struggling to rule over nature and at other times skulking in fear of it. However dimly, each of us senses that this world is not our home. Created to live in another, happier state, we chose (perhaps foolishly) to be here, where every day we eat of the Tree of Knowledge of Good and Evil, and where we earn our bread in the sweat of our brows and give birth in pain.

Yet the situation is not as grim as it may seem. While some versions of Christianity teach that the punishment for the Fall is damnation to an eternity in hell, this is not what the Bible says. The punishment (if it can be called that) for the original act of disobedience was banishment to the life we know here on earth. We are not laboring under a primordial curse that will consign our souls to perdition after a brief and uncertain life. Moreover, as Christianity has always taught, there is a way out of this fallen state, a means of overcoming the world. For the outer Christian, it comes at death, and involves *salvation*. For the inner Christian, it can come in this life, and it has to do with *gnosis*.

3

Salvation and Gnosis

I N LIGHT OF THE INNER TRADITION about the Fall, the human condition looks poignant and even grotesque. We struggle to preserve individual identity at all costs, exhausting our energies on survival and status, and yet this individuality, based on the premise of an existence separate from the human collectivity, is the very source of our difficulties. Hence the paradoxes in the teachings about escape from this plight: "Whosoever will save his life shall lose it: but whosoever will lose his life for my sake, the same shall save it" (Luke 9:24).

But like all great spiritual traditions, inner Christianity not only describes the problem but provides a means of solving it as well. On the outer level this is seen as *salvation*. The best way to approach esoteric Christian teachings about salvation is through some diagrams. Before turning to them, however, I must stress that diagrams are metaphorical, and metaphors are powerful but dangerous tools. They are a simple and effective way of conveying ideas that may enlighten the mind. Unfortunately, the mind has a tendency to attach itself to such metaphors, regarding them as reality itself rather than as simple signposts. This is the inner meaning of the commandment against idolatry. In the days when the Mosaic Law was written, people were more literal-minded than they are today, so they may have actually confused stone and wooden images with actual gods. Today, with our greater capacities for abstract thought, we are unlikely to make this mistake, but we are more likely to indulge in the idolatry of ideas and conceptual systems, forgetting that they are merely means of freeing the mind rather than freedom itself.

I stress this point here not only because it is one of the most common traps on the spiritual path but also because it may help prevent confusion as this book progresses. At various points I will discuss different schematic pictures of the worlds visible and invisible. Soon it will be obvious that not all of them can be integrated into one visual picture. In fact, each of these schemas provides a different window upon inner realities. You may find some of them more appealing and comprehensible, others alien and difficult. Some may mean nothing to you until years after you first see them. Everyone's mind has its own unseen and unknowable rhythms and timings, and what may be opaque at one point may be transparent at another.

THE THREE-DIMENSIONAL CROSS

Let us begin with the concept of space.[1] Although space as we know it is composed of three dimensions, for the sake of simplicity let us represent it in the form of a single line:

Then there is time, which we can depict as a vertical line intersecting it:

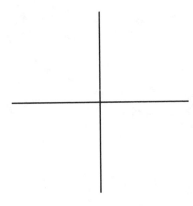

Thus we have the central symbol of Christianity, which is not only the cross of the historical crucifixion but the "cross" of time and space on which each of us is crucified. This familiar cross, however, is not the ultimate version of this symbol. A fuller representation is a three-dimensional cross. To imagine it, you would have to think of the two-dimensional cross lying flat. Then draw a third line perpendicular to this cross and going through its center. On a two-dimensional page, it can be represented thus:

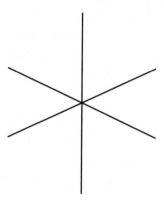

If the first two lines are time and space, what is the third? We could say that it is consciousness, interiority, the sense of an "I" experiencing, which is eternal, undying, and omnipresent. We customarily associate this with the head, so sometimes in the tradition a small semicircle is placed at the top of this line to indicate its true nature:

At this point this symbol will be familiar to most Christians. It is the *chi-rho*, so called because it is a monogram of these two Greek letters, chi, X, and rho, P, which are the first two letters of the name of *Christos*, Χριστός in Greek.[2] This gives an idea of how esotericism works. To view the Chi-Rho as a simple monogram is not in itself wrong, but the understanding of this symbol can be taken further. Most people would be satisfied to know that this symbol stands for two Greek letters, but there are always a few who suspect that something more is concealed in such images, and to these the inner tradition is addressed.

This central line, then, refers to the level of consciousness. Like all lines, it contains an infinite number of points. Each point corresponds to a state of consciousness, which in turn may be visualized as a horizontal plane. Human incarnation on earth is only one of these states or planes. Although it is the one we as humans are most concerned with, there is nothing especially privileged about it; there are many others both above and below. We can portray these planes as circles. So let us take one circle as the level of the human plane:

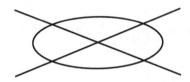

There is an ancient teaching of *evolution*. This should not be confused with the Darwinian sense of the term. Esoterically, *evolution* refers to the idea that as consciousness progresses, it passes through a virtually infinite number of different planes, or different levels of being. This process can be represented as a spiral on this three-dimensional cross:

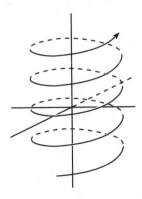

Each turn on this spiral can be viewed as a lifetime, with each of the points at either end symbolizing birth and another death. Thus, as has been commonly taught, birth in this life is death to another, previous life, which we usually do not remember. And death to this life will involve birth to another life. If we grant that there is something in human consciousness that survives death—an idea that is universal in human religion and which makes a great deal of intuitive sense as well—there are three possibilities. The consciousness can pass to a higher state, a lower state, or to one more or less like the one it knew in its previous life.

VISIONS OF THE AFTERLIFE

If you have ever gone into the Egyptian gallery of a museum, you may remember seeing a representation of the weighing of the heart after death. In these scenes, which are common in ancient Egyptian art, the heart is shown on a pair of scales; the gods are weighing it. The Egyptians believed that if the heart was heavier than a feather—that is, if it had anything on its conscience—it was consigned to a baleful afterlife. This idea has been inherited by Christianity, where the judging of the soul is usually imagined as facing an angel with a ledger book recording one's good and bad deeds—a kind of spiritual double-entry accounting. Whether one's debits or credits in the moral arena prove to be preponderant is said to determine one's fate for eternity.

Today it would be more helpful to view this individual day of judgment—the "particular judgment," as theologians call it—as a matter of a person's own predispositions rather than as an external sentence carried out by a God who is reckoning moral accounts. By this view, after bodily death a person naturally gravitates toward the level of being to which he or she is best suited.

What does this mean? Throughout our lives we are subject to conditioning of various forms: social, cultural, even religious. Much of this is, strictly speaking, exterior to the true "I." As a result, it is not likely to survive death. Many traditions hold that there is a period after physical death—forty days is a common number—during which time this exterior aspect of the self gradually dies. In essence it means that the vast majority of what we take to be ourselves—our hopes, dreams, wishes, opinions—will not long outlast the physical shell in which we are incarnated.

This may seem to contradict what Christianity teaches about the immortality of the soul. But a large part of the soul—that is, the psyche—is not and cannot be immortal. To see why, simply examine the thoughts and feelings that course through your mind during a typical day. Nearly all of them relate either to the body itself—its appetites and aversions—or to your social life in the world: your job, status, friends and family, and so on. There is no reason to believe that much, if any, of this part of your nature will survive your body's demise. You will not be worried about your health when you are dead, nor will you care about your career or your social position. Your tastes in food and sex, your manners and habits, your political and probably even your religious convictions will all be gone.

Nonetheless, *something* will survive. And, it is taught, the period after death is the time when this sorting of the eternal from the transitory will take place. This is the weighing of the soul. The British esotericist W. G. Davies puts it this way: "When a man dies he will, if he fears, burn in the flames of his terror. He will be torn by the dogs of his unfulfilled desires, cut to pieces by his guilt, until all that he has tied to himself is purified, and a little, just a little, metal—it may be gold, or copper, or mercury, or silver, or even lead—be left."[3]

This "metal," the consciousness or "I," is what endures. Its nature—what Swedenborg calls its "love" or "intention"—determines its fate. As he puts it, "After death, a person is his love or intention."[4] Swedenborg's description of hell bears this out:

> In milder hells one sees something like tumble-down huts, crowded together rather like a city, with sections and streets. Within the houses are hellish spirits, so there are constant brawls, hostilities, beatings, and clawings. There are robberies and holdups in the streets and districts.
>
> In some hells there is nothing but brothels that look disgusting and are full of all kinds of filth and excrement. There are dense forests too, where hellish spirits roam about like wild beasts, and there are underground caves in them where they flee when others are after them.[5]

Hell is not a place of punishment. Instead, it is a place that is evil because the inhabitants are evil. They are there because they want to be there and because they would not be comfortable anywhere else. The apocryphal *Gospel of Philip* tells this story:

> An apostolic man in a vision saw some people shut up in a house of fire and bound with fiery [chains], lying in flaming ointment

....And he said to them, "[Why are they not able] to be saved?" [They answered], "Because they did not desire it."[6]

C. S. Lewis expresses the same idea in his allegory *The Great Divorce*, which tells of a bus that runs daily between heaven and hell. The inhabitants of hell are free to go to heaven at any time, but they cannot stand it. It is too real for them; the blades of its grass cut their feet. As one of the inhabitants of heaven says, "All that are in Hell, choose it. Without that self-choice there could be no Hell."[7]

Anyone who has gone into a disreputable bar can understand this idea. The stranger who enters such a place, whether from curiosity or by mistake, is usually struck by the impulse to leave at once. He finds darkness, the odors of stale cigarette smoke and sour, evaporated beer, and a collection of people who seem menacing, lost, or broken. There is something unquestionably hellish about the scene. And yet a bar is a place of recreation. No one is kept there by force, and anyone who wants to leave can go at any time. Even those who work there are free to walk out and find another job. Swedenborg and Lewis are suggesting that hell is like that, as is heaven; we are free to leave these states as we choose, and it is only our own choice or "ruling love" that determines our place.

Origen has a slightly different view of these nether realms: that they are realms of correction and atonement rather than eternal damnation. Following Clement, who taught that there are many worlds before and after our own and that souls transmigrate from one to another in different lives, he suggests that "for the correction and improvement of those that need it there will be yet another world, either similar to the one that now exists, or better than it, or possibly much worse."[8]

Christ says, "In my Father's house are many mansions" (John 14:2). Visionaries over the centuries have been granted many glimpses of these "mansions" in the higher planes of existence. Often they are envisioned as realms of pleasure, where all suffering ceases and only joy is experienced. But of course such a garden of perpetual delight would soon prove boring. Swedenborg suggests that life in heaven is different, that it consists of pursuing an industrious life. Even in heaven, he says, "there is no happiness . . . apart from activity."[9] He also portrays life in heaven as a process of growth; as a spirit grows in wisdom and goodness, it moves closer and closer to the source of all wisdom and goodness, which is the Lord.

A similar perspective appears in the works of Daniel Andreev (1906–59), a Russian visionary who had rich and intricate visions of other dimensions while serving a sentence in Stalin's gulag. He too suggests that there are higher planes of reality and that we progress through them as part of our development in our lives after death. Here is his description of a realm he calls Gotimna:

> Entire forests of the enormous flowers of Gotimna bob up and down, swing and sway, making sounds of unimaginable rhythm. Their rustling is like the softest of music, never wearying, as peaceful as the sound of forests on Earth. Yet it is full of inexhaustible meaning, affectionate love, and concern for all those living there. . . . There, in sky-blue meadows and next to huge, softly glittering gold petals, we were visited by those who descend to Gotimna . . . to prepare us, their younger brothers and sisters, for the next legs of our journey.
>
> Gotimna is called the Garden of Higher Fate, for the destiny of souls for a long time to come is decided there. I arrived at a crossroads, one that lies on the path of all who ascend to that plane. For many centuries afterward it is impossible to change one's decision in any of the many worlds that are preordained there.

Andreev goes on to say that in Gotimna he had been given the choice, before his birth in Russia, to ascend to higher planes or to return to earth to carry out certain specific missions. He chose the latter.[10]

We on earth inhabit a middle realm. There are levels above and below ours; at death we have the occasion either to progress on the spiral, rising to higher levels, to descend, or to stay more or less on the same plane. This last possibility entails reincarnation. Those who are neither so pure that they have an affinity for the heavens nor so corrupt that they are drawn toward the hells stay on this round. Others, like Andreev, may choose to return to this life to accomplish a special mission.

Christian teaching has not laid much stress on reincarnation, but there have always been those like Origen who have understood that it remains a possibility. Its recent surge in popularity in the United States can be attributed not only to the influence of Eastern mysticism but also to the fact that it seems like a plausible and even desirable outcome compared to the eternal hell with which conventional Christianity has threatened people over the centuries.

Christianity's customary reticence about reincarnation seems to be inspired by three motives. In the first place, the religious authorities have believed the fear of hell to be an effective form of social control.[11] In the second place, fixation on past and future lives can present a kind of spiritual trap: a person may become fascinated or obsessed by glimpses of her past lives and even start to take a vain pride in them. (One self-proclaimed guru in the 1980s even used to give a résumé of his past incarnations on his posters.) Or there may be a temptation to put off spiritual work to the next incarnation, just as we procrastinate with the tasks of everyday life. Finally, reincarnation is not regarded as a desirable outcome for the afterlife. While returning to another human existence is not as dismal a fate as those that impel individuals to descend to hells, it is far from ideal. Christianity has ignored or downplayed reincarnation because the tradition has always offered salvation—a means of helping the individual progress to a higher plane after death.[12]

In essence, salvation consists of asking God for help so that you will not be dragged down to lower levels at the hour of death. While the Fall does not automatically condemn us to these levels, it does generate a downward momentum that must be counteracted by help from above; in Christianity, this is the salvific work of Christ. This help is given as soon as it is requested. It is not conferred by sacraments, which are mere outward signs of grace. Nor does it require adherence to a long list of beliefs. It need not even take on a specifically Christian aspect. Otherwise, we would find ourselves confronted with the dilemma that occurs to every thoughtful nine-year-old in catechism class: what about the people in the jungles of Africa who have never heard of Christ? Are they damned?

Some of the grimmer versions of Christianity decree that such people are indeed damned. But the finest and most authentic part of the tradition holds that if a person, no matter where she is, leads a good, decent, sincere life and honors God in the ways she best understands, God's help will be granted to her. Furthermore, the higher power that is God can, in its infinite compassion, assume many different guises, since no one of these will appeal to all. It can certainly assume a feminine form, as the perennial popularity of devotion to the Virgin suggests.[13] It can even take on aspects that seem weird or grotesque. We may be tempted to laugh at the bizarre religion that has formed around the memory of Elvis Presley, but this may be the most effective way by which God can address the sensibilities of certain people. Or conversely, it may be the form their own minds give to the unfathomable reality of the sacred.[14]

Salvation is not, however, merely a matter of the afterlife. God's help is offered not only at the hour of our death but among the difficulties and hardships of life in the world as well. As we know, this help does not always automatically remove such problems, but it does make them easier to bear. The skeptic may sneer at this benefit as a kind of narcotic, a self-induced palliative, but as the experiences of many indicate, help from above is real enough. Moreover, people have glimpses of divine revelation far more often than is usually believed. Some teachers say that an experience of "cosmic consciousness" is vouchsafed to everyone at least once in a lifetime, however fleetingly.

THE TWO GREAT COMMANDMENTS

What responsibilities does salvation entail? Nearly the entire New Testament, including the sayings of Christ and the writings of Paul, stresses to the point of redundancy that it is not a matter of "the Law," of merely following the rules. At the same time, there are principles to be observed, summarized in the two great commandments: to "love the Lord thy God with all thy heart, and with all thy soul, and with all thy mind," and "to love thy neighbor as thyself" (Matt. 22:36–39).

In regard to the first, God's love and mercy are beyond measure and are extended to all indiscriminately: "He maketh his sun to rise on the evil and on the good, and sendeth rain on the just and on the unjust" (Matt. 5:45). Consequently, worshiping God is not indulging his vanity or appeasing his wrath. "Loving the Lord thy God" has to do not with groveling but with opening ourselves to his beneficence. It is enjoined upon us, not as a means of ingratiating ourselves with the Deity, but as an essential form of nourishment for our own being. The services, sacraments, and prayers of the Christian faith are simply a means to this end. They are useful insofar as they nourish a sense of connection with God and keep it alive. If they do not achieve this aim, they are useless and are best discarded.

What of the second great commandment: "to love thy neighbor as thyself"? For an individual, salvation is a beginning of the reversal of the Fall. At some level, however unconscious, it involves the realization that you are not separate from the other human beings but share something vital with them. Thus you love your neighbor as yourself because essentially your neighbor *is* yourself.

If you have been blind to this truth before, indifferent to the welfare of others and usurping whatever small advantage you can take wherever you can take it, you may well feel some remorse at this insight. Remorse usually stems from the recognition that others feel the same kind of joy and pain as you do, and helps you to see the suffering you have caused others. Remorse in turn leads to repentance—the resolution to make amends for the damage done in the past and to avoid it in the future. At the same time, remorse and repentance have to have limits. If they lead to a masochistic self-loathing and self-punishment, they have gone beyond their proper bounds. It is best simply to acknowledge your mistakes, take steps to put them right, ask forgiveness, and move on.

Remorse, incidentally, has nothing to do with sins against God: God is beyond any harm or offense we can give. Ethical injunctions have their meaning and place in a human context. Even if, as the holy books say, they were granted from above, they are nonetheless designed for human beings, to make our lives together more bearable and satisfying. They are rooted in a profound awareness of how the universe is. When we transgress these rules, we are not inflicting some injury on God; it is our own happiness that is at risk.

One example has to do with *karma*. This is a Sanskrit term, imported from the East during the past century and now in common parlance. But the principle, if not the name, of karma has always been acknowledged in the Christian tradition, typically using the metaphor of sowing and harvest: "Whatsoever a man soweth, that shall he also reap" (Gal. 6:7). "For they have sown the wind, and shall reap the whirlwind" (Hos. 8:7). There is something fundamental in the nature of the world whereby an effect is like its cause and will inevitably return to its progenitor: "For he that soweth to his flesh shall of the flesh reap corruption; but he that soweth to the Spirit shall of the Spirit reap life everlasting" (Gal. 6:8). While it is true that bad things sometimes happen to good people, there is more justice in the universe than is commonly admitted, and most people most of the time receive their due.

The ethical teachings of Christ acknowledge this truth. Although we may not immediately experience the consequences of our hatred and greed, sooner or later they will come back to us. This is not a matter of divine wrath but a consequence of the structure of things; the law of karma is as implacable as the law of gravity. You cannot cause discord without experiencing ill effects yourself. Even when there is no apparent retribution, you will register a subtler but deeper response in your very nature. Evil actions make a person's "ruling love" become twisted and corrupt. This is a far worse fate than outward loss or punishment.

The moral commandments of the Gospels have another purpose as well. The Christian wins freedom of the spirit as much by interacting with others as by inner meditation. As one of the Desert Fathers said, "Unless thou first amend thy life going to and fro amongst men, thou shalt not avail to amend it dwelling alone."[15] Obedience to ethical teachings provides a means of liberating the true "I" in daily life. Christ urges, "Whosoever shall smite thee on thy right cheek, turn to him the other also" (Matt. 5:39). No one can do this without being free, at least to some extent, from identification with reactions, emotions, and other internalized aspects of the world.

All this may seem to be making salvation sound terribly simple. But salvation *is* terribly simple: "My yoke is easy and my burden light" (Matt. 11:30). Salvation is available to all for the asking. It is a free gift; it confers on us no obligation other than to receive it and to try to live a decent life. Nothing could be easier or more self-evident.

Yet there is something incomplete about personal salvation. It does not entirely counteract the effects of the Fall, for the simple reason that it is an individual matter, and individuality as we know it is the consequence of the Fall. If a given portion of the human race has been redeemed from suffering after death (a body traditionally known as the "communion of the saints"), many still have not. As long as the collectivity of Adam remains divided, "groaning and travailing in pain," the redemption is incomplete; in the end we cannot be saved alone. It is taught that the final culmination, known as the Last Judgment, will mark the end of this process of reintegration of the cosmic Adam. Until then, personal salvation contains an element of hope. As Paul writes, "We are saved by hope. . . . if we hope for that we see not, then do we with patience wait for it" (Rom. 8:24–25).

THE PEARL OF GREAT PRICE

Unlike salvation, gnosis is *not* available to all for the asking. It is rare and precious, and even those who seek after it rarely receive it fully. There are few reliable guideposts: the teachers of the present and the texts of the past offer valuable clues, but the way is completely individual and may manifest itself very differently for one person than for another. If some seem to attain it spontaneously by grace, others may work and study for a lifetime only to remain at the outer gates.

If this seems unjust, it may be helpful to remember that attaining gnosis does not ward off the terrible fate of damnation. It is salvation, offered freely and at no cost, that provides this help. Gnosis is simply a means of attaining the highest knowledge of God possible in this life. It does not confer any special reward; it is its own reward, and those who seek after it do so only because it is the deepest longing of their being, which nothing else will satisfy. Christ likens it to a "pearl of great price," which a merchant "sold all that he had" to buy (Matt. 13:46).

To see how gnosis differs from salvation, it would be helpful to go back to the spiral in the diagram at the beginning of this chapter. Remember that this spiral is wound around three axes, with the up-and-down axis representing consciousness. This consciousness is the true "I," the Logos, the center of our being. Ordinary awareness is only remotely connected with this Logos; we live at the periphery, in the "world." This life at the periphery is what I have already described as the ego, but it has other names as well; in many old Christian texts it is called the "self" with a small *s*. Gurdjieff referred to ego-consciousness as "personality" and to the true "I" as "essence";[16] Jung used the terms "ego" and "Self"; other teachings use other words. At any rate, there are these two poles of consciousness: that of the true "I" and the attenuated version of self in which we customarily live. This explains the strange but common impression that we are somehow alienated from ourselves or do not know ourselves.

Attaining gnosis or liberation in the ultimate sense means uniting one's outer consciousness with the inner, as Christ said: "When you make the two one, you will become the sons of man" (*Thomas*, 106). In terms of the diagram, it entails a journey from life at the periphery to life at the center. This is symbolized by a radius; the journey along this radius is esoterically known as the *way*. "The way" was the earliest name given to Christianity (Acts 9:2).

Traditionally, reaching the state of illumination symbolized by the center bestows a different fate from that of the ordinary person who accepts salvation. For the latter, life after death will persist in many different planes of being—higher ones, no doubt, where existence is less painful and burdensome and where spiritual aspiration faces less resistance. But those who attain gnosis are freed from this spiral entirely. They can choose to return to manifestation for a special purpose or can dwell in absorption into God—known in the Christian tradition as the "beatific vision." They are, to use T. S. Eliot's famous words in *Four Quartets*, "at the still point of the turning world."[17]

In the Gospels, one name for this still point is "the eye of the needle."[18] As Christ says, "It is easier for a camel to go through the eye of a needle, than for a rich man to enter the kingdom of God" (Mark 10:25). This means that the "I" has to be very fine and subtle to reach this still center of being. A "rich man"—one who is encumbered not only with property but with the heavy baggage of a pompous self-image—is too big to make it through. Obviously, this is an inner condition and so does not necessarily refer to all rich people, though in practice it probably applies to most. Francis de Sales, a Catholic spiritual teacher of the early seventeenth century, observes:

> A man is rich in spirit if his mind is filled with riches or set on riches. The kingfisher shapes its nests like an apple, leaving only a little opening at the top, builds it on the seashore, and makes it so solid and tight that although waves sweep over it the water cannot get inside. Keeping always on top of the waves, they remain surrounded by the sea and are on the sea, and yet are masters of it. Your heart . . . must in like manner be open to heaven alone and impervious to riches and all other transitory things.[19]

Money—"mammon," as Christ called it—is only one of the forms the force of the world takes. There are people for whom money holds no allure but who are beguiled by sex, pleasure, or power. And for those who are indifferent even to these temptations, there is always the trap of apathy (*accidie* or *acedia*, derived from a Greek word meaning "not caring," are names sometimes used in the tradition). There are many variations, which will take on slightly different forms in everyone. Freeing oneself from the world requires overcoming these drives in oneself, however they appear.

What are the characteristics of those who have reached the "still point"? The *Theologia Germanica* describes them thus: "The illumined ones live in freedom. This means that they are free from fear of pain or hell. They have abandoned hope of reward or heaven. They live in pure surrender and obedience to the eternal Good, in love that frees."[20]

Very few attain this level. Perhaps no one on this earth is able to maintain a state of perfect illumination from moment to moment. Even fairly advanced practitioners probably reach a glimpse of gnosis and then fall back into the preoccupations of the world; this may explain the experience of "dryness" or "aridity" that is described in so many spiritual texts. When one notices this has happened, one picks oneself up and begins again. Thus vigilance and watchfulness are always essential, and complacency always dangerous. As Christ says, "Watch ye therefore, and pray always" (Luke 21:36).

But there are said to be a few who attain this consciousness to a degree that their being is totally transformed, becoming pure and luminescent, far surpassing the limits of what we understand as embodiment.

The Transfiguration of Christ, in which "his face did shine as the sun and his raiment was as white as the light" (Matt. 17:2) is a prototype of this experience. The Orthodox tradition says that those who reach this goal have attained *theosis* or deification; the individual literally becomes divine. As the fourth-century Church Father Athanasius the Great put it, "God became man so that man could become God."

For those of us in the battlefield of daily life, *theosis* may seem a distant and elusive goal. Yet human capacities—and divine grace—reach far beyond what is commonly believed possible. A story from the Desert Fathers gives a hint of what such transformation may be like:

> There came to the abbot Joseph the abbot Lot, and said to him, "Father, according to my strength I keep a modest rule of prayer and fasting and meditation and quiet, and according to my strength I purge my imagination; what more must I do?" The old man, rising, held up his hands against the sky, and his fingers became like ten torches of fire, and he said, "If thou wilt, thou shalt be made wholly a flame."[21]

4

The Second Birth

W_{E KNOW, AND HAVE BEEN REMINDED} often, that the Christian life centers around being born again. In outer Christianity, this rebirth is a comparatively simple matter: a person chooses to accept salvation and reorients his life around God; the church marks this decision with the sacrament of baptism. Rebirth in inner Christianity is not so easy. Salvation is a starting point only; the goal beyond is gnosis. This rebirth on a higher octave is a long and arduous process; like the pearl of great price, a person literally has to "sell all he has" to attain it.

To explore the esoteric view of rebirth, we might begin with the celebrated passage in the Gospel of John:

> Jesus answered and said unto him, Verily, verily, I say unto thee, Except a man be born again, he cannot see the kingdom of God.
>
> Nicodemus saith unto him, How can a man be born when he is old? can he enter the second time into his mother's womb, and be born?
>
> Jesus answered, Verily, verily, I say unto thee, Except a man be born of water and of the Spirit, he cannot enter into the kingdom of God.
>
> That which is born of the flesh is flesh; and that which is born of the Spirit is spirit.

Marvel not that I said unto thee, Ye must be born again.

The wind bloweth where it listeth, and thou hearest the voice thereof, but canst not tell whence it cometh, and whether it goeth: so is every one that is born of the Spirit (John 3:3–8).

Here Christ mentions three different levels in human nature: "the flesh," "water," and "the spirit." There is also a fourth level, above all these: the "kingdom of God."

The first three correspond to the three parts of human nature as seen in esoteric Christianity: the body, the soul or psyche, and the spirit. These can be best understood directly by going back to the exercise at the beginning of chapter 2. If you did this exercise observantly, you no doubt noticed that that which you experience—the world—has two different aspects, or one might almost say flavors. The first is that of bodily sensations and impulses. This is what Christ and the New Testament authors are talking about when they speak of the "flesh." Another term used for this is the *carnal* nature: "carnal" is derived from the Latin *caro*, or "flesh."

The second form of experience consists of mental images, thoughts, and emotions. They differ from carnal impulses in that they do not arise from any immediate or obvious physical stimulus. A carnal impulse comes directly from the body; hunger, for example, is the body's cry for food. Emotions like sadness or joy usually do not have any apparent physical cause (even if, as we now know, there is some neurological component to them). The same is true of the ceaseless flow of images that pass before the mind's eye.

I use the term *flow* deliberately, for there is a long custom of likening this part of the human mind to liquid. There is the "stream of consciousness" technique in literature, and in ordinary language we often use similar metaphors, speaking of a "torrent of emotions" or of someone as being "adrift" or "at sea." Jung noted that in dreams and myths the psyche is often symbolized as a body of water. And in the "Hymn of the Pearl" we have seen how the pearl is guarded by a monster at the bottom of the ocean.

Thus the psyche or soul—the thoughts and emotions that flow ceaselessly, and usually uncontrollably, through our being—is known symbolically as "water." This is almost certainly what Christ is referring to in the passage from John. And as any reader of the Gospels will recollect, the theme of water recurs constantly in many contexts.

There are, then, two aspects to experience: the physical and the psychological—"flesh" and "water." Finally, there is the third level, the most subtle and mysterious—the spirit. Even many religious writers do not seem to know what this term means, or how, for example, it differs from the soul. But as we have already seen, the "spirit" refers to the ground of consciousness, the "I" that experiences.

Christ says the spirit "bloweth where it listeth." That is to say, it cannot be limited by any particular type of experience. You can feel ecstasy or grief, pleasure or torment; whatever arises in the course of existence, there is always something that perceives it. And, the inner traditions say, this is immortal, indestructible, and ultimately unaffected by what it experiences. Even death changes the content but not the fact that there is something that perceives this content.

Here is one of the central truths of religion the world over. It is also known intuitively even apart from religion. One of the simplest but most eloquent expressions of this knowledge comes from Thornton Wilder's play *Our Town*:

> Now there are some things we all know, but we don't take'm out and look at'm very often. We all know that *something* is eternal. And it ain't houses and it ain't names, and it ain't earth, and it ain't even the stars . . . everybody knows in their bones that *something* is eternal, and that something has to do with human beings. All the greatest people ever lived have been telling us that for five thousand years and yet you'd be surprised how people are always losing hold of it. There's something way down deep that's eternal about every human being.[1]

This "something eternal" is the true "I," the spirit. In the state in which we now live, this "I" is submerged in the forces of "water" and the "flesh." It is not harmed thereby, but it remains more or less inaccessible and its potential is not realized. It is the "seed" of which Christ speaks in his famous parable (Matt. 13:3–8), which addresses the fate of these sparks of consciousness in different individuals. Some of it falls by the wayside, some of it is eaten by the "fowls of the air," and so on.

Gnosis is the complete liberation of this "I" from its immersion in the physical and psychological worlds; it is the reversal of the Fall. In essence it consists of mastering each of these levels of being: the physical, psychological, and the spiritual. This is what it means to be "born again." This rebirth gives entrance to the "kingdom of God," the fourth and highest level of experience of which we as humans are capable.

CHRIST'S THREE TEMPTATIONS

For an individual, the way of inner mastery is set out symbolically in Christ's temptation in the wilderness. Christ is baptized by John in the River Jordan, and "being full of the Holy Ghost returned from Jordan, . . . was led by the Spirit into the wilderness, being forty days tempted of the devil" (Luke 4:1–2).

This verse suggests that the entire purpose for Christ's retreat into the wilderness was to be tempted. After the spirit is quickened in a human being—whether by a conversion experience or simply by the quiet movement of an inner longing—he or she must then proceed to face down the forces of the world. They can be seen as three major challenges.

The first has to do with the flesh. Christ's first temptation comes after he has fasted for forty days. The number forty has considerable esoteric significance, as we can see from the forty days of rain in Noah's Flood, the forty years the Israelites wandered in the wilderness, and the forty days between Christ's resurrection and ascension. In essence it refers to a full completion of a cycle. Here, however, it also has a more straightforward sense, since forty days are roughly the maximum length a person can live without solid food. Jesus has thus completed a cycle of purification; he is also at the end of his physical endurance.

At this point the Devil, the personification and embodiment of all the world's forces, suggests that Jesus turn the stones around him to bread. Jesus refuses, citing the verse from Deuteronomy, "Man shall not live by bread alone, but by every word of God" (Luke 4:4; cf. Deut. 8:3).

This passage suggests that the first level of mastery has to do with the body and its appetites; as Paul writes, "I keep under my body, and bring it into subjection" (1 Cor. 9:27). Essentially there is nothing all that arcane about this aspect of the work. Much of the socialization of ordinary life has to do with controlling the body's impulses. You may be famished, but you wait until everyone's plate has been served before you begin to eat. You want to doze off in the middle of the afternoon, but you drink a cup of coffee and go on with your job. Or you feel a strong sexual pull toward someone, but you refrain from showing it.

Most of us in fact govern the body by means of social expectations—usually an internalized sense of "other people," often imagined as an impersonal "they." This internalized social construct, of which one's own ego is a part and which even in a sense constitutes the ego, exists at the level of the psyche, which rules (or should rule) the body, the level below it.

Certain people never reach this stage. They are restrained only by the direct fear of punishment—the presence of the policeman, the threat of jail, the realization that the person whose wallet they are eyeing is bigger and stronger than they are. They are known in the tradition as "carnal" people. Another term that sometimes appears is *hylic*, from the Greek *hyle*, or "matter." Sociopaths are an extreme example of this type.

Life at the carnal level is brutal and unpleasant. It is a human imitation of animal life, although what is perfectly natural and appropriate for animals becomes repulsive in human beings. Swedenborg evokes it in his description of hell, with its crime, quarreling, and squalor. Paul refers to this level when he addresses the Corinthians: "For whereas there is among you envying, and strife, and divisions, as ye not carnal?" (1 Cor. 3:3). This is slavery in the esoteric sense: the inability to act of one's own initiative, reacting only to stimuli from the outside, always covetous, resentful, suspicious. None of this, of course, has to do with intellectual attainment or social class. "Carnal" people are found among the rich and well educated, just as those who are spiritually advanced often appear on the margins of society.

Nor is it a matter of graduating permanently from the carnal level, so that one need not concern oneself with these urges or feel the need to watch over them. It is true that some esoteric Christians, the Gnostics in particular, took the idea of levels of inner development to the point of saying that the teachings of Christianity were different, even the opposite, for the spiritual elite than for the ordinary run of believers: spiritual or "pneumatic" Christians did not need to pay attention to moral rules, having transcended them.[2] But the tradition has generally repudiated this view. There *are* people who are more advanced than others, but no one is so advanced that he cannot easily descend to lower levels at more or less any moment. This helps explain the strong stress Christianity lays on humility and watchfulness.

Christian masters in fact often mention the need for bodily self-control as an aid to vigilance. The body is kept on a tight rein, neither indulged nor victimized. Regarding diet, John Cassian observes, "At times the body becomes enervated through the undue lack of food and sluggish over its spiritual exercises, while at other times, weighed down by the mass of food it has eaten, it makes the soul listless and slack." Cassian adds, "When the Apostle said, 'Make no provision to fulfill the desires of the flesh' (Rom. 13:14), he was not forbidding us to provide for the needs of life; he was warning against self-indulgence."[3] Similar exhortations are made about sleep. Many monastic orders have a tradition of rising at night for worship in obedience to the verse, "At midnight I will rise to give thanks to thee because of thy righteous judgments" (Ps. 119:62), although again this is not to be pursued to excess.[4]

Similar demands appear in ordinary life. Few of us live as monks today, but most of us have to pay some attention to what food we eat. For many, duty makes it necessary to rise in the night. If you work as a baker, you may have to get up at three in the morning for your job; a mother has to do the same for her baby. The chief difference between the esoteric approach and that of outer life is that for the esoteric Christian, this self-discipline is subordinate to the central goal of gnosis.

Control of sexuality is one of the most fraught and ambiguous aspects of this need to "keep the body under." Sex differs from other basic bodily needs such as food or sleep in at least two respects. In the first place, it at least ideally requires the participation of another human being. This heightens the possibility for enjoyment, but it also raises the prospect of emotional confusion and pain, which few manage entirely to avoid.

In the second place, unlike food or sleep, sex is not absolutely necessary for individual survival. Many people live perfectly well as celibates. These considerations have led many in the inner Christian tradition to turn away from sex entirely. Paul seems to have done this. So did the Desert Fathers and the Cathar *parfaits*. Although some scholars, such as Morton Smith, point out that there has been something of a libertine tradition in Christianity that may well go back to Christ himself—"a friend of publicans and sinners" (Matt. 11:19)—most of the tradition has been extremely negative about sexual expression.[5] Exhortations to purity are countless, and the war with the Devil often seems to have centered around a struggle with unwanted sexual impulses.

Today Christianity is excoriated from many sides for promoting sick and damaged attitudes toward sexuality—a charge that has much truth to it. This tendency is probably best understood by recognizing that Christianity, like any religion, was to some extent the creation of its formative years. It grew up in the late Roman Empire, when sexuality had become brutal and compulsive. (We need not take the Christians' word for this; the testimony of pagan authors like Tacitus, Suetonius, and Juvenal is ample.) The young religion no doubt overreacted to its surroundings, becoming rigidly puritanical and promoting sexual standards that it has never been completely able to enforce. While it is important to recognize this fact, such recognition need not commit us to repeating the mistakes of the past. At the same time the essential point about mastery of the carnal level still stands, because even if you do not choose a life of celibacy, you still have to control your desires to some degree. Sexual urges arise constantly; it is not wise or even feasible to indulge them all.

Given that some kind of impulse control is essential to any adult life, how does an esoteric attitude toward the flesh differ from that of society at large? For the most part, social control is a matter of repressing desires and impulses. If for one reason or another they cannot be expressed or satisfied, one tends to push them behind the screen of consciousness. Esotericism has a different approach. Rather than repressing the passions, the trick is to feel them as fully as possible without yielding to them or becoming identified with them.

This can be practiced in almost any setting. Take the quintessentially American irritation of being cut off in traffic. A common response is to react—to honk or curse at the person or at least mutter under your breath. If you do *not* react, it is usually a matter of habit—the good manners inculcated from childhood—or fear of retaliation. In these cases, you may have a sense of what colloquial language calls "putting a lid on it," stifling the energy and letting it simmer underneath.

To turn this experience into an esoteric practice, when you are cut off in traffic, you can restrain the impulse to react *while feeling the irritation fully*. It is most helpful to feel it somatically as much as possible. If you do this, you may even notice a kind of subtle "burning" or effervescence in some part of the body, say, the limbs or abdomen. If you keep some attention on this sensation, you may notice that the irritation exhausts itself and that its energy is somehow recycled into your system. You have burned up the emotion instead of carrying it around.

There is more to this practice than simply getting rid of an annoyance. Although the theory of this esoteric transformation can become quite complex, in essence it involves two forces that have become entangled with each other.[6] You have become identified with a passion: the "I" is enmeshed in the world. The method above is a way of liberating the "I" from this entanglement. You can practice it on a moment-by-moment basis with any irritation that may come up. Pragmatically you will find that you need a certain amount of effort and attention simply to remember to do this practice. Even if you resolve to carry it out, often enough at first you will probably forget until well after the impulse has passed. At a later stage you may remember the practice while the passion is arising, but you may somehow find yourself unable to do it. Eventually, however, if you persist, you will succeed. It is essentially no different from learning any other technique: a certain amount of failure is to be expected at the beginning. Very likely as a baby you were not able to walk the first time you tried.

Nonetheless, the effort is worth making. In the language of the old alchemists, such a practice will help transmute the "lead" of ordinary experience into the "gold" of consciousness. Such a process requires heat—the "burning" that you may have experienced. In esoteric Christianity, this is sometimes called the "fire." As Christ says in Revelation, "I counsel thee to buy of me gold tried in the fire, that thou mayest be rich" (Rev. 3:18).

At first it is best to use this technique with small and simple things, such as being cut off in traffic, dealing with a surly store clerk, or feeling a sexual thrill when someone attractive passes by on the street. Ephemeral feelings like these come and go all the time and can easily be dealt with. When it comes to more powerful and long-lasting passions—a sexual attraction to a friend's spouse, a deep-rooted anxiety, or a long-standing grudge against someone in your family—you may need to bring other approaches into play.

MASTERY OF THE SOUL

This takes us into the level of the soul or psyche, the second stage of esoteric mastery. The psyche is the structure of thoughts and emotions that constitutes inner life in human beings. Paul speaks of it as the "natural body" (1 Cor. 15:44–46). Here the word "natural" is used to render the Greek word *psychikos*, which means "having to do with the psyche." This translation suggests that we are dealing with the level of what is "naturally" human as opposed to the carnal level, which we share with animals and even to some degree with plants.

The level of the psyche is reflected in the second temptation of Christ (by Luke's account; Matthew's order is different): "And the devil, taking him up into an high mountain, shewed unto him all the kingdoms of the world in a moment of time." The Devil promises him "all this power and . . . glory" if Jesus will worship him. Jesus refuses, saying, "Get thee behind me, Satan: for it is written, Thou shalt worship the Lord thy God, and him only shalt thou serve" (Luke 4:6–8).

Now we are no longer at the level of carnal or animal urges. Animals do not build "kingdoms of the world." And humans cannot build such kingdoms unless they have some mastery over their immediate physical impulses. To build a civilization requires a great deal of work as well as forethought. One has to face many obstacles, physical and internal, and overcome them with patience and insight. These are essentially human virtues. Moreover, no one can build a civilization alone: to rule over a kingdom requires the help and cooperation of other people. To be an effective leader means guiding and even manipulating the psyches of others, and one cannot do this unless one has achieved some mastery over one's own. While there may be leaders whose self-control in private life is far from perfect, in practice almost all have the ability to contain themselves in matters pertaining to their ambitions. Reactions of anger, fear, desire, and personal dislike are subordinated to a higher goal of power. This dynamic operates in business and the military as well as in politics; in fact, it is indispensable to success in all structures of authority. Here the carnal level obeys the psyche, which is itself centered around a ruling impulse: the desire for power or glory.

This is a higher stage of development than many people achieve in their lives. It is quite true, of course, that nearly all of us in some way or another lust for success. We dream of power and esteem, luxury and wealth. But in most of us these desires are poorly coordinated; they conflict with each other, they are stymied by fears and anxieties, and they are impeded by the carnal self, with its greed for immediate satisfaction. Often we simply prove too lazy to accomplish our own aims. Gurdjieff took this idea to the point of contending that, as we are now, we are not one unified "I" but a mass of swarming, struggling, little "I"s, each of which is king for a minute. "Man is a plurality," Gurdjieff said. "Man's name is legion."[7]

Those who have mastered the psychological level are not quite so dissociated. In their case an overwhelming urge to achieve has managed to subordinate the other aspects of their being—at least temporarily. This urge could be linked to the "evil servant" in the parable I discussed in chapter 2. Yet often enough the other "servants" manage to get their own back sooner or later. We see this in public figures whose careers are subverted by their own malfeasances. Probably in these cases the little "I"s have sharpened their swords beneath the surface of consciousness and waited to take vengeance at their leisure.

Hence mastery of the "natural" level in itself has little or nothing to do with spirituality. In fact, it may serve as an obstacle, as the temptation of Christ suggests. If he had wanted worldly power, he would have bowed to the "prince of this world": he would have made ambition his god and gone no further. It is a bargain that many would willingly make and have made for much smaller recompense. Such a bargain is not a matter of having Satan appear with a contract to be signed in blood, but rather of long and persistent (though often subtle) compromise of one's own inner integrity for the sake of power or gain. Those who do this close themselves off to higher development, chiefly because they cannot see its value: "The natural man receiveth not the things of the Spirit of God: for they are foolishness unto him; neither can he know them, because they are spiritually discerned" (1 Cor. 2:14).

The parable of the evil servant in Matthew 24 speaks of the "lord," who finally takes charge over the household. The "lord" is the spirit, the true "I." It is the right and proper ruler of the household that is the human self. Unlike the evil servant, it holds its authority by right, and the other, little "I"s will submit to it. But when the lord returns, he may find that, like Odysseus, he has some work to do to put his house in order. Some of these subpersonalities, rebellious and self-willed, may be in need of subjugation; in the language of the parable, "there shall be weeping and gnashing of teeth" (Matt. 24:51). This process involves the extremely important and difficult task of mastering the thoughts and emotions—a subject that has received much attention in inner Christianity.

A crucial step lies in recognizing that we are not our thoughts and emotions. Although in exterior life, we are completely identified with these things, believing that they are ourselves, they are not, as you may have discovered from the exercise at the start of chapter 2. If there is something in you that can see the contents of your psyche as upon a screen, it must necessarily follow that you are not these contents—at least not entirely. Once you realize this, you can gradually begin to free your consciousness from them.

Esoteric Christianity stresses that these mental events are ultimately extraneous to us, and even gives them names that emphasize this exteriority. Emotional disturbances are in Greek called *pathe* (*pathos* in the singular)—literally, "passions."[8] The word *passion* is a curious one. It can refer to strong desires like love, but we also use it to speak of suffering, as in the Passion of Christ. Both of these usages point to the root meaning of the word, which comes from the Latin *pateri*, "to suffer." (*Pathos* in Greek has exactly the same connotation.) Christ's Passion involved suffering inflicted from the outside, but the use of this word, which has a long heritage in the Christian tradition, indicates that our emotions and desires too are something that are inflicted from outside the true Self. The old texts make countless references to temptations by the Devil. This may seem a quaint manner of speaking, but in essence the Devil is the personification of the attractive power of the world. The Hindus refer to something similar in speaking of *maya*, or "illusion." This force generates the emotions that pull consciousness away from its center.

The passions take on manifold forms. The classic list of the Seven Deadly Sins provides a catalog: pride, gluttony, anger, lust, sloth, envy, covetousness. Note that these are not external offenses like murder or theft; they are all internal states. The Christian tradition has always stressed that in order to do an evil deed, one must first have an inner predilection to do so: "Ye have heard that it was said by them of old time, Thou shalt not commit adultery: But I say unto you, That whosoever looketh on a woman to lust after her hath committed adultery with her already in his heart" (Matt. 5:27–28).

Like the passions, mental images are regarded as ultimately external to the true "I." In Eastern Orthodoxy, they are called *logismoi*, which roughly means "products of the creative mind," or *logos*.[9] *Logismoi* are frequently portrayed as intrusions by the Devil or his minions, but again they are perhaps best seen as spontaneous creations of that primordial force known as the world. They are not in themselves evil, but they possess an allure that distracts and beclouds the "I." (In the Russian Orthodox tradition, the word for this allure is *prelest*, or "illusion.")[10] Although we normally regard such images as arising from the exterior—as the marks that physical objects make on the senses—esotericism teaches the opposite: that the mind spontaneously generates these images, which in turn undergird the physical universe.

We can even be affected by the *logismoi* generated by others. Just as we disgorge the spontaneous productions of our minds—the ceaseless and unstoppable flow of images, thoughts, and impressions—into the ocean of the psyche at every second, so does everyone else, and it can sometimes be hard to tell which is whose. "There are no private thoughts," says *A Course in Miracles*.[11] A bad mood is far more contagious than a virus and often as dangerous. The late Stylianos Atteshlis, known as "Daskalos," the Cypriot

Christian magus made famous by the books of Kyriakos Markides, focused much of his healing practice on freeing his patients from harmful and alien *logismoi*.

How does one master the psyche in a sane manner? This is one of the most important questions that faces every human being. Even if one is indifferent to spiritual life, it soon becomes quite clear that these pieces of psychological furniture clutter up the house of the mind, making movement in life difficult and causing frustration and unhappiness. Moreover, the psyche is not like the body, which, after some preliminary training, often tends to enjoy a tight rein, like a well-trained dog that takes pleasure in doing what it is told. The psyche is far more intractable, and simple commands are harder to give. Vigilance is certainly a key: "Watch ye therefore, and pray always" (Luke 21:36). Or, in the words of *A Course in Miracles*, "You are much too tolerant of mind wandering, and are passively condoning your mind's miscreations."[12]

This vigilance requires walking an extremely fine edge. If you give too much attention to these passions, you begin to feed them and give them power; ignoring them, you run the risk of pushing them into the recesses of the mind, where they can wreak far more havoc than if they rest on the surface. This sort of repression can itself, as we have seen, become a kind of "evil servant."

A basic technique is one I have already discussed in dealing with carnal impulses: to feel the emotion fully—or to see the thought clearly in the mind's eye—without becoming identified with it. This approach is in and of itself quite powerful, since this effort in its own right creates a crucial distance between the "I" and what it is experiencing. Sometimes this very act can be enough. But not always, since some tendencies of mind are deep seated and hard to change. At other times, the passion will recede and return shortly, sometimes even after only a couple of seconds. Other approaches may be called for.

In some cases the passions involve deep-seated inner conflict. One "I" wants something; another does not. Generally the ego chooses one course or another, usually on the basis of maintaining its own self-image, leaving the other parts of the psyche frustrated and hostile. One way of dealing with this is a variant of the first practice: to stand back as much as possible from these conflicting emotions and to feel them simultaneously as intensely as possible without going along with any of them. If you persist, you may have a sense of a consciousness that is able not only to detach itself from these passions but in a strange way reconciles them.

In practical terms you may still have to choose one course or another, but the two quarreling aspects of your nature will no longer be as dissociated or as hostile, like warring states who have managed to sit down at a table and talk. Over time they are likely to become better integrated and less at odds with one another. Moreover, the aspects of your nature that you had ignored have now received attention, and this in itself may satisfy them: attention is the food of the psyche.

Sometimes, however, even this practice does not work. When assailed by unwanted thoughts and feelings, you may have to revert to a time-honored practice of the tradition, which is to strenuously refuse such thoughts and to call upon God for help. Francis de Sales offers this advice:

> As soon as you are conscious of being tempted, follow the example of children when they see a wolf or bear out in the country. They immediately run to the arms of their father or mother or at least call to them for help and protection. Turn in the same way to God and implore his mercy and help. This is the remedy our Lord himself has taught us: "Pray that you do not enter into temptation" (Matt. 26:41).
>
> If you find that the temptation still continues or even increases, run in spirit to embrace the Holy Cross as if you saw Christ Jesus crucified before you. Insist that you will never consent to the temptation, implore his assistance against it, and continue steadfastly to protest that you will refuse consent as long as the temptation continues. When you make such protestations and refusals of consent, do not look the temptation in the face but look solely at our Lord. If you look at the temptation, especially when it is strong, it may shake your courage.

De Sales makes another recommendation: "The sovereign remedy against all temptation, whether great or small, is to open your heart and express its suggestions, feelings, and affections to your director."[3] He means a spiritual director. Nearly everyone who makes any progress in spiritual life—as in any other sphere of endeavor—at some point comes to rely on the guidance of a mentor.

While there are geniuses and luminaries for whom the heavens open and divine light floods down unbidden, they are rare, and one cannot count on being among them. For most of us, having a teacher at some point is of paramount importance, and good ones are not common. Even fewer are those who are knowledgeable about inner Christianity.

At present there is a growing category of individuals who style themselves spiritual directors.[14] Here as elsewhere, one should exercise caution and intelligence—at least as much as when choosing a doctor or a psychotherapist. Two general guidelines could help: first, be extremely cautious about those who charge money for their services. Spiritual guidance should cost little, and in my experience, the best do not charge anything at all. "Freely ye have received; freely give" (Matt. 10:8). Second, fame is of little value as a criterion. Many spiritual celebrities are little more than artful self-promoters, ingeniously packaging small fragments of knowledge, while those with real depth are usually indifferent to the public eye and sometimes make efforts to avoid it.

Even apart from the issue of spiritual guidance as such, many people today feel the need of conventional psychotherapy to deal with emotional issues. If you feel the need for a therapist, make sure to choose one who does not regard spiritual interest in and of itself as a sign of dysfunction (as some analysts, notably Freudians, do). Furthermore, therapists are not spiritual teachers, so you can expect to pay handsomely for the services of one who is competent.

Mastering—or, if you prefer, integrating—the psyche is the work of a lifetime, and it is a task no one finishes, except perhaps the wisest of people, and then only at the very end of their lives. This mastery is not holding the psyche in rigid subjugation (which is impossible in any case), nor is it a matter of having a maniacally religious ego lording it over the emotions and the body. Rather, it is being centered in the still, small voice that is the true "I" of the spirit. Here the silent consciousness looks out over its terrain, internal and external, lovingly and inclusively, governing mildly though sometimes firmly, as a good ruler should. Ironically, this bestows far more power than holding sway over the "kingdoms of the world."

THE PINNACLE OF THE TEMPLE

This consideration leads to the next level of spiritual attainment, symbolized by the third temptation of Christ. The Devil sets him up "on a pinnacle of the temple," and says, "If thou be the Son of God, cast thyself down from hence: For it is written, He shall give his angels charge over thee, to keep thee: And in their hands they shall bear thee up, lest at any time thou dash thy foot against a stone. And Jesus answering said unto him, It is said, Thou shalt not tempt the Lord thy God" (Luke 4:9–12).

The setting of this episode gives an important clue to the level it is discussing. The Temple in Jerusalem was revered as the place where God made contact with his people; the Shekinah, the immanent divine presence, was said to dwell in its Holy of Holies. Thus the pinnacle of the Temple represents the highest level of spiritual attainment. Here the individual has mastered the cravings of the body and the undulations of the psyche. This gives access to tremendous power, and it is a stage at which the miraculous begins to manifest.

How? For all its apparent solidity, the world is a far more fluid thing than we normally believe. Even the most conventionally minded person can recognize that time and space themselves are plastic: they can shrink and stretch depending on psychological conditions. Waiting in line seems to take an eternity, while a fascinating conversation that lasts for hours can feel as if it has only taken minutes; a journey to an unaccustomed place seems to stretch out over vast expanses, while a routine trip of the same length feels as if it covers hardly any distance at all.

While these, of course, are subjective experiences, religious traditions teach that spiritual accomplishment can give one actual mastery over the physical world. Nature itself seems to obey such a person, as we can see from a story told of the death of Paul, not the Apostle but a hermit who was among the first of the Desert Fathers.

Upon Paul's death, his disciple, the famous Anthony, is dismayed to discover that he does not have a spade to bury the old man's body. He is at a loss for what to do until suddenly two lions come bounding toward him. Anthony is afraid, but he calls upon God, and the lions crouch at his feet, roaring in lament of the dead hermit. Finally they begin to scratch at the ground with their paws, throwing up the sand until there is a hole big enough to bury the corpse. They then come to Anthony, licking his hands and feet. "He saw that they were begging for his blessing; and pouring out his soul in praise to Christ for that even the dumb beasts feel that there is God, 'Lord,' he said, 'without whom no leaf lights from the tree, nor a single sparrow falls upon the ground, give unto these even as Thou knowest.'"[15]

A mere legend? Possibly. But there is some truth to the idea that the borders between us and other beings are thin and permeable, so if we can master the animal nature in ourselves, we may find that this power extends to the external animal kingdom as well. At any rate, this mastery has a hidden trap in it, as the story of Christ's temptation indicates. Say one does start to becomes endowed with amazing powers—or, more likely, the occasional serendipitous or even miraculous event happens: things fall into place, small signs of grace appear, and one starts to feel the radiance of divine favor. This is a critical juncture. It may be the "narrow gate" of which Christ speaks.

Up to now this book has spoken of the "I" in referring to the spirit of consciousness that is the true Self. And this is correct: this principle is that in each of us which says "I" at the deepest level possible, beyond all thought and desire and even beyond ordinary waking consciousness. But if one stops at this point, a cosmic egotism springs up, a spiritual pride that is the deadliest of the Seven Deadly Sins. Legend even says that Lucifer fell because he dared to say "I" in the presence of the Holy One.

Following the way of inner Christianity to its full conclusion means stepping past the constraints of this "I," which in its turn must take its rightful place in the cosmic order. And this requires an awareness of the central mystery of Christianity, which could rightly be said to enable one to "enter into the kingdom of God."

It is simply this: *the "I" is ultimately the same in all of us.* We are collectively one great being, the Son of God, which is known in its fallen state as Adam and in its unified state as Christ. "For as in Adam all die, even so in Christ shall all be made alive" (1 Cor. 15:22). This thought, so crucial, so often stated yet more often misunderstood, is difficult to approach, even difficult to state in ordinary language. How can English, with its neat system of three persons expressed in tidy pronouns, do justice to the idea that what is most truly "I," what is most innate and private and essential to myself, is precisely what I share with all other beings?

Yet this is the truth to which the teachings of Christ ultimately point. "When you make the two one, you will become the sons of man" (*Thomas*, 10). "But he that is joined to the Lord is one spirit" (1 Cor. 6:17). "The Son of Man" is one esoteric name for this Christ principle; "the Son of God" is another. *A Course in Miracles* expresses this idea most clearly: "God has only *one* Son. If all His creations are His Sons, every one must be an integral part of the whole Sonship. The Sonship in its oneness transcends the sum of its parts."[16] This is why we are to "love thy neighbor as thyself"— our neighbors are literally ourselves.

Some souls understand this truth intuitively. Their acts are invariably marked with kindness; they do good of their own accord, without any thought to personal advantage, and for them compassion comes as spontaneously as a heartbeat. Such people evoke a natural respect; even those who look down on them as foolish or naïve grudgingly admire their sublime disdain of self-interest. These radiant souls are rare, but not all that rare, and most of us can remember at least one or two such people in our lives. While their innate nobility puts them far ahead of most of us, there is a level that is still higher.

The way is ultimately a journey in consciousness. It is about being aware of truths to which we are usually oblivious, and so it is a process of awakening. The highest level of development, perhaps the final expression of the kingdom of God as we can know it in earthly life, includes those who not only possess this innate capacity for kindness but who understand the reason for it. They know clearly what others only sense dimly—that there is an underlying unity of being of which we are all part. This is gnosis in the fullest sense.

This understanding is not merely a matter of conceptual knowledge; if it were, it could be realized by simply reading a book. Perhaps the best way to describe it is to say that you become aware that your own life and perception are part of a much larger field, the common life of consciousness that is esoterically known as the Son. Sometimes it may feel as if you and your whole body and soul are merely a sort of telescope through which something much larger and wiser and more powerful is peering out at the world. As such realization grows and deepens, you may increasingly sense that you know certain things without knowing *how* you know them. You begin to have access to the knowledge that is common to the whole human race. Christ advises his disciples to make use of this capacity: "But when they shall lead you, and deliver you up, take no thought beforehand what ye shall speak, neither do ye premeditate: but whatsoever shall be given you in that hour, that speak ye: for it is not ye that speak, but the Holy Ghost" (Mark 13:11).

For some, this awareness comes through mystical realization, often spontaneous and unsought. Jacob Boehme was illumined by gazing on a glint of light from a pewter dish; Paul's vision on the road to Damascus is an even more famous instance. Compare also the awakening of George Fox, the founder of Quakerism, who wrote, "I saw into that which was without end, things which cannot be uttered, and of the greatness and infinitude of the love of God, which cannot be expressed by words."[17] But mystical fireworks are not necessary for such illumination. Some people have this type of experience; others do not. In fact, Christianity has a long tradition of warning about mystical experiences, since even the most beautiful of these can be nothing more than "glamour" or illusion produced by the Devil.

In the end, those who know, know. They come to this knowledge through many approaches, multifarious, and often idiosyncratic: the paths are as diverse as humanity itself. Some people seem to be born with this knowledge; others receive it unasked and do not always regard it as a blessing. For most of us, however, such illumination must be nurtured by a life-long program of prayer, meditation, and study, along with the inevitable rigors of trying to lead a decent and ethical life.

5

Cosmology

TODAY WE KNOW MORE about the universe than human beings ever have. Each day science penetrates further into dimensions of reality that far outstrip those of the imagination, and its accumulating knowledge gives us ever increasing power to shape the visible world. In this context, to speak of esoteric cosmology may seem outmoded. What could its quaint old systems possibly offer in an age when physics and biology are revolutionizing our lives daily?

There is a lack that science, for all its accomplishments, does not fill but rather makes more acute. Each advance in scientific knowledge seems to exact a cost in reducing the meaning and purpose of human life. The closer we come to seeing the universe as a whole, the further we feel from having any significant place in it. Diminished by our own achievements, we have constructed a cosmos in which we ourselves are irrelevant.

It is this need, so excruciatingly felt in the modern soul, that the esoteric worldview can help meet. For esotericism, the physical universe, as vast as it is, is only an infinitesimally thin slice of a much larger cosmos. And yet this increased sense of scale does not diminish the human role but enhances it. For esotericism says each of us is a microcosm of the universe. We can come to know ourselves by contemplating the grand scheme of things, and conversely we can understand the universe by exploring our own inner makeup. Moreover, this very exploration serves a central cosmic function: our experience of these different levels is essential to the life of the universe itself. Consciousness is the lifeblood of this universe; our own explorations of the inner and outer dimensions help this blood to circulate. The universe does not inherently lack meaning. If it seems to do so, it is because we were created to provide this sense of meaning and are failing to do our job.

Esoteric cosmology also suggests that each level of scale in the physical universe corresponds to a level within. The earth corresponds to the body, the planets of the solar system to the psyche, the stars and galaxies to the spirit, and the universe as a whole—and what is beyond the universe—to the divine. The old esoteric schemes, found in Plato and Dante and the Hermetic texts, provide such a picture, but in a more rudimentary form: they were based on the universe as understood in those times. We need not be shackled to these perspectives in their old forms, but we can take them as starting points. We can use the knowledge of the physical world developed by modern science to enhance our knowledge of ourselves as microcosms.

A JOURNEY OUT

It may be easiest to convey a sense of this perspective through a meditative exercise. You may find it easier to do this practice if you refresh your sense of the stars and planets by visiting a planetarium or looking at a book on astronomy, or simply by going out into your backyard at night and gazing up into the sky. If you find it hard to remember the following instructions in detail, you can tape-record them, reading them aloud at a slow pace, and play them back to yourself, or ask someone to read them to you.

Sit in a comfortable but erect position in a place where you will not be disturbed for twenty minutes or so. Allow your eyes to close and bring your attention to your breath. As your mind begins to settle, become aware of your body sitting in the room you are in. Feel your body as fully and completely as you can. See if you can have a sense of the body as a single, unitary whole. You may be aware of the breath, the heartbeat, and other rhythms and processes in your body.

Now shift your attention to the stream of thoughts, images, and emotions that are passing before the inner eye of your consciousness. Watch them alertly but impartially, allowing yourself to become neither dazed and sleepy nor preoccupied with any of these images.

At this point become aware of what *is* aware in you: bring your attention to the consciousness that is the true "I," the awake, unsleeping watcher that is your essence. Now feel as if you are lifted up out of your body. You are at the top of the ceiling of your room. You rise further, above the roof of your house, above the city or town you are in. Allow yourself to see this scene as vividly as if you are looking out the window of an airplane making its ascent.

Venture further, until you can look down upon the earth like an astronaut gazing from a spaceship. Your mind continues to take you beyond the limits of our planet. You go past the luminaries of the solar system—the moon, Mercury, Venus, the sun, Mars, Jupiter, Saturn, Uranus, Neptune, Pluto. Imagine yourself going past these bodies as if you are in a spaceship. As you pass by, you may have a sense of them, not as dead balls of matter, but as living, active intelligences like yourself. Indeed, you may have the sense that they are far larger and more powerful than you. Allow yourself to observe these entities without becoming either frightened or attracted by them.

In your mind's eye you proceed further now, outside the solar system, into the realms of interstellar space. You find yourself receding from our solar system at a tremendous speed, and the sun itself now seems like nothing more than another of the stars in the firmament. You become aware of the great stellar masses, the stars and nebulae of the Milky Way galaxy. You go beyond the Milky Way itself so that you see it as only one of countless other galaxies in the sky. Here too you are aware of these galaxies, not as inanimate objects made of flaming gas, but as living, growing beings in their own right—which is what they are.

Now you go to the bounds of the universe and beyond. You reach a level now where the entire universe is itself only one of countless other universes, some of which you can imagine, some of which you cannot. And you realize that our entire universe is itself also an active, dynamic being among other such beings.

Here, in this space of profound quiet, you realize that there is an intelligence that unites all of these universes. It is the principle of consciousness—though far beyond consciousness as we experience it as humans. If you are very still and attentive, you may sense that there is something even beyond this consciousness, something that you cannot know directly but which you can glimpse out of the corner of your mind's eye, a nothing that is nonetheless not empty but profoundly alive. Unimaginably vast, it can never be known in full. You cannot give it a name, because it cannot be named.

Now you begin to return. You move into the realm of our known universe as if you were in a spaceship returning home. Among the unfathomable number of galaxies in our universe, you find yourself drawn toward one as if you are a homing pigeon that knows exactly which way to fly. And indeed you find that this is our home galaxy, the Milky Way. Here you look around, and of the many stars and solar systems you see, you are again attracted to one in particular. At almost unimaginable speed you move toward it, and you find yourself at the edges of our solar system. You go further, through the realms of the planets, until you find yourself in the vicinity of the earth. You descend into the sphere of our planet. You find your country, your town, your home, and you return to the room in which your physical body is waiting for you. You descend into your body and you fully feel your own physicality.

Make sure you have totally returned. You may want to stretch, stamp your feet on the floor, or do some other simple exercise to reestablish full contact with your body. If you are the sort of person who is easily disconnected from physicality, you may need to walk around or eat a little food to reinforce the sense of contact. The main objective of this exercise is not to precipitate out-of-body experiences or to teach "astral travel," but to have a sense of some of the different levels of the universe, which correspond to the same levels in ourselves.

THE GROUND OF BEING

The levels of experience in the exercise can be broken down in terms of scale. In the first place, there is the earthly, bodily experience with which you began and ended. Next is the level of the solar system—the sun and the other planets we know. Beyond this is the level of the stars and galaxies. In traditional systems like Dante's, this was known as the realm of the "fixed stars." Our knowledge of it differs from theirs in that we have a much more detailed sense of these stars and galaxies than they did. We also know that these entities are not "fixed" in the sense that they are immovable. They *do* move, but on a vastly larger scale than those of our individual lives.

We can go further and recognize that the universe is only one of many, perhaps infinitely many, possible universes. These may be built on such different premises from our own that we will never be able to know or encounter them directly. Nor can we ever be entirely sure that they exist. Nonetheless, it seems likely that our own universe is only one small branch of an immeasurable tree of life that includes dimensions of which we can scarcely dream.

Uniting all these unfathomable dimensions is consciousness, or mind. Why consciousness? Why not some natural force such as gravity or light? Light is the quickest thing known to science: it travels at a speed of 186,000 miles per second. But as fast as this may seem, it is really not all that fast when one considers the immense distances in the universe; even the light of our own sun takes about eight minutes to reach us.

There is only one thing we know of that is faster than light: thought. You proved it yourself in doing this exercise. In your mind you were able to travel across millions of light-years in the course of a simple visualization that lasted only a few minutes. This does not, of course, mean that you literally made the journey, or that the consciousness that unites the countless universes is identical to human consciousness. It simply suggests that mind is, of all the things we know, the closest to this primal force.

This primal level of consciousness is what esoteric Christianity calls the Son or the Word. "All things were made by him; and without him was not any thing made that was made" (John 1:2). It is the deepest part of us, as it is of everything that exists: "In him was life; and the life was the light of men" (John 1:3). To use theological terminology, it is the *immanent* aspect of God: the part of the divine nature that is active and present in the world. And so it is called in the Bible: "And they shall call his name Emmanuel, which being interpreted is, God with us" (Matt. 1:24; cf. Isa. 7:14).

But there is something even beyond this Word. It is the silent vastness out of which everything, even the Word, arises. It neither exists nor does not exist. We cannot even say it is unknowable, for if it were completely unknowable, we would not even be aware of it at all. To say anything about it is to lie, for it encompasses all opposites. It has given rise to many of the most profound and paradoxical expressions of mystics and visionaries. It is the *transcendent* aspect of God. Meister Eckhart spoke of it as the "Godhead"; the Kabbalists call it the *Ain Sof* (which is Hebrew for the "infinite") or the "Ancient of Days." In esoteric Christianity it is the Father.

How do these two, the Father and the Son, interact with each other? What enables them to have any connection at all, while still in some way remaining distinct? There is, it is taught, a principle that makes this interaction possible. It is called the Comforter, or the Holy Spirit.

Here, in essence, is the Christian Trinity. At the deepest level we can even glimpse is the unfathomable Father. Out of the Father proceeds the Son, the level of consciousness or mind that begets all things, and without whom there "was not anything made that was made." Between them is the Holy Spirit, the divine principle of relatedness, which accomplishes perhaps the most astonishing of all miracles: uniting two separate entities while still allowing them to be separate. The seventh-century monk Thalassios the Libyan writes, "The Father is the sole origin of all things. He is the origin of the Son and the Spirit as Their begetter and source, coeternal, coinfinite, limitless, coessential, and undivided. He is the origin of created things, as the one who produces, provides for, and judges them through the Son in the Holy Spirit."[1]

In this brief summary we can see two basic truths about the divine as we know it and can know it. In the beginning is the sole, unique, irreducible One. Out of this primordial Oneness proceeds a dynamic of three. Gurdjieff, in his magnum opus *Beelzebub's Tales to His Grandson*, called this process the "Sacred Triamazikamno" and connected it with the Christian Trinity. He equated God the Father with the force "Holy Affirming," or the "'Pushing-force' or simply the 'Force-plus.'" God the Son is "Holy Denying" or the "'Resisting-force' or simply the 'Force-minus.'" God the Holy Ghost is "Holy Reconciling," or "'the Equilibrating-force' or the 'Neutralizing-force.'"[2]

Papus describes this sacred ternary in a different way:

> The Ego cannot be realized except through its opposition to the non-Ego. The assertion of the Ego is scarcely established, when we must instantly realize a reaction of the Ego, Absolute, upon itself, from which the conception of its existence will be drawn, by a kind of division of the Unity. This is the origin of *duality*, of opposition, of the *Binary*. . . . But the opposition of the Ego and the Non-Ego immediately gives rise to another factor; this is the *Affinity* existing between this Ego and this Non-Ego.[3]

Papus equates these forces with the Hebrew letters י (*yod*), ה (*heh*), and ו (*waw*)—the three letters that make up יהוה, the Tetragrammaton, the most potent of God's names. *Yod*, which means "hand," is the active force; *heh*, which in Hebrew is used as an ending to mark feminine nouns, is the passive force; *waw*, which connotes a link or a tie (*waw* at the beginning of a Hebrew word means "and"), is the reconciling. (The final *heh* is not a fourth force but a kind of result or consequence of the first three, leading to a new process in its own right.) The *yod* would, then, be the Father, the first *heh* the Son, and the *waw* the Holy Spirit.

The sacred ternary is far more universal than Christianity. The ancient Egyptians venerated the trinity of Osiris, Isis, and Horus; in Hinduism there is Brahma, Vishnu, and Shiva; Chinese religion has the triad of Heaven, Earth, and Man. Buddhism expresses this idea in the "three poisons"—ignorance, desire, and anger—that produce conditioned existence, as well as in the Triple Gem in which the seeker takes refuge—the Buddha, the teacher; the Dharma, the teaching; and the Sangha, the community of practitioners. Triads can also be found beyond the boundaries of religious thought per se: Hegel's philosophy is based on the dialectic of thesis, antithesis, and synthesis. Ironically, the same triadic structure underlies the most militantly atheistic philosophy in human history: dialectical materialism, created by Karl Marx as a way of stripping Hegel's ideas of their spiritual emphasis.

Certain Christians claim that these other systems are inferior or degenerate views of the central truth of the Christian Trinity. They contend that Christianity has always stressed the radical personhood of God, arguing that the Father, Son, and Holy Spirit are not forces or powers but persons united in a loving relationship.

This is a notable difference but should not be overemphasized. If God is the ultimate ground of being out of which all arises, it must necessarily follow that God is not a person or persons as we customarily understand the term.

Consider the following analogy. Suppose two cells in your bloodstream possess a certain measure of self-consciousness. They begin to reflect on the nature and purpose of their existence, and they dimly begin to suspect that they are part of a larger whole. What is this larger entity? they ask each other. Is it a living thing, a cell like themselves? Does it know of them, care about them, love them? Does it respond to their needs and hopes and wishes?

What could one say to them? How could two cells, no matter how precociously endowed, ever really understand the human organism that is their universe? Is this entity a cell like them? Yes and no. Like individual cells, a human organism has life and purpose and intention. But it is far more than a mere cell. On the other hand, the life force that courses through us is supremely conscious of each of these cells. It cares for them, feeds them, protects them, even if our conscious minds have no part in this process.

Such reflections should inspire a certain reticence in discussing the personhood of the divine entity in whom we live and move and have our being. This is not to say that we are forbidden to reflect or speculate about it but that we should not be too arrogant about our conclusions. On the other hand, there seems to be some truth in the Christian insistence on the personhood of God. Whether or not God is ultimately personal in the sense that we humans understand it, the tradition suggests that *we* are persons, and God can address us in ways we can understand personally. To return to the analogy of the blood cells, the greater being of which they are a part is not a cell but can interact with them in a way that is appropriate for them, furnishing them with care and sustenance as they require it. So God provides for us and for all creatures. "Are not five sparrows sold for two farthings? and not one of them is forgotten before God?" (Luke 12:6).

THE ANGELIC REALM

Traditionally, the highest level of existence apart from the divine is the realm of the angels, who govern the operations of the planets and the fixed stars. The sixteenth-century Christian Kabbalist Johannes Reuchlin writes:

> Every [heavenly] sphere has, in addition to its own essential form, an accompanying Intelligence which keeps it moving in its orbit. This Intelligence is called an "angel" because it has been sent to perform this duty. It is endowed with intelligence and has a will of its own, and fulfills the command of the Creator like a mediating power between God and nature.[4]

We no longer regard the stars as living intelligences, but maybe we have missed the mark. Astronomers tell us the stars have their own lives— they are born, grow, age, and die, just like the living creatures we know on earth. Rudolf Steiner even says that in the past, human beings possessed a clairvoyant capacity that enabled them to perceive this inner life: "Man, when gazing into the starry heavens, saw not merely the physical stars but still saw the spiritual beings united with these stars."[5]

These angelic entities are vibrant, dynamic, and intelligent cosmic powers—not so much the physical entities we know as stars but the consciousness that animates them. This would of course include our own sun. We live in the world they make as our cells live in our bodies. Reflecting on these matters, the biologist Rupert Sheldrake observes, "Nature is organized by fields, and these fields are the realms of activity that bind and order the energy or power. . . . The angels are, as it were, the consciousness of the fields operating at all levels of nature."[6]

In this sense, we can say, rather prosaically perhaps, that these angelic beings are a second-tier product of the interaction of the primordial divine energies. As such, they still remain considerably simpler than we as humans customarily understand intelligent life to be. But they are not simple in the sense of being stupid; quite the opposite. Our human intelligence is as intricate as the folds of our very brains; complex and often self-contradictory, the mind stumbles over itself and countermands its own directives. The angelic nature, like that of God, is not only supremely aware and intelligent, but unconflicted and for that very reason supremely potent. This may explain why fire is one of the most common symbols of the angelic essence. God "maketh his angels spirits; his ministers a flaming fire" (Ps. 104:4).

There are said to be angels of different levels and different functions. The most famous system is set out in the *Celestial Hierarchy* of Dionysius the Areopagite.[7] He describes a hierarchy of nine types of angels, divided into three triads of three. Bonaventure, a Franciscan monk of the thirteenth century, describes it poetically:

Note, lastly, what the Truth must be.
In the first Hierarchy:
    evoked by the utterance of prayer,
        work of the Angels;
    heard in study and reading,
        work of the Archangels;
    announced through example and preaching;
        work of the Principalities.
In the second Hierarchy:
    joined with as refuge and place of indulgence,
        work of the Powers:
    apprehended through zeal and emulation,
        work of the Virtues:
    conjoined with in self-deprecation and mortification,
        work of the Dominions.
In the third Hierarchy:
    worshipped through sacrifice and praise,

work of the Thrones;
admired through ecstasy and contemplation,
work of the Cherubim;
embraced in kiss and dilection
work of the Seraphim.
Note diligently what I say here,
because this is a fountain of life.[8]

A number of these are known from the Bible, including angels proper as well as archangels, cherubim, and seraphim. Ephesians refers to principalities and powers but regards them as enemies of humankind: "For we wrestle not against flesh and blood, but against principalities, against powers, against the rulers of the darkness of this world, against spiritual wickedness in high places" (Eph. 6:12). It was this aspect of early Christianity that helped inspire Gnosticism, which portrayed the archons, the invisible administrators of the universe, as evil. Paul suggests that worship of these intermediate powers was the source of paganism: "For though there be that are called gods, whether in heaven or in earth, (as there be gods many, and lords many,) but to us there is but one God, the Father, of whom are all things, and we in him; and one Lord Jesus Christ, by whom are all things, and we by him" (1 Cor. 8:5–6).

Thomas Aquinas says the angels were given free will at their creation. When Lucifer rebelled, they had the choice to join with him or with God. After they decided at that point, their position in the universe was fixed.[9] They are cosmic functionaries, and it is their job to serve as gatekeepers, keeping out the unworthy, as the cherubim do who stand guard at the east of Eden (Gen. 3:24).

Ritual magic calls upon angels to serve in a similar role. Usually at the start of a ritual, the four archangels Michael, Gabriel, Raphael, and Uriel are invoked to serve as the guardians of the cardinal directions. Their invisible (but often quite palpable) presence carves out the boundaries of a sacred space so that divine influences can descend without either dissipating or suffering interference from negative entities.

Angels are also sometimes seen as the souls of departed human beings who have returned to give help or guidance to those on earth. Swedenborg claimed to have had many conversations with such beings, and he insisted that all angels were human in form, except that they do not have material bodies. He also repudiated the view I have mentioned above, which sees angels as primordial forces: "Some honest spirits I talked with on this subject were heartsick at the existence of this kind of ignorance in the church about the condition of heaven and about spirits and angels. They maintained indignantly that I ought to go right back with the message that they were not formless minds, not ethereal gases, but people to a T, that they could see and hear and feel just as well as people on earth."[10]

Thus the term *angel* can refer to primordial forces of the universe; intermediate powers between the Absolute and us; messengers that convey and express the will of God; and the spirits of departed humans. What unites these many views is the idea that there are unseen beings that stand between us and the unfathomable divine, not as barriers, but as helpers. It is in this form that angels have had such appeal to many. Some experience them in dramatic and vivid ways, as the countless cases of angelic apparitions remind us; I know one woman who said she saw an angel while driving on the Bay Bridge between San Francisco and Oakland. For others, they can hide their true identity with a human guise; "some have entertained angels unawares" (Heb. 13:2). For still others, they are present not as bodies or as visions but as a small voice of inspiration or a flash of protection in the face of an instant's danger. At any rate, these mysterious beings seem to be as much in our minds as ever. Matthew Fox, an ex–Dominican priest and founder of the movement known as Creation Spirituality, says that 60–80 percent of the people at his lectures claim to have encountered angels in their lives, and he cites polls in which about a third of the general American population say the same.[11] And mass culture, as evidenced in books, movies, and TV shows, suggests that we continue to believe in or at least hope for their presence.

THE PLANETS AND THE PSYCHE

Now we can begin to see how cosmology mirrors the composition of an individual human. The universe as a whole corresponds to the divine Son who abides in each of us; the stars and the angelic hierarchy correspond to the spirit, the "I." These realms are vast and impersonal; though they have their own rhythms and cycles, by an ordinary human time frame they seem practically eternal, just as a sense of "I" persists unchanging throughout a lifetime, no matter how a person's external circumstances may shift and alter. The next level, that of the planets of the solar system, corresponds to the level of the soul or psyche.

How does this work? Imagine it this way. In the beginning there is nothing. In this nothing, in what Dionysius calls "the dazzling obscurity of the secret silence,"[12] empty yet vibrant and fertile, a divine spark of inspiration appears. At first it is only the slightest glimmer and has no substantial existence. This impulse then proceeds into the realm of the angelic intelligences, who clothe it with specific qualities. At this level certain potentials begin to manifest while others are excluded: to be big is not to be small; to be red is not to be blue. Plato described this as the realm of *forms* or *ideas*, abstract types to which all individual members must conform. Say this spark of inspiration is to take form as a human being. To be human means to have a certain shape, a certain type of intelligence and not others: a human being cannot breathe under water but is capable of rational thought, and so on.

This entity, still extremely abstract, exists not in actuality but in potential. It then descends through the spheres of the planets, which impart their own qualities to it, creating the psyche. Jupiter bestows expansiveness and growth; Mars, rigor and severity; Venus, desire and the capacity to reproduce itself; Mercury, the capacity to think and reflect. These characteristics are further modified by the planets' relative positions at a particular moment—in the case of a person, at the moment the newborn draws its first breath. Natal astrology, which casts a person's chart from this moment, thus paints a picture of the individual soul as it is fixed at the moment of its entry on earth.

Conversely, returning to the realm of the divine is often portrayed as an ascent through the spheres of the planets. Dante describes it this way; so does the Hermetic text known as the *Poimandres*, which describes the bad qualities the soul must shed after death in each planetary zone:

> Thence the human being rushes up through the cosmic framework, at the first zone [the moon] surrendering the energy of increase and decrease; at the second [Mercury] evil machination, a device now inactive; at the third [Venus] the illusion of longing, now inactive; at the fourth [the sun] the ruler's arrogance, now freed from excess; at the fifth [Mars] unholy presumption and daring recklessness; at the sixth [Jupiter] the evil impulses that come from wealth, now inactive; and at the seventh zone [Saturn] the deceit that lies in ambush. And then, stripped of the effects of the cosmic framework, the human enters the region of the ogdoad [the spiritual realm]; he has his own proper power, and along with the blessed he hymns the father.[13]

Eastern Orthodoxy picturesquely calls these spheres the cosmic "toll-houses": the seventh-century monk Maximus the Confessor exhorts believers to reflect on how after death "the harsh keepers of the toll houses will bring before us one by one the actions, words, and thought which they suggested but which we made our own."[14]

The influence of the planets (which today would have to include Uranus, Neptune, and Pluto, unknown when the Hermetic texts were written) extends to everything on earth. The Renaissance Hermeticists devoted much attention to examining which plants and stones manifested the properties of each planet, sometimes using them as means of healing or psychotherapy. We have already seen how Marsilio Ficino tried to cure his own melancholia through such means. But each moment, each event, on earth is also regarded as a reflection of the relations of the planets in the heavens. This has given rise to the ancient practice of electional astrology, so called because it is used to "elect" the best moment to begin a certain activity.

Astrology is now regarded as the province of dreamy mystics, New Agers, and other faddists; science, it would seem, has no interest in such foolery. It was not always so. Although the truth of astrology has long been disputed, the battle lines have often been drawn differently than one might expect. Many of the greatest luminaries in science, including Kepler, Newton, and Tycho Brahe, took this art very seriously indeed, often practicing it professionally, while such esoteric philosophers as Plotinus and Pico della Mirandola derided it.

The truth, as often happens, seems to lie somewhere in between. The planets do influence events on earth; the activity of solar flares and the pull of the moon on the tides are the most obvious, though far from the only, examples. On the other hand, there is a danger in becoming preoccupied with astrology, as happens with some enthusiasts who dwell obsessively and superstitiously on the planets, blaming them for all evil and hoping upon them as the source of all luck. Spiritual teachers' numerous warnings against this trap deserve to be taken seriously. Astrology is not an exact science: it gives a general but by no means perfect idea of what is to come. Furthermore, becoming fixated upon the planets limits one's awareness and aspiration to the level of the psyche. While this is higher and more comprehensive a view than that of ordinary life, which restricts itself to the physical arena, in the long run it is still stifling.

Nevertheless, esoteric teachings, including those of Christianity, say that the planets are intimately connected with the ebbs and flows of our own lives as well as forming a filter for the divine presence of God. God is envisaged as radically "outside" our universe. The divine energies penetrate the universe first through the galactic and stellar realms and then through that of the planets. At each step the divine light and power is stepped down. It reaches the earth only in an attenuated form.

This idea may provoke some indignation. Why has God put himself so far away from us? Why are we not nearer to him? Conventional Christianity would say that we have placed ourselves apart from God through the Fall. Esoteric Christianity would add that even so, we continue to exist and function on all these levels. If we open ourselves to these higher dimensions, we can have contact with them.

NATURE AND CORRESPONDENCE

Finally, there is nature, the physical world proper. Here esotericism differs radically from modern science, which regards consciousness as an epiphenomenon, a kind of side effect, of neurological processes. For the esotericist, consciousness is primary; matter comes after. The different levels of being, from the most rarefied to the most substantial, are simply a set of sheaths in which consciousness swathes itself, and the natural world, the rocks and trees and buildings that seem to us so real, are all nothing more than the thinnest film on the surface of being. Moreover, this material realm echoes unseen dimensions. Charles Baudelaire gave this idea one of its most sublime and celebrated expressions in his poem "Correspondences," which begins:

> Nature is a temple whose living pillars
> Sometimes let confused words come forth;
> Man passes here through a forest of symbols
> Which observe him with familiar glances.[15]

This sonnet, first published in 1855, is one of the most influential poems of modern times, giving rise to the entire Symbolist movement in nineteenth-century art. Baudelaire owed his inspiration to the esoteric doctrine of correspondences, which says that everything on earth has its counterpart in the celestial realms. It is the ancient Hermetic idea "as above, so below" restated in modern terms; Baudelaire learned it from reading Swedenborg.[16] And it entails the idea that even the part of nature that is apparently inanimate has its own hidden life and awareness, partaking of the "I" that is common to us all.

The French scholar Antoine Faivre regards the concept of living nature (along with the doctrine of correspondences itself) as one of the central themes of esotericism.[17] Faivre adds that nature itself is often seen as needing redemption, a view evoked by these words of Paul's: "For the earnest expectation of the creature waiteth for the manifestation of the sons of God. . . . Because the creature itself also shall be delivered from the bondage of corruption into the glorious liberty of the children of God." Nature fell with the human race, not through nature's own fault, but because the primal Adam was no longer able to hold his post in "dressing the garden and keeping it"—in uniting heaven and earth. Since then, Paul continues, "the whole creation groaneth and travaileth in pain together" (Rom. 8:19, 21–22).

Humanity, then, has a responsibility to nature: to provide it with the conscious link with the unseen that it otherwise lacks. Despite its importance, this idea has not played a central role in Christianity for centuries; a cruel antipathy to the natural world has been far more prominent. The famous verse from Genesis has often been quoted as justification: "And God said, Let us make man in our image, after our likeness: and let them have dominion over the fish of the sea, and over the fowl of the air, and over the cattle, and over all the earth, and over every creeping thing that creepeth upon the earth" (Gen. 1:26).

An esoteric understanding of this verse sheds another light on the matter. In esoteric terms the "air" is the dimension of the spirit, the "water" that of the psyche, the "earth" the physical world per se. God's granting humanity dominion over these realms is not so much a license for exploitation as a command to master the forces of consciousness, thought, emotion, and action in ourselves. If we can bring ourselves into this state, a spontaneous harmony arises naturally not only within ourselves but with nature, as symbolized by the story of the lions who buried the hermit Paul. Francis of Assisi, who counted the birds and animals as his friends, is perhaps the most famous instance of this attitude in Christianity. The Swedenborgian John Chapman, better known as Johnny Appleseed, is another—a man so compassionate that he once put out his campfire because he pitied the mosquitoes flying into it.

THE COSMIC OCTAVE

Such, at any rate, is a brief capsule of esoteric cosmology as understood in the Christian tradition. One theme particularly worth noting is that of scale. Each of these realms—the physical, psychological, spiritual, and divine—follows an order of increasing size and scope. As a level's scale increases, its energies become subtler and more rarefied. The earthly is the densest; it is what we can smell and see and touch. The realm of the planetary, corresponding to the psychological level, is the next. Not coincidentally, the material of this realm is known as the *astral light*. It is, in Shakespeare's words, "such stuff as dreams are made on"—the mind-stuff that forms the substance of thoughts and dreams, and which can make its presence felt across long distances: such paranormal phenomena as telekinesis and clairvoyance are possible consequences of its activity. The substances of the spirit and the divine operate at levels that are eternal and universal relative to an individual human life; they extend throughout the universe and beyond. Their manifestations in the physical world, as rare and sporadic as they are, are regarded as miraculous.

Some may object that this view of the universe cannot be taken seriously in the light of current knowledge; shouldn't we go beyond antiquated views that portray the earth as the center of the universe? But the geocentric view is not as outdated as it may appear. While the earth is not the center of the universe, it remains the center of *our* universe. And we are principally examining cosmology as it affects us as we are here on earth.

Moreover there are other perspectives on this question. One esoteric Christian tradition depicts the universe as a grand cosmic octave. The names for the notes of the musical octave reflect this teaching:

Do	*Dominus*	The Lord
Si	*Sidereus Orbis*	The starry world
La	*Lactea Via*	The Milky Way
Sol	*Sol*	The sun
Fa	*Fatum*	Fate (the realm of the planets)
Mi	*Mixtus Orbis*	The "mixed world" of good and evil: earth
Re	*Regina Astrorum*	The moon, "Queen of the Stars" [18]

This cosmic octave is in some ways closer to the scientific view in that it goes beyond a geocentric universe. It starts with the universal scale, the divine, and proceeds down to more and more narrow spheres of existence, ending not with the earth but with its satellite, the moon. It suggests that the moon is the point of growth of our part of the universe, and so far from being dead, will someday be a living planet like ours. (This is said to be the hidden meaning of the prophecies that the moon will be turned to blood: Acts 2:20; Rev. 6:12.) Gurdjieff made this idea a central part of his teaching, holding that organic life on earth, including man, was nothing more than a means of transmitting certain cosmic energies to the moon to help its growth. "Humanity is *food* for the moon," he said.[19]

While most Christians would not agree with Gurdjieff's view as thus stated, a closer examination of his views in *Beelzebub's Tales to His Grandson* suggests that in a broader sense he does not differ from the esoteric Christian tradition as a whole. He teaches that through certain cosmic mishaps, humanity came under the sway of the forces of illusion and fragmentation and thereupon became unable to sustain its role as a link in the cosmic chain. Consequently, we are paying the price, not only in the miseries engendered by our own inner conflicts, but also in large-scale calamities such as war.

Gurdjieff's ideas, like those of the Bible itself, are clearly mythic: they attempt to speak metaphorically of truths that do not lend themselves to ordinary language or thought. As for humanity serving as food for the moon or the moon turning to blood, the old esoteric maxim holds good: "Neither accept nor reject." There is an attitude of mind whereby one can entertain and contemplate ideas like these dispassionately and openmindedly without falling into the traps either of credulity or of reactive skepticism. This is not an evasion or an attempt to deflect legitimate criticism: rather, it is meant to cultivate a certain freedom of thought that can go beyond the boundaries of dualistic yesses and nos.

A JOURNEY IN

There is, then, something valuable to be found in the old frameworks of Christian cosmology. But we need to remember that these cosmic forces are also inside us. They are not thousands of light-years away but are embodied in our being; they literally make us up at levels that science cannot discern. As Elisabeth Vreede, a disciple of Rudolf Steiner, says, "The whole human being is born out of the cosmos. He or she builds himself or herself up from the forces of sun, moon, planets, and stars. The planets bestow as their contribution what human beings carry within them as the seven 'organs of life'—the spleen, liver, heart, and so on."[20] What appears to us on the surface as physical organs is, on a deeper level, the actions of the planets, the stars, and the universe itself.

Another meditative exercise may illuminate this idea. As you will see, it is simply the inverse of the exercise at the beginning of this chapter. Again you may want to read the instructions aloud slowly into a tape recorder and play them back to yourself while actually doing the practice, or have someone read them to you.

Find a place and time where you will not be disturbed for twenty minutes or so. Sit quietly, in an erect but comfortable position, and allow your body to settle into stillness. Close your eyes and let your attention focus on the breath. Breathe naturally and comfortably. You may want to take two or three deep breaths as a way of relaxing and centering yourself.

Now bring your attention to the sensations of the physical body. Feel your back against your seat and your feet on the floor. Most likely you will find your attention moving spontaneously to feelings in different parts of the body. This is fine, as long as you keep your attention on the body.

Now imagine yourself going further within yourself. It is as if the body and all its experiences and processes are simply the outermost layer of what is you. You have the sense of going to a deeper layer of yourself. See if you can imagine the sky and the stars and the planets inside you, as if you were seated on the inside of an enormous hollow bowl. And you begin to journey into this internal sky.

You begin with the moon; it is as if you can feel the moon somewhere inside yourself, in one part of your body or another; see if you can find where it is. In such exercises, it is always more important to note clearly and objectively what you experience rather than trying to have any *particular* experience. Do the exercise patiently and attentively, without a sense of strain.

You now proceed on this journey inside yourself, going past the realm of the moon and seeing the other planets: Mercury, Venus, the sun, Mars, Jupiter, Saturn, Uranus, Neptune, Pluto. It is as if there are vast realms of interplanetary space within your own being that you are beginning to experience and explore. Take note of anything you see there. If you encounter living beings—humans, animals, or other creatures—again note them clearly without becoming distracted or detained by them.

You now seem to have reached the bounds of this solar system that is inside you, and you discover that you are on the bounds of interstellar space. It is a place that is immeasurably vast, dark, and alive—*and it is within you*. Go further now, into the realms of stars and galaxies, which you can see and encounter as if you were going by them in a spaceship. Here too you may have the sense that these entities that you are passing are living and conscious beings.

As you make this journey further and further, you may become aware that all this time you have been proceeding to the center—to your own center. And this center is somehow beyond the confines even of this vast space inside yourself. The realm of the planets and the stars and the galaxies are all layers of yourself, and they all surround an inner core. So at this point permit yourself to go beyond this final barrier—the limits of time and space themselves, however you conceive them—and allow yourself to enter the realm of the divine. You may experience it as a realm of utter light, utter darkness, or something completely different. Quite possibly you will understand that it is beyond all pictures and images you can make of it.

At this point you may have a sense of the divine presence that is at the very center of your own nature. It is the place where you, as you, meet God. Allow yourself to experience this as fully as you can. You may feel reverence, humility, joy, love, awe, even dread. But you also know that you have the right to be here and to engage in this most profound and most intimate of communications.

At this point words will not be adequate for what you experience. So allow yourself for two or three minutes to dwell here in absolute silence. You will know what to do and where to go.

At length you realize that it is time to return. You detach yourself from this divine presence while recognizing that it is always within you and that you can return here at any time. You go back by the way you came. You move away from the divine core of your own being. Now you are passing through the expanses of interstellar space, past the spirals of galaxies and nebulae.

You continue to proceed outward until you find yourself encountering the borders of our solar system. You reenter it. You find yourself moving at tremendous speed past the planets—Pluto, Neptune, Uranus, Saturn, Jupiter, Mars, the sun, Venus, Mercury, the moon—until you reach the earth, the physical realm that is the outermost shell of your own nature. And as in your mind's eye you proceed toward earth, you become aware again of the sensations and processes of the body. You plant your consciousness again firmly in this exterior part of yourself. You feel your back against your seat and your feet on the floor. You are aware again of your breathing. Allow your ordinary consciousness to reestablish itself, and after a minute or two, open your eyes and make contact again with the external world with which you are familiar.

WITHIN AND WITHOUT

In the Hebrew Bible, the first letter of the first verse of Genesis is the letter ב or *bet* for בראשית, *Bereshit,* or "in the beginning." The Jewish sages have made much of this fact. In the first place, ב is the second, not the first, letter of the Hebrew alphabet. Why doesn't the Bible begin with the first letter, which is א, or *aleph*?

Many answers to this question have been offered. In the first place, *aleph* is a silent letter. If you say an English word that begins with a vowel, like "at" or "ask," you will notice that your throat catches slightly before you say the vowel. This sound—which is not exactly a sound—is the *aleph*. Symbolically it is the silence out of which all proceeds. It is beyond speech or thought, so a mere text, no matter how sacred, cannot begin with this letter. Thus the Bible begins with the second letter, *bet*.

The *bet* has meanings of its own that relate it to the world of manifestation. It literally means "house." In addition, when placed in front of a word in Hebrew, *bet* means "in." These two apparently disparate facts point toward the same truth. For the essence of a house is that it possesses an inside and an outside, and to say "in" of course also means that there is such a thing as "out." Thus we are at the level of the primordial duality, the in/out, the yes/no, the light/dark that define all things insofar as they are things. (Using this same truth, computer scientists have devised the strings of 0s and 1s that make up all the content of artificial intelligence.)

What this all means in this context is that the mystery of the inner and the outer is perhaps the linchpin of the universe as we know it and can know it. God is radically outside the cosmos, and his light penetrates to us only through the countless filters of the spheres of the stars and the planets. Yet he is at the core of our own being as well, and the levels of the spirit and the psyche are subtle shells that encase this divine light and both hide and reveal it to the world. The truth of God is beyond inner and outer, beyond yes and no, even beyond good and evil. We will never plumb the depths of this mystery. Rather, it is something to be contemplated for a lifetime. When a truth like this becomes sufficiently embodied in one's consciousness, it becomes a wellspring of internal life and inspiration, bestowing wisdom and understanding as needed. To reflect on these ideas—and indeed on all esoteric cosmology—is not to amass mere information, but to allow a seed of insight to be planted in the field of the mind.

6

The Gospels and the Work of Christ

FOR MANY CHRISTIANS, what is most central to Christianity is Christ himself. The story of this great and unfathomable man, who taught a gospel of love and awakening for two or three years before being put to death by the powers of his day, is all the more compelling for its enigmas. Christ wrote only once, upon sand; yet he has inspired more books than any other human being. He was executed in an ignominious fashion, but the torture stake upon which he died has become the most widespread religious symbol in the world. He is surrounded by mystery, and yet the central fact about him, asserted by his disciples from the very beginning, is precisely the one that is most incredible: that he rose from the dead.

Christ the man is usually an object of faith. Regarded as the fully incarnated Son of God who took on the sins of humanity, he is seen as a bridge between the divine and the human, the Redeemer who has come to deliver us from our bondage to wickedness. He is the font of salvation. This is the exoteric Christ, the Christ of the outer circle.

Whatever we choose to make of this figure, there is also the Christ of the inner circle. This Christ is not the man Jesus, but the "I," or Logos, that lies at the center of each of us. The story of his life, his sufferings, his death and glorification is the story of this Logos in us. This is the esoteric Christ, the Christ who is not an object of faith but of knowledge. We come to know him—or it—not only by poring over Scripture but by cultivating the life of the spirit in ourselves.

THE JESUS OF HISTORY

Before we can get to this point, however, we seem to confront an enormous obstacle in the person of the historical Jesus. The quest for this elusive figure has proved to be one of the great intellectual enterprises of the past two centuries. Although Christians have always been fascinated by this subject, it did not gain center stage until the Enlightenment, when an increasingly skeptical intelligentsia began to ask awkward questions about the miraculous healings and exorcisms in the Gospels, as well as about the palpable discrepancies among the accounts of the four Evangelists.

The decisive step in this discourse took place in 1835–36, when a German scholar named David Friedrich Strauss published a life of Christ that made the radical but entirely plausible assertion that, in addition to factual history, these texts contained myths that had accrued around the figure of Jesus. Ever since then, scholars have been sifting and resifting the Gospels to find the grains of literal truth among the husks of legend. The Jesus Seminar, a collection of some seventy liberal New Testament scholars, is among the most famous: it has published versions of the Gospels in four colors to distinguish shades of likelihood in what Christ may have actually done and said.

The Jesus Seminar and similar efforts have been widely criticized, not only by fundamentalists but also by moderates who are troubled by the apparent arbitrariness of many of the Seminar's decisions and by the fact that the Jesus that remains after the editing is a nebulous figure. But in fact there is nothing really new about the Jesus Seminar's approach: Albert Schweitzer's *Quest of the Historical Jesus*, first published in 1906 and still a classic in the field, shows that theologians at the dawn of the twentieth century were just as ruthless in cutting out pieces of Scripture that they found implausible. On a less academic plane, it has long been an engaging hobby to pick and choose the parts of the Gospels that suit one's own predilections. One of the most famous examples was Thomas Jefferson, who literally cut out and pasted down the parts of the Gospels he found inspiring, leaving out the more "superstitious" elements: facsimiles of this work are occasionally reprinted as *The Jefferson Bible*. Stephen Mitchell's *Gospel According to Jesus* is a more recent example.

Yet all these versions of Jesus, both popular and academic, pose one problem that has never been solved: there is little or no evidence about

Jesus' life and teaching apart from the Gospels themselves. We learn something additional from Paul's writings as well as from extremely brief passages in non-Christian authors such as Tacitus and Josephus, but none of these are detailed or informative enough to tell us, say, whether Jesus really cast moneychangers out of the Temple or told people to cut off their right hand if it offended them. And for all we can learn about Jesus' historical context from archaeology and from contemporary texts such as the Dead Sea Scrolls, so far they have informed us only about his milieu. About the man himself they are silent. There is no way of really determining how much of what the Gospels say about him really happened and how much was legend.

Consequently, Jesus has become a Rorschach blot. We do not have to read many books about him to realize that the authors are telling us far more about themselves and their own interests than about the carpenter of Nazareth. Jefferson saw him as the exponent of a rational system of ethics; Morton Smith, as a folk magician; Albert Schweitzer, as a street-corner prophet of doom; and in a 1920s best-seller entitled *The Man Nobody Knows*, an ad man named Bruce Barton even portrayed Jesus as "the greatest salesman of all time."

Probably it was always so. "Tell me what I am like," Jesus asks Peter, Matthew, and Thomas in *The Gospel of Thomas*. Peter says he is like a righteous angel; Matthew, that he is like a wise philosopher. Thomas says, "Master, my mouth is wholly incapable of saying whom you are like." Jesus replies, "I am not your master. Because you have drunk, you have become intoxicated from the bubbling spring which I have measured out" (*Thomas*, 13).

The disciples themselves did not know who Jesus was. They knew he was not like other men; they saw that he came from a higher level of being, but they did not understand what it was. He never gave them a clear answer. The entire history of Christianity, its creeds, controversies, orthodoxies, and heterodoxies, consists of an attempt to deal with this issue.

In this book, as must already be clear, I have chosen to disregard historical issues of what Jesus may or may not actually have done or said and to take everything in the Gospels more or less at face value. This is partly because, for better or worse, the Jesus we know is the Jesus of the Gospels. Whether he himself did and said all these things, they are so ineradicably bound to him that it seems both pedantic and highly subjective to try to sort out his actual words and deeds from what was made up about him later. Moreover, the inner tradition has another perspective on Scripture.

Here the inner meaning of the Gospels has to do with the illumination of one's own soul.

Deep down, perhaps, all thoughtful and sincere readers of the Gospels sense this, and this quality may be the prime source of their appeal. The Gospels can be likened to Zen koans: they are not so much meant to be understood as to be felt. Their differing accounts, even their apparent discrepancies, strike at our minds and hearts from different angles. If we are attentive to these texts, they will convey their message to our deepest essence, awakening and stimulating it as a seed is quickened by the warming days of spring. Rational examination and critical inquiry are not to be excluded from this process, but are only one aspect of it. Boris Mouravieff observes: "The depth of Jesus' words is very great. . . . the Gospel is still very little 'exploited,' perhaps up to 5% or 10% of its depth. Doubtless even this estimate is optimistic."[1]

THE FOUR LIVING CREATURES

If what I am saying is true, it should somehow be reflected in the Christian tradition. And it is—in symbolic form. For centuries the four Evangelists have been represented by four living creatures. On the exoteric level this has to do with how each begins his Gospel. Matthew opens with the human lineage of Jesus, hence his symbol is a man. Mark starts with John the Baptist, "the voice of one crying in the wilderness" (Mark 1:3), so he is represented by a lion. Luke begins with Zecharias the priest performing his duties in the Temple; thus Luke's symbol is an ox, an animal used for sacrifice. And John commences in heaven, with the divine, preexistent Word, so his image is an eagle.

These symbols are older than Christianity. They appear in the first chapter of Ezekiel, in which the prophet has a vision of these four creatures. "As for the likeness of their faces, they four had the face of a man, and the face of a lion, on the right side; and they four had the face of an ox on the left side; they four also had the face of an eagle" (Ezek. 1:10).

Ezekiel's vision is a complex and highly compacted symbolic picture. It is difficult to visualize as described; no doubt the prophet saw something that was not easy to express in language as he knew it. But the general form is clear. There are four living creatures: the ox, lion, eagle, and man. Above them is a throne upon which a man sits. Usually this image is regarded as a theophany—a visible manifestation of God—but it could be equally well understood as a revelation of the nature of a human being, suggesting that there are four essential elements to each of us. The ox, with its strength and bulk, symbolizes the body. The lion, with its pride and its urge to dominate, represents the emotions. The man symbolizes the mind or reason, which is what makes us distinctively human. The eagle, with its power of flight and its sharpness of vision, is associated with the spirit, the transpersonal aspect of the human character. Above these four is a throne with a man sitting on it. Perhaps Ezekiel is trying to say that in order to be fully human, we need to have access to, and to master, these four dimensions of ourselves.

Astrologers will recognize these symbols as the four fixed signs of the zodiac. There is Taurus the bull, Leo the lion, and Aquarius the water bearer, who is portrayed as a young man. Scorpio is the fourth, and while the creature usually associated with this often-maligned sign is the scorpion, esoteric astrologers say that Scorpio, which is peculiarly well adapted to self-transcendence, is also symbolized by the eagle.[2] The zodiac, with its twelve signs associated with twelve fundamental human types, encompasses the range of human experience and expression. The four living creatures—that is, the four fixed signs—are the anchoring points of this array of twelve types and so serve as a symbolic abbreviation for them all.

How does this symbolism help us approach the Gospels? Boris Mouravieff has some interesting suggestions in this regard.[3] He says that the three synoptic Gospels correspond to three different types of individuals. At the outset of esoteric development, each of us is biased toward one of the basic facets of our nature: the mind, the emotions, or the body. The three synoptics are addressed to these: Matthew speaks to the one who is oriented toward thought (which may be why Matthew, in the verse from *Thomas* quoted above, tells Jesus he is like "a wise philosopher"). Matthew is concerned with thought as the Jews understand it, which is centered on the Torah. Matthew is extremely scrupulous in rooting Jesus' words and deeds in precedents and prophecies from the Hebrew Bible.

Mark is the shortest and most direct of the Gospels. It is addressed to those who are centered on the emotions. In a conventional sense, Mark is not a very emotional gospel. It is direct, abrupt, and elliptical. But our understanding of this part of our being is different from what it has traditionally been. We tend to associate the emotions with a vapid sentimentality, a fuzziness and softness that is the opposite of the way they are in fact. In their deepest essence the emotions are swift, direct, and ruthless—like a lion. They can size up a situation instantaneously, much more rapidly than can the rational mind. This is why a gut feeling about a person one has just met is generally faster and more accurate than rational evaluations, which are usually running to catch up. It is this aspect of the emotions to which Mark speaks.

Luke is addressed to those oriented toward the body. Luke is more concerned with Jesus' growth and development—those fundamental bodily concerns—than are the other Evangelists. Although his anecdote of Jesus' teaching in the Temple at the age of twelve gives only a brief glimpse into Christ's boyhood, it is really the only picture we have. Luke is also the only one who tells us that in his youth "Jesus increased in wisdom and stature, and in favour with God and man" (Luke 2:25). The ox or cow is a common and perhaps universal symbol of the body, which sustains us and helps us grow in the physical world—a consideration that casts light not only on Christian symbolism but also on the Hindu veneration of the cow as well as on the celebrated Zen ox-herding parable. And for Luke, the mother of Jesus, the personification of nurturing in the Christian tradition, looms much larger than in the other Gospels, where she is a shadowy figure and where we never have any sense of her internal responses to her role in her son's drama. It is Luke that tells us of the Annunciation and has Mary sing a hymn of praise in her joy at the news.

Finally, there is John, the Gospel that is different. It does not talk about Jesus' birth, it does not show him speaking in parables, and it says little about his preaching in Galilee, which probably occupied the greatest part of his public career. The Gospel of John takes place mostly in Jerusalem, and this detail, while apparently inconsistent with the synoptics, offers an important key to what John is trying to accomplish. His Gospel does not speak to the three lower aspects of our natures, as the others do; it addresses the highest part, the spirit, or "I," which unites and harmonizes these three; it rises above them, which is why it is symbolized by the eagle. In the Bible this part of the human makeup is symbolized by Zion or Jerusalem, the seat of the Temple, where Israel makes contact with the presence of the living God. John does not show Jesus as speaking in parables because at this level analogies and stories are unnecessary and possibly unhelpful; what is disclosed in encrypted form by the synoptics is uttered openly there.

There may be some value, then, in approaching the Gospels not as if they were newspaper articles giving contradictory accounts, but as sacred texts presenting the same truths in a manner that speaks to different types of individuals as well as to different levels of our own being. Such a perspective may help us step beyond the apparent discrepancies that have dogged so many readers of these texts. If we can open the manifold aspects of our natures to the Gospels, they can disclose themselves to us in our fragmented state and can help to integrate it.

TWO NATIVITIES

This approach can be applied to Gospel texts with some fascinating results. One example may be found in the nativity accounts. There are only two, in Matthew and Luke. And these two accounts show some serious divergences from a historical point of view. Chronologically, for example, Matthew has Jesus born during the reign of Herod the Great, who died between 6 and 1 B.C. But Luke says that Jesus was born when his parents went to Bethlehem for a census that took place "when Cyrenius was governor of Syria" (Luke 2:2). Cyrenius, or Publius Sulpicius Quirinius, was governor of Syria in 6 A.D.[4] This discrepancy has troubled scholars since antiquity. Some argue that Quirinius must have had another, earlier term as governor of Syria, but there is no evidence for this claim, and it is merely special pleading.

Another difference is the tone of the two accounts. Matthew's is overshadowed by the menace of Herod's enmity toward the infant Jesus, culminating in the slaughter of the innocents; Luke's is quite peaceful. Here too these versions are at variance with the historical context, since there is no outside evidence of the slaughter of the innocents, while the census under Quirinius caused a revolt in Judea (Luke himself mentions it in Acts 5:37).

An esoteric understanding of these texts will not try to force some reconciliation at the literal level; perhaps, as Origen said of Genesis, "these passages, by means of seeming history, though the incidents never occurred, figuratively reveal certain mysteries." But they may cast some light on the birth of the spirit in the flesh as seen through the lenses of the mind (represented by Matthew) and the body (represented by Luke).

To begin with Matthew: The birth of the divine child is the birth of the "I" in the individual, the first glimmer of higher consciousness. In Matthew (as in Luke) it is a *virgin* birth; that is to say, it is a juncture of the unseen essence of the individual combined with his situation in time and space. Even in an ordinary nativity there is the combination of the earthly elements—protein, water, the parents' genes—with an indefinable something else, a consciousness and presence that comes from beyond; many parents say they were able to recognize this essence as soon as their children were born. In this sense every birth is a virgin birth.

The newborn Christ child is a king; that is, this "I" is the rightful ruler of the realm that is a human being. Hence the oldest and wisest elements of the psyche, symbolized by the Three Magi, come to pay it reverence, but in so doing they unintentionally endanger it by alerting King Herod to the birth.[5] Herod symbolizes the false king, the ego. In symbolic language Matthew is suggesting that the mind is a dangerous entity, and its capacity for forethought (depicted by the magis' ability to divine the meaning of the star of Bethlehem) often willy-nilly ends up at the service of the lower self. This false king does its best to destroy the child by killing all the newborns—that is, all the fresh impulses toward life and awakening that arise in the psyche.

But the true "I" cannot be killed. Its parents, the forces that sustain and foster it, take it into Egypt—the "black land" (as its name means in the ancient Egyptian language) that in the Judeo-Christian tradition has always symbolized the darkness of material immersion. These are the years of spiritual silence, of preoccupation with the world, often of indolence and aimlessness. As the fourteenth-century Friend of God Johannes Tauler says, only a call from a higher level can summon it back again, as Joseph is called back to Egypt by an angel in a dream.[6]

Luke's account has quite another flavor. It has given us some of the most familiar images of the nativity: the journey to Bethlehem, Joseph and Mary finding no room at the inn, Jesus laid in a manger. Viewed in light of the symbol of the ox, the symbol of the bodily consciousness, many of the details achieve a striking clarity. Here there are no kings and wise men, but simple pastoral people peacefully returning to their hometown. We hear nothing of the revolt against the census or other momentous events; the journey sounds as placid and uneventful as the return of a flock to its fold. And in fact Christ's birth is announced not to astrological adepts but to shepherds "keeping watch over their flock by night" (Luke 2:8).

The body has often been loathed and despised in the Christian tradition, but this passage in Luke symbolically casts another light on it. Esoterically shepherds "keeping watch over their flock by night" refer to those who are able to keep some control over their bodily impulses. Like sheep, these impulses will stray if left on their own, but if guarded with a firm but mild hand they will respond devotedly. The fact that the shepherds are keeping watch "at night" reinforces this point: to keep a vigil is to conquer the desire for sleep. What Francis of Assisi called "Brother

Ass" is not as recalcitrant as often believed; it likes and responds to guidance. Only when this bodily mastery is achieved, Luke is suggesting, can the messenger of higher consciousness arrive.

THE VOICE OF THE EAGLE

John's Gospel has no nativity at all. It begins in heaven with the divine Word. In a celebrated homily on this Gospel, the ninth-century Irish sage John Scotus Eriugena writes:

> The blessed theologian John . . . flies beyond not only what may be thought and spoken, but also beyond all mind and meaning. Exalted by the ineffable flight of his spirit beyond all things, he enters into the very arcanum of the one principle of all. There he clearly distinguishes the superessential unity and supersubstantial difference of the beginning and the Word—that is, the Father and the Son—both incomprehensible, and begins his Gospel saying: "In the beginning was the Word."[7]

In his arcane philosophical language, Eriugena is trying to express the paradox of divinity: the essential unity of the transcendent aspect of God, the Father, with the immanent aspect, the Son, and indicates that this mystery, the source and origin of all that was made, extends to the furthest reaches of being. The Gospel begins at this point because it is the point at which everything begins.

John the Evangelist has traditionally been identified with John the beloved disciple. Whether or not this is so, Eriugena also says that John serves as a symbolic figure in his own Gospel. He is juxtaposed with Peter in a manner that sharpens the contrast between the outer religion of faith and the inner tradition of knowledge: "Peter is always presented as the model of faith and action, while John portrays the type of contemplation and knowledge. The one leans on the bosom of the Lord, which is the sacrament of contemplation, while the other often hesitates, which is the symbol of restless action." Eriugena points out that both Peter and John run to the empty tomb on the morning of Jesus' resurrection, but Peter enters first. "If Peter symbolizes faith, then John signifies the intellect. Therefore, since it is written, 'Unless you believe you will not understand,' faith necessarily enters first into the tomb of Holy Scripture, followed by the intellect, for which faith has prepared the entry."[8] As this passage suggests, faith has an important role to play in the life of the spirit, but there is something ignorant and blind about it as well. It is a prelude to knowledge, not a substitute.

One episode in John's Gospel illuminates with special clarity the relation between the "I" and the world. Christ meets a woman of Samaria at a well and asks her for water. She refuses on the grounds that he is a Jew, and Jews have no dealings with Samaritans. In response he offers her living water and tells her to go and bring her husband back with her. She replies: "Sir, I have no husband. Jesus said unto her, Thou hast well said, I have no husband: for thou hast had five husbands; and he whom thou hast is not thy husband: in that thou sayest truly" (John 4:17–18).

From earliest times the woman of Samaria has been understood as a personification of the soul. She has had five husbands, meaning the five senses (the number five in esoteric terms often has this connotation). She is living with another man, who is "not her husband." Maurice Nicoll suggests that this indicates a state where the soul has begun to detach itself from the external world; "at this point the 'soul' vaguely turns to other interests—perhaps to some sort of philosophy or to different forms of so-called occultism, to opinions, theories and imagination and so on, in an endeavour to satisfy its thirst with truth other than the truth of the senses."9

At this stage, if it is open enough, it can encounter the true "I," the Logos, at the well. This true "I" offers it living water—which, Nicoll says, symbolizes truth. Her reluctance to take it on the grounds that he is of another nation reminds us that truth often takes a form different from what we expect. But in the end she relents and tells her husband that she has met the Christ; "then they went out of the city and came unto him" (John 4:30). To come out of a city, in esoteric terms, means to leave behind all that is known and familiar and comfortable. God's command to Abraham to go forth from his father's country (Gen. 11:31–12:1) has exactly the same meaning.10

But the esoteric backbone of John's Gospel—and the aspect that most clearly illumines the central truth of inner Christianity—consists of seven pronouncements Christ makes: "I am the vine" (John 15:5); "I am the way, the truth, and the life" (14:6); "I am the door" (10:9); "I am the bread of life" (6:35); "I am the good shepherd" (10:11); "I am the light of the world" (9:5); and "I am the resurrection and the life" (11:25).11

Taken at face value, these are grandiose and improbable utterances. But viewed from an inner level, they constitute extremely powerful statements about the relation of the "I" of the self to the greater, collective "I" that is the true Christ. "I am the door," for example, is to be understood not as a claim made by the man Jesus, but rather as saying that "I am" is the door through which we enter into higher consciousness. "I am the vine; ye are the branches" means that this greater Christ, who is the restored Adam, is the core of our identity as individuals. And "I am the way, the truth, and the life; no man cometh to the Father but by me" is not a narrow sectarian claim but a mystical utterance of the truth that the ineffable, transpersonal Father cannot be encountered except through this inner Christ. Viewed in this light, these utterances no longer seem arrogant or exclusionary. Rather, they remind us that by penetrating to the core of our own being, we can make contact with the consciousness at the center of the universe.

THE GREAT SACRIFICE

Although it would be possible to go through the Gospels line for line in light of this understanding, there is not the space to do so here. Instead, it might be more valuable to focus on the inner meaning of the Gospels' central drama: the passion, death, and resurrection of Christ. While the details of this event vary among the Gospels, the basic story is the same in all of them, and it is one of the best-known stories on the face of the earth.

God came down to earth. He was made man. He was born and grew up in a particular time and place. He contributed to the life of his era; he made friends and enemies. Even so, the world "knew him not." He suffered and died in a painful and ignominious fashion. Yet in the end it did not matter. Nothing that was ultimately true or real about him was lost. He continues to live in a new and transfigured form.[12]

This is the story of Christ. It is ours as well, and its deep truth, not only about a particular man who lived two thousand years ago but also about ourselves in our most intimate essence, is the greatest source of its appeal. The myth is saying that in its pristine state, consciousness, the "I" that is the true Son of God, is totally free and unconditioned; it is not encumbered by being bound to a particular body in a particular time and place; it does not suffer from the impediments of specificity. But for reasons that must always remain somewhat obscure to us, it chooses to descend into the realm of matter, of constraint, of limitation. Consciousness is no longer absolute but relative; it is no longer pure and collective but is apportioned into yours and mine. It is crucified on a cross known as time and space. We have chosen to "know good and evil" by isolating ourselves from God and from each other. And this is an experience of terrible suffering and privation, impelling Christ to cry out in his final agony, "My God, my God, why hast thou forsaken me?" (Matt. 27:46).

If this were the whole story, it would be a tale of despondency indeed. We would be nothing more than the sum of nervous impulses that make up the consciousness of the body, and when the body dies, that would be the end. But it is not the end. The crucified Christ rises on the third day. So far from facing extinction with the demolition of the body, the Son of God lives again in a new and sublime but perhaps unfamiliar form. Mary Magdalene does not recognize the risen Christ at first, "supposing him to be the gardener" (John 20:15—an allusion, perhaps, to Adam, who was put in the garden "to dress it and to keep it"). Nor do the disciples on the road to Emmaus.

Such is one meaning of the story of Christ's passion viewed from a human perspective, but it has a cosmic perspective as well. The immanent aspect of God has to limit itself to enter into manifestation; by doing so, it debases and degrades itself (Luke expresses this truth by portraying the newborn as being laid in a manger). Once it has made this great sacrifice, it is subject to the laws of the realm it enters. It takes on the life of a particular type of being, with its limitations and restrictions. This polarity—the infinite bound in the finite, the absolute in the relative—engenders a tension that can never be fully resolved. Once it reaches a breaking point, again symbolized by the extremity of the Crucifixion, the embodied form shatters in death, only to rise again in a transfigured state, its dissipated elements giving rise to new combinations and forms.

This process takes place on all scales, from the birth and death of a galaxy to the life of a fly. It was long recognized in the vegetative cycle of the seasons and underlay the old fertility cults. Its profound and perplexing truth has inspired myths from the Egyptian tale of Osiris to Joyce's *Finnegans Wake*. No doubt it was initially inspired by the recognition of death. The first human who looked upon another dead person and realized that this same fate lay in store for her was perhaps the first philosopher and the first religionist. Provoked to ask what awaited her beyond this gate, she may have recognized that that in her which saw this situation was itself what is immortal and would long survive the dispersion of his form. Sometimes this immortal force has been personified externally, in the gods of all pantheons; but the wise have always known that these are only figures, pictures we create as a way of seeing the truth more clearly, and that the true divinity is the being that peers at the world through each of us as through so many telescopes.

REDEMPTION AND RESURRECTION

Seen this way, the story of Christ's passion and resurrection is a myth like other myths, and its essential similarity to these has long been recognized: a hundred years ago, J. G. Frazer caused a shock in the Victorian world by suggesting as much in his classic *Golden Bough*. New Testament scholar Gregory J. Riley even believes that this was why Christianity spread so rapidly in the Greco-Roman world: the story of Christ was identical to the hero myths people already knew. Gnostics past and present tend to focus on this mythic aspect of Christ's life, holding that what is most important is the truth that it symbolizes and leaving the factual side of the matter an open question.

But most esoteric Christians have not been content to leave the story of Christ a myth. Rather, they tend to stress that with Christ, what the myths were alluding to actually happened in the flesh. As Rudolf Steiner says, "the secrets of the Mysteries became manifest in Christianity."[13] What was this work that Christ enacted?

The teaching about Christ's Redemption that is most current today (as it has been for many centuries) is that of the vicarious atonement. By this account the fallen human race sinned so grievously against the will of the Father that the only possible recompense could be the sacrifice of a perfect human life. But since the whole human race had been tainted by Adam's fall, no ordinary individual could constitute this acceptable sacrifice, so the Son of God himself had to incarnate and offer himself as the price for Adam's sin.

There is a certain sublimity to this doctrine, but what, in the end, is it trying to say? That the human race so irked the Supreme Being by trespassing a minor command that it was completely alienated from him, and that God's wrath could be quenched only by having a part of himself come down and offer itself as a sacrifice to another part? Put this way, the absurdity of this doctrine becomes apparent. There *are* such things as divine mysteries, things that cannot be fully comprehended by the human mind, but there is also such a thing as nonsense, and one should not be mistaken for the other.

In fact, the doctrine of the vicarious atonement is a comparatively late one; it was more or less unknown in the early centuries of Christian history and became official doctrine only in the eleventh century. As the Theosophist Annie Besant reminds us, "The general teaching in the Early Church on the doctrine of the Atonement was that Christ, as the Representative of Humanity, faced and conquered Satan, the representative of the Dark Powers, who held humanity in bondage, wrested his captive from him, and set him free."[14] This is now known as the "ransom theory" of salvation.

The Fall inverted the right relationship between the "I" and the world; to use the old language, humanity was enslaved to the Devil. Christ's redemptive act set it free. This liberation could not be carried out in the unseen spiritual world: the bondage existed on this earth, on the level of reality in which we live and breathe, and the redemption had to take place here as well. Once Christ's work was completed, consciousness could be freed from bondage to its own experience, and a new life of freedom was possible. Rudolf Steiner goes so far as to say that the earth itself was transformed and spiritualized by the redemptive act of Christ.

Christ's victory over the "Dark Powers" is generally acknowledged to have been complete not with the Crucifixion but with the Resurrection. This leads us back to the issue of the historical Jesus, because to accept this perspective is to accept at least the possibility that Jesus rose from the dead. Although this has often been regarded as a later legendary accretion, in fact the Resurrection is one of the earliest documented parts of the Christian tradition.

In the New Testament as we have it now, the letters of Paul come after the four Gospels and Acts, but scholars almost universally believe that Paul's letters were written first.[15] Paul was executed in Nero's persecution of the Christians in 64 A.D. (the emperor blamed them for the fire during which he allegedly fiddled), so his Epistles had to have been written before this date; the Gospels are generally dated to between 70 and 90. First Corinthians is generally thought to have been written in the 50s, and it contains the earliest written reference to Christ's resurrection:

> For I delivered unto you first of all that which I also received, how that Christ died for our sins according to the scriptures; and that he was buried, and that he rose again the third day according to the scriptures: and that he was seen of Cephas, then of the twelve: after that, he was seen of above five hundred brethren at once; of whom the greater part remain unto this present, but some are fallen asleep. After that, he was seen of

James; then of all the apostles. And last of all he was seen of me also, as of one born out of due time (1 Cor. 15:3–7).

Here Paul is identifying his own experience of the risen Christ—his famous vision on the road to Damascus—with Christ's appearances to the Apostles after his Crucifixion. Whatever one wishes to make of this, it is impossible to say that the Resurrection is a legend that grew up around Christ long after he lived: Paul knew the Apostles intimately and heard their stories from their own lips. Thus, as Christians have claimed from the earliest times, the risen Christ is the basis of their faith, and Christianity would not exist without it. We do not really know what the Apostles saw. But clearly they saw *something*, and what they saw led them to change not only their own lives but the life of the whole world as well.

How we deal with these considerations will depend on our own predilections. The credulous take it on faith; the skeptics deny it equally mechanically. Inner Christianity is not about either selling this teaching or explaining it away, but about leaving it for each person to examine and explore with the inner organ of intuition. Gnosis is verification—not exterior, factual verification, but the ability to penetrate a mystery like this with the deeper reaches of one's own spirit and to evaluate it accordingly.

WHO WAS CHRIST?

Who, then, was Jesus? Was he the preexistent Son of God, born of the virgin, fully divine and fully human? Was he a divine being slightly lower than God, as the fourth-century bishop Arius, some Unitarians, and sects such as Jehovah's Witnesses contend? Was he a man upon whom the "Christ-consciousness" settled at the time of the baptism (a view known as adoptionism)? Was he just a good, wise teacher who was later deified by his followers? All of these options have been espoused by different groups and individuals. In his book *The Tree of Gnosis*, the Romanian scholar Ioan P. Couliano ingeniously argues that, taken together, these doctrines represent a kind of logical working-out of the various combinations.[16]

The dynamic underlying this issue is a profound and mysterious one, and it would be wise not to become high-handed about any conclusions we might reach. But one way of understanding this issue can be teased out from what we have seen already. The Father is the ineffable, transcendent aspect of God; the Son is God's immanent aspect. This divine spark or Logos is the first sounding-forth of existence from the depths of infinity:

"All things were made by him; and without him was not any thing made that was made. In him was life; and the life was the light of men" (John 1:3–4). Christ is the embodiment of this immanent aspect of God.

So are we. "Without him was not any thing made that was made." Nothing comes into existence unless this divine spark of consciousness, no matter how faint or dim, lies at its center. This was true of Jesus, it is true of me, and it is true of you who read this book. We may not be as exalted as Christ or the other great beings of the cosmos; we may not be as good or as wise. But at the core we are the same.

Of the texts of esoteric Christianity, *A Course in Miracles* sets out this truth most clearly. The Fall (which the *Course* calls the "separation") happened not because God became angry with humanity but because the human race chose to "know good and evil" by seeing itself as isolated from God. This is the cause of all unhappiness, and as soon as it occurred, God ordained a remedy called the Atonement—a process, long in terms of time but instantaneous in eternity, by which human beings will again come to recognize their unity with God and one another. The man Jesus was the first human being to fully realize his part in this plan. "The name of *Jesus* is the name of one who was a man but saw the face of Christ in all his brothers and remembered God. So he became identified with *Christ*, a man no longer, but at one with God." For this reason Jesus says in the *Course*, "I am charge of the process of Atonement, which I undertook to begin." [17] This does not mean that Jesus is essentially different from the rest of us; the *Course* insists he is not. In it Jesus says:

> There is nothing about me that you cannot attain. I have nothing that does not come from God. The difference between us now is that I have nothing else. This leaves me in a state which is only potential in you.
>
> "No man cometh unto the Father but by me" does not mean that I am in any way separate or different from you except in time, and time does not really exist. The statement is more meaningful in terms of a vertical rather than a horizontal axis. You stand below me and I stand below God. In the process of "rising up," I am higher because without me the distance between God and man would be too great for you to encompass. [18]

Another part of the *Course* says about Jesus, "Is he the Christ? O yes, along with you. His little life on earth was not enough to teach the mighty lesson that he learned for all of us. He will remain with you to lead you from the hell you made to God." [19]

As I have said, it is impossible to say whether the *Course* was dictated by the being known as Jesus Christ or not; no criterion that could establish it one way or another could possibly be agreed upon. But the *Course* does take what had been a hidden teaching and presents it in clear English, showing that what is divine in Christ is what is divine in each of us. The *Course* is not the only work that presents this teaching; it is implicit in many Christian texts, even, as we have seen, in the Gospels themselves. But it has been expressed darkly and covertly because people were not ready to hear it in the open. Now, as a new understanding arises, what was formerly concealed is newly disclosed. As we come to see it more clearly, we will tend to regard the divine less as an external being to be worshiped and adored and more as something within to be drawn out of ourselves and made manifest. As Christ said to the woman of Samaria, "The hour cometh, and now is, when the true worshippers shall worship the Father in spirit and in truth" (John 4:21, 23).

7

The Feminine Face of God

T HE RECENT UPHEAVALS IN GENDER RELATIONS have come to pervade theology. Many feminist critics of Christianity argue that the long-held image of God as Father and King has subtly or overtly upheld a cultural pattern of male dominance. As this structure has begun to break down, they are saying that feminine images of God should receive equal homage.

While it is true that the Christian hierarchy has been male-dominated since its earliest centuries, it cannot be said that the tradition as a whole has offered no reverence to the feminine aspects of the divine. Feminine images of the sacred are practically as numerous as masculine ones. The great church of Hagia Sophia in Istanbul, built by the Byzantine emperor Justinian the Great in the sixth century, is devoted to Sophia, the Wisdom of God, and the great Gothic cathedrals of Western Europe are dedicated not to Jesus or the Father but to Mary. Icons, paintings, and statuary represent Mary and female saints as often as their male counterparts. The power of the divine feminine has even made itself felt in paranormal occurrences, especially the Marian apparitions in such places as Guadalupe, Lourdes, Fatima, and most recently in Medjugorje in Bosnia-Herzegovina. For many Catholic and Orthodox Christians, the Virgin is as numinous a figure as Christ himself. Often she is seen as far more immediate and accessible.

The figures of Mary and Sophia, one omnipresent and the other enigmatic and often forgotten, constitute the two chief female images of the divine in Christianity. Each of them, representing a different aspect of the human makeup, has a great deal to teach about the inner tradition.

Before we look at these figures, however, it may be necessary to restate a point that is both obvious and too often overlooked: The Deity does not have a gender, or, if it does, it is an androgynous gender, as the Bible suggests: "God created man in his own image, in the image of God created he him; male and female created he them" (Gen. 1:27). To refer to God as masculine, feminine, or even neuter is only a manner of speaking. We have to use such manners of speaking, because language does not permit us to utter thought in any other fashion, but the constraints of speech can easily lead us astray.

English assigns gender to nouns on the basis of sex. A man is a "he," a woman, a "she"; things without sex are called "it." This is not so in most other European languages, which assign gender on the basis of a word's form. This is known as *grammatical gender*, and it is found in modern languages such as French and German as well as in ancient tongues such as Latin, Greek, and Hebrew. The gender of a given abstract noun may vary from language to language. The word for "spirit," for example, is masculine in Latin (*spiritus*), feminine in Hebrew (*ruach*), and neuter in Greek (*pneuma*).

This apparently pedantic point has had tremendous consequences for how individuals and indeed whole civilizations have viewed the divine. The fact that *spiritus* is masculine in Latin makes the Western Trinity entirely male. In Greek theology, the Holy Spirit (*pneuma hagion*) has a more impersonal quality, while in Syriac (a language like Hebrew that was spoken by much of the ancient Eastern Christian world) the feminine gender of the word for "spirit" makes it seem as if the Third Person of the Trinity is female. Because the human mind thinks in concepts, and concepts are dictated and structured by language, there is the inevitable danger of turning these words into absolutes. One may be tempted to think that the spirit of consciousness really *is* masculine or feminine, depending on the language one speaks.

THE DIVINE SOPHIA

Nowhere is this problem so evident as with Sophia. Sophia means "wisdom" in Greek, and Sophia is the hypostasis, or personification, of divine Wisdom. *Sophia* is in fact simply the Greek word for "wisdom"; the

Hebrew equivalent is Hokhmah, the second of the ten *sefirot* on the Kabbalistic Tree of Life.

Our earliest glimpse of Sophia is in the Book of Proverbs, where wisdom and understanding are frequently paired, as in the verse "How much better it is to get wisdom than gold! and to get understanding rather to be chosen than silver!" (Prov. 16:16). Often wisdom and understanding are regarded as abstractions, but sometimes they are personified (as women, because these nouns are grammatically feminine): "Say unto wisdom, thou art my sister; and call understanding thy kinswoman" (Prov. 7:4). On still other occasions, Wisdom alone appears in a more active capacity, as in the famous verse, "Wisdom hath builded her house, she hath hewn out her seven pillars" (Prov. 9:1). This tendency reaches its climax when the personified Wisdom speaks:

> The Lord possessed me in the beginning of his way, before his works of old. I was set up from everlasting, from the beginning or ever the earth was. When there were no depths I was brought forth; when there were no fountains abounding with water. . . . When he prepared the heavens I was there; when he set a compass on the face of the depth: when he established the clouds above: when he strengthened the foundations of the deep (Prov. 8:22–24, 27–28).

Wisdom here has a pivotal role in the creation itself. But how? This passage suggests an answer in saying that God "set a compass on the face of the depth." This is more than a poetic utterance; it shows how consciousness creates a world around itself. This principle operates in us individually, in each moment, so you can catch a glimpse of it in ordinary cognition. As you look around you in the room you are in, you recognize familiar objects. You see, perhaps, a desk, a chair, a table, a sofa. You can also observe that as you recognize these things *as* these things, you are picking them out from an initially indistinct landscape of shapes and colors, which then immediately recede into the background.

This action of "picking out," which is essential to recognition, usually goes on unconsciously and automatically. It happens so fast that it can even be hard to become aware of it. Yet this "picking out" enables us to create a familiar world around ourselves and to function in it. This process is esoterically called "setting a compass upon the face of the depth." It is cognition in the purest sense; perhaps it would not be amiss even to translate *hokhmah* as "cognition" rather than "wisdom." The British esotericist W. G. Davies writes:

> We live in a created world. That world is shown forth by division and so it multiplies its parts. The appearance of things is as the grains of sand in the desert. They show to us small and great, evil and good, upper and lower, before and after. It is our duty as brothers to both see and instruct. Without wisdom we can do neither. Therefore we are told by our teachers that there is no wisdom without seeing, no seeing without wisdom.[1]

One modern philosopher who seems to have understood this process was Martin Heidegger, who discusses it in a lecture on the Greek thinker Heraclitus. Heidegger suggests that Heraclitus described this process of cognition as "picking out" and even used a term for it—*logos* (from the Greek *legein*, "to gather" or "to pick out").[2] *Logos* is usually translated as "word." Although it has an enormous range of other meanings as well, it can accurately be described as the "word," because as consciousness goes through its experience and picks out some special feature of it—an object, external or internal—it instantly appends a name to it, a word. In this sense it is the "word" that brings the world into being. The ancient Hebrews made this fact the centerpiece of their worldview. They believed that the name for a thing was identical to the thing itself: as one Kabbalistic aphorism says, "God and his name are one." Philo of Alexandria, who lived around the time of Christ, incorporated the term *logos* into the Jewish tradition. It was brought into Christianity in turn through the Gospel of John, where we read that through the Word "all things were made . . . and without him was not any thing made that was made" (John 1:3).

But the Word is usually considered to be masculine (*logos* is a masculine noun in Greek), while Sophia is feminine. What, then, is the relation between the two? The tradition in its earliest times saw an extremely close connection between Sophia and Christ—the Logos—so it would not be mistaken to see them as essentially the same principle. In the apocryphal Book of Sirach or Ecclesiasticus, Wisdom is literally the Word of God: "I came forth from the mouth of the Most High," she proclaims (Sir. 24:3, Revised Standard Version). As some New Testament scholars point out, the Gospels draw strong parallels between Christ and Sophia: Christ's use of bread and wine echoes Sophia's cry "Come, eat of my bread, and drink of the wine which I have mingled" (Prov. 9:5), and in the Last Supper his

The Way to the Sabbath of Rest, *by Thomas Bromley, a follower of Jacob Boehme (here reproduced from an eighteenth-century German edition), sets out a basic schema of the human being as seen by esoteric Christianity. The three overlapping circles represent (from the bottom) the body, the psyche, and the spirit. The lowest realm is "Sathan" or Satan, representing the downward pull of the world. In the small circle at the center of the diagram are the numbers 1 through 12, symbolizing the zodiac, which rules the psyche. The eye in the heart at the center of the circle at the top indicates the spirit illumined by Sophia or the Logos, the "I that is we."*

call to eat of his body and drink of his blood echoes Sophia's call in Sirach: "Come to me, you who desire me, and eat your fill of my produce. . . . Those who eat me will hunger for more, and those who drink me will thirst for more" (Sir. 24:19, 21, RSV). Paul himself equates Christ and Sophia, calling Christ "the wisdom of God" (1 Cor. 1:24).[3]

Sophia, then, is the same as the Logos, the principle of consciousness, the transcendental "I" that experiences the world in and through us. This parallel was explicit in the early years of Christianity. The fourth-century church historian Eusebius writes, "This is in truth a Being, living and subsisting before the world, who assisted the Father and God of the universe in the fashioning of all created things, namely the Word of God and Wisdom."[4] But later the identification of the Logos with Sophia was covered over and practically lost. The Logos was increasingly identified with the historical Jesus, who was male. Consequently, it was believed, the female Sophia had to be something different—but exactly *what* became increasingly unclear, and Sophia became a shadowy figure.

THE FALL OF WISDOM

The Logos, or Sophia, as the principle of consciousness that creates the cosmos, is connected with the descent into manifestation. Most of inner Christianity regards this as a positive process—bringing a world into being that is essentially good. But some strains of the tradition have held that Sophia was debased by this descent. They include the Gnostics, for whom she is a fallen figure in need of redemption. The various Gnostic cosmogonies are intricate and idiosyncratic, and each teacher had his own system, so there is no single one we can turn to as the epitome of Gnostic thought. But in broad outline the story is the same. The Gnostic myth of Sophia is at its core the tale of the fall of consciousness and its redemption.

A characteristic version of this myth appears in a text known as the *Apocryphon of John*. Here Sophia is an Aeon, a primordial being like an archangel in later Christian theology. Like the other Aeons—of whom there are twelve, arranged in pairs—she is begotten by the unknowable, primordial, beneficent Father.

At a certain point, however, the text tells us, "Our sister Sophia . . . thought a thought of herself." She chooses to have an offspring without her partner, and begets a monstrous being named Ialdabaoth, the Demiurge, whose nature partakes of the selfish impulse that led to his engendering. He begets a cosmos of his own, inferior and imprisoning, and when it is done, he cries, "I am a jealous God; apart from me there is none." The text dryly comments, "Thereby he indicated to the angels under him that there is another God; for if there was no other, of whom should he be jealous?" Eventually Sophia repents of her action, and her consort comes to rescue her from the plight into which she has fallen. She is not, however, restored to her former place, but is assigned the role of serving as a bridge between the higher world and the Demiurge, until she manages to set right the aborted universe she has spawned.[5]

Regarded as cosmology or theology, this account is difficult to swallow; viewed as an allegorical portrayal of human cognition, it is quite astute. Sophia's name, as we have seen, means "wisdom"—"a paradoxical name in view of the history of folly of which she is made the protagonist," as Hans Jonas comments.[6] But it is not quite such a misnomer if we realize that the Greek word *sophos*, or "wise," also has the connotation of cleverness. The name may be suggesting that this principle of primordial consciousness is occasionally too clever for its own good. It creates a world by picking objects out, but then "falls" by becoming fixated upon them. It loses its own identity, or rather forges a fictitious identity for itself by perceiving itself as an object among other objects. Sophia "thought a thought of herself," indicating that this story has to do with the arising of self-consciousness—the creation of a self-aware ego that sets itself apart from the world. This is symbolized by Ialdabaoth, who cries, "I am a jealous God; apart from me there is none." This is usually taken as a jibe at the Old Testament God, who tells the children of Israel, "I the Lord thy God am a jealous God," but it is more apt as a characterization of the ego, which is profoundly uneasy with its own self-aggrandizing yet self-isolating stance.

Ialdabaoth spawns a monstrous set of beings identified with the seven planets, as well as such entities as "Divinity," "Lordship," "Fire," and "Kingdom," which will ultimately give humans their mental powers. As Hans Jonas has suggested, these "principalities" and "powers" (as they are called in the *Apocryphon of John*) are not evil entities lurking in the stratosphere but are the fundamental lenses through which we see the world. We could even identify them with the categories of Kant's philosophy— such modes as time, space, and causality, without which our experience is inconceivable.[7]

To simplify these reflections, the Gnostics seem to be saying that the principle of consciousness takes a stance and so creates an "I." By the very act of creating this "I," it also brings into being a world as well as the categories by which this world is experienced. But it is overwhelmed by this world and its own modes of experience. Consciousness is buried in and subjugated to them—particularly to the ego, the tyrannical sense of "I" experienced in isolation and in opposition to all else. This is the bondage of unredeemed human life, from which consciousness must be rescued by its "consort." This is the aspect of consciousness that at some level continues to recognize that it is free from the world and superior to it.

Some Gnostic myths explicitly connect Sophia's consort with Christ. In another text known as the *Pistis Sophia* ("Faith-Wisdom"), it is Christ who makes it possible for Sophia to be liberated. In these contexts, the two mythic figures stand for two deep impulses in consciousness. Sophia represents the part that is prone to immersion in and subjugation to the world, the part that surrenders itself indiscriminately to its own experience; for this reason some Gnostics called her *Sophia Prunikos*: "Wisdom the Whore." Christ, on the other hand, is the part that remains free and makes total liberation possible through gnosis. Here the Gnostics again differ from the mainstream esoteric tradition, which equates Christ or the Logos with Sophia, and in which Christ's descent is not a fall but a redemptive act.

Even so, certain Gnostic texts portray the dual aspect of consciousness as residing in Sophia herself. In the Nag Hammadi text known as *The Thunder: Perfect Mind* an unnamed figure who is clearly Sophia proclaims, "I am knowledge and ignorance."[8] The primordial consciousness thus contains at the same time the impulse toward its own downfall and toward its own liberation. Its dual motion—inward, toward unity, and outward, toward manifestation—furnishes and propels the lifeblood of the cosmos.

SOPHIA TODAY

Although the myth of Sophia casts a powerful light on the nature and destiny of consciousness, this light is a subtle one. Consequently, after the early centuries of Christianity, Sophia became an increasingly remote figure, particularly in the West. Only in the last 125 years has there been a widespread renascence of interest in this divine figure. This impulse was launched by the Russian mystical philosopher Vladimir Solovyov (1853–1900), who had several visions of her during his life. For Solovyov, Sophia is "the world soul, or ideal humanity . . . which contains within itself and unites with itself all particular living entities." He regards the Logos and Sophia as practically identical. The Logos is the "primordial unity," the condition of humanity before its descent into multiplicity. Sophia is "a second, produced unity," created by the reintegration of the many parts of creation into one.[9] Although Solovyov stops short of actually equating the Logos with Sophia, he comes close to doing so, making his views very much resemble those of primordial Christianity.

Solovyov set out these ideas in his extremely influential "Lectures on Divine Humanity." Delivered between 1878 and 1881 and attracting an audience that included Tolstoy and Dostoyevsky, they inspired a whole current of Sophiology in Russia. The twentieth-century theologian Sergei Bulgakov, for example, saw Sophia as the very essence of the Godhead—the Being that the three Persons of the Trinity share among them. For another theologian, Pavel Florensky, she was the primordial nature of creation, the creative Love of God. The visionary Daniel Andreev held that since Christ was "begotten of the Holy Spirit," the Father and the Holy Spirit were in fact the same Person of the Trinity. Sophia was properly the third, so that the Trinity should really consist of the Father/Holy Spirit, the Son, and Sophia.[10]

However ingenious these explanations may be, in the end they seem rather overcomplicated and factitious. It is simpler and clearer to see Sophia as she seems to have been originally—as the principle of consciousness that was also known as Christ.

The past generation has seen a further revival of interest in Sophia. This is due partly to a powerful grassroots impetus to recover traditional images of the divine feminine, partly to a resurgent interest in Gnosticism as a result of the work of Jung and the publication of the Nag Hammadi scriptures. Today Sophia seems to be enjoying an ever widening circle of admirers. She is the subject of an increasing number of books, and even in mainstream American denominations women's groups have developed rites and prayers to honor this haunting and elusive figure.

THE VIRGINAL WATERS

Over the centuries the form of the divine feminine that has commanded the most allegiance is not Sophia but the Virgin Mary, so it is reasonable to ask if there is any connection between the two. Some modern authors say there is, even making a blanket equation between them. But this does not really make sense. If Sophia is the Word, she cannot be the same as Mary, by whom the Word was made flesh. They must represent two different principles.

This leads us back to the fundamental dichotomy, discussed in chapter 2, between "I" and the world, between that which *experiences* and that which *is experienced*. Sophia, the Word, primordial consciousness, symbolizes the former; the Virgin, the latter. The Virgin and Sophia rarely appear together in the iconography, which tends to portray this fundamental polarity in terms of the sexes: it is the male Word that is portrayed as "knowing" the female world and bringing a new life into being.

To understand further what the Virgin Mother symbolizes, we might return to the image of Jacob's ladder with angels "ascending and descending" to heaven. Much of this book has been occupied with the ascent: how consciousness can emancipate itself from the world. This is because the story of Christ (like that of Sophia) is essentially about this liberation. But there is also the opposite: the descent into manifestation. It is this to which the mystery of the Virgin points.

Not surprisingly, this process is reflected in the creation account of Genesis. "In the beginning God created the heavens and the earth. And the earth was without form, and void, and darkness was upon the face of the deep. And the spirit of God moved upon the face of the waters" (Gen. 1:1–2). Initially there is a dual creation: "the heavens and the earth." These two forces correspond to the spirit and the world respectively. Arising out of the same source, which is God, eternal and unfathomable, they remain intermingled and indistinct, "without form, and void," until the next phase, when "the spirit of God moves upon the face of the waters." At this stage there is a differentiation between the two: the "spirit of God" moves upon the face of the "waters," the astral light, the still indeterminate primordial matter of experience. Consciousness arises and differentiates itself from its surroundings, thus giving rise to a world. After this, existence can begin.

The Virgin symbolizes the "waters," the prime matter of the world. There is no good term for this matter in English because modern thought does not admit that it exists; even so, those who work with meditation or some other introspective practice can acknowledge that it is real. This primordial substance is like the matter of physics in one sense: it is undifferentiated. No one ever sees matter in its raw form; matter is always experienced in the specific, as a tree or a rock or as atoms or particles. Similarly, no one ever encounters the "waters" of the world in their pure form, but always *as* something, whether it be a thought, an emotion, or a sense impression. These "waters" of which Genesis speaks are unlike physical matter, however, in that they are the stuff of the internal as well as of the external world and give rise to both. As Éliphas Lévi says, the astral light "is the common mirror of all thoughts and forms; the images of all that has been are preserved therein and sketches of things to come."[11] The astral light, symbolized by the Virgin, is that which *is experienced*; hence she is the "vessel," the "receptacle of all things."

Christian iconography often links the Virgin with water. *Mem*, the first letter of her name in Hebrew, was originally an ideograph for "water," and Maria, her name in Latin, literally means "seas." Even her principal colors are the blue of the ocean with its whitecaps. But a nexus of other symbols is connected with her as well; they do not form rigid equivalences, but, like poetic metaphors, form a chain of associations that cast light on different aspects of this archetype. Jung writes, "The prima materia in its feminine aspect . . . is the moon, the mother of all things, the vessel, it consists of opposites, has a thousand names. . . . it contains the elixir of life in potentia and is the mother of the Saviour. . . . it is the earth and the serpent hidden in the earth, the blackness and the dew and the miraculous water which brings together all that is divided."[12]

Why, though, must this universal mother be a virgin? Virginity implies purity, and in a cognitive sense this means that for something truly new to be born, the waters of the mind must be still; they must not be agitated, nor can they have been "defiled" by being shaped into any other form. This is one of the chief aims of most meditative practices. The oscillations of the mind must cease if the spirit is to light on them, just as the waters of the Flood had to recede before the dove sent out by Noah could land. This stillness is "virginity" in the esoteric sense. It suggests why creative flashes so often come in reverie, when ordinary preoccupations have come to rest, however briefly; the mind is at rest and ready for inspiration to settle upon it.

Curiously, many of the most ancient and venerated images of the Virgin—some of which are said to work miracles—show her as black. The author Ean Begg, in his book *The Cult of the Black Virgin*, says that there are over 450 of these enigmatic figures, counting only those in the Mediterranean littoral and north, where people are light-skinned and hence would not be simply fashioning these works in their own image.[13]

Several explanations have been given for the darkness of these images. Some say the artisans must have thought the people of Palestine were black; others say the images were charred by centuries of candle smoke.

These explanations may account for some examples, but there are others that are unmistakably black and must have been meant to be so; moreover, the images often come from areas that had considerable interpenetration with Jews and Arabs and where the artisans would have had a more or less accurate picture of how people in the Holy Land would look.[14]

This imagery of the Black Virgin makes most sense in light of the consideration that the substance of the world, with which Mary is connected, is itself seen as archetypally black. She represents what the alchemists called the *prima materia*, the "prime matter," that is the foundation of the Great Work of making gold. (Alchemy is not ultimately about making gold in the literal sense. The "gold" the alchemists sought was gnosis.) Often this prime matter is portrayed as dark or black, because that which *is experienced* has no light of its own but requires the light of awareness to illuminate it. Many of these images are accompanied by an infant Christ who is black as well; from an esoteric point of view, this would indicate that the newborn consciousness is closer to the darkness of the world than to the light.

Richard Temple, a British authority on icons, points out that the *iconostasis*, or icon screen, which in Orthodox churches separates the altar from the congregation, intersperses scenes from the life of Mary with those of Christ. In fact, the scenes begin with the Nativity of the Virgin and her presentation at the Temple; similarly, they end with her Dormition (or, as it is called in the Catholic Church, her bodily Assumption into heaven). The life of the Virgin thus surrounds and encapsulates the life of her Son. This reminds us that the awakening of the Son of true consciousness, in the context of our life here, as we can know it, takes place in the matrix of the world; it is not separate or apart from it.[15] Ultimately, the world is sanctified and elevated by this process, a truth symbolized by the Virgin's Assumption into heaven. As Jung points out, this dogma "does bridge over a gap that seems unfathomable: the apparently irremediable separation of spirit from nature and the body."[16]

Jung's comments bring up an important point about spiritual transformation. Much of this process involves—and indeed heightens—the basic polarity between spirit and matter. This differentiation is necessary, but if it stops here, life begins to freeze and die: "I" and the world become rigidly oppositional, and dualism sets in. Only if this duality is ultimately transcended and the final unity of "I" and the world is realized can full illumination take place. As Jung says, this is symbolized by the Assumption. In another context, this culmination is suggested by the "resurrection of the body" mentioned in the creeds.

MARY PAST AND PRESENT

After the Nativity, Mary is a somewhat shadowy figure in the canonical Gospels. During their encounters, her son is frequently curt with her. At the wedding of Cana, he addresses her contemptuously as "woman" (John 2:4), and later, when he is teaching, he keeps her and his brothers waiting, saying, "Whosoever shall do the will of God, the same is my brother, and my sister, and my mother" (Mark 3:35). Only when he is dying on the cross does he take some thought of her, commending her to the care of the beloved disciple (John 19:26–27). The Bible tells us nothing of her later fate, although legend says the beloved disciple took her to Ephesus in Asia Minor, where she finished her days. Whether or not this story has any truth, it is striking that Ephesus was a cult center of Artemis or Diana, the Greco-Roman virgin goddess; Paul himself fell afoul of a mob there for challenging her primacy (Acts 19:23–41).

Mary's comparatively minor role in the biblical narrative led the founders of Protestantism, with some justice, to eliminate her cult entirely from their reformed religion. In fact, there is little evidence for any devotion to Mary in the church's first centuries. While some of the early Church Fathers lauded her as an example of perfect faithfulness and purity, there is little or no evidence that she received any special veneration in the earliest part of Christian history.

By the fifth century, however, the Virgin's status in the Christian faith had begun to soar. In 430 a synod convened in Rome promulgated the doctrine of Mary as Theotokos ("Mother of God"). In theological language, she was entitled to *hyperdulia*—a term that is difficult to translate (literally it means "overservitude") but basically means a degree of worship greater than that given to the saints but less than that owed to God.

Two forces converged to bring this reversal about. In the first place, in the century after the Edict of Milan in 313, in which the Emperor Constantine ordered toleration of Christianity, the church established itself as the official religion of the Roman Empire. This meant that the Christian faith had to undergo a radical change. In the first three centuries of its life it had in a sense been the religion of a spiritual (though not necessarily a social) elite. To be a Christian meant facing the very real possibility of being called to suffer torture and death for one's beliefs. While many Christians yielded to pressure, many others did not, and all who entered the faith did so knowing they might have to face these extremes.

The new status of the Christian faith changed the situation completely. It meant that now Christianity had to have much wider appeal, particularly if it was to supplant the old pagan religion (as it had every intention of doing). Thus in this period we see many features of paganism incorporated into Christianity; December 25, for example, the old feast of Sol Invictus, the Unconquerable Sun (a favorite god of Constantine's), was made the birthday of Christ. There is some evidence too that the rite of baptism was modified to make it more closely resemble the initiatory rites of the pagan mysteries. This era also saw the rise of the cult of Mary, who came to receive much of the devotion lavished on the now discredited pagan goddesses. Many features of the goddesses were transferred to Mary, not only those of the virginal Diana, but especially those of Isis, the compassionate Egyptian mother venerated all over the Roman world. Even incidental features of Isis's cult were brought over into Christianity: her priests, for example, wore white surplices and black cassocks, much like their Catholic successors.[17]

The fourth and fifth centuries were also the time when the great theological controversies about the nature of Christ came to a head. There were intense and intricate debates about whether Christ was God first and a human only secondarily, a man who was deified by divine adoption, or something in between. The accounts of these disputes leave the modern reader amazed that there could be such widespread and passionate feelings about such abstract theological issues; they were even the themes of popular songs. Eventually the controversy culminated in the official teaching of the dual nature of Christ: that he was fully God and fully man.

These disputes brought the role of Mary into greater focus. If Christ was fully God and fully man, was Mary mother to the man only? Some objected that this would create too much of a detachment of the two natures of Christ. Eventually this issue was settled (at least for the mainstream church) by the proclamation of Mary as Theotokos.[18] Remarkably, this happened only four years after the imperial decree of 426 that finally closed all pagan shrines and temples, suggesting how closely the Virgin's new status was bound to a need to supplant the worship of the old goddesses. (A similar thing happened after the Spanish conquest of Mexico. The Virgin of Guadalupe appeared on the ruins of a temple to Tonanzin, the Aztec goddess of the earth, a circumstance that caused the ecclesiastical authorities at first to regard the vision with some misgiving.)

Over the centuries since then, Mary's status has increased incrementally, culminating in the papal promulgation of the doctrine of the Assumption in 1950. At that point Pope Pius XII established it as a dogma of the Catholic Church that the physical body of Mary had been taken into heaven after her death. (Previously this teaching was nothing more than a "pious option" for Catholics, although its Orthodox equivalent, the feast of the Dormition, has been celebrated since at least the sixth century).[19] More recently, Pope John Paul II has taken the liberty of dedicating not only the third millennium but the earth itself to Immaculate Heart of Mary. Presently a movement is afoot to have her proclaimed Co-Redemptrix with her son.

Devotion to the Virgin has not been imposed from the top down; it is very much a grassroots affair. In the twentieth century there were hundreds of reports (386, by one count) of miraculous appearances of Mary in locations as far-flung as Nigeria, China, and the Philippines, but mostly in Western Europe.[20] While a few apparitions over the centuries, including those at Guadalupe, Lourdes, and Fatima, have been granted more or less legitimate status by the Catholic Church, the vast majority have not. Unaccredited encounters with Mary range from weeping statues and icons to more commonplace manifestations, such as her image seen in glints of light on windows and even on household appliances. In 2000, residents of a Houston apartment complex began to venerate a puddle of spilled ice cream they believed had congealed in the shape of the Virgin of Guadalupe.[21]

While the esoteric themes associated with the Virgin are clear enough, they are unlikely to be grasped by someone without at least a certain amount of inner training. They do not really explain the fervor that her worship inspires in so many believers, the vast majority of whom have never heard of esotericism and would probably have little interest in it if they had. The popularity of Mary's cult must stem from another source.

To help explain it, I should perhaps repeat an idea that I have already mentioned: God is beyond all gender, beyond all personhood. We, on the other hand, live both as persons and as beings with gender. While the divine is not limited to either of these modes of manifestation, it *is* capable of expressing itself through them, and may choose to do so as the best way of communicating with us. Or, to view it from the other side around, the human mind, in encountering that which is beyond all its known experience, still has to make use of that experience in framing and expressing such encounters to itself. When we experience a force of transcendental compassion and limitless love, it is only natural that it should take the human form that most resembles it, and the closest thing to unconditional love that most of us experience is mother's love. For the Mary's innumerable devotees, her image is the one that most powerfully evokes the limitless love that has brought us into being—just as for many others this same love is personified in Jesus.

The divine Son, the immaculate Mother—these archetypes have always been known to humanity. As Mary's earthly incarnation recedes from us in the historical distance, her personal presence fades and she becomes ever more the glass through which we see the shimmering and fecund waters of the world and the infinite compassion that gave them birth.

PART THREE

Expressions

8

Spiritual Practices

"G OD IS VASTLY QUICKER TO POUR OUT His grace than man to take it in," said Meister Eckhart.[1] Christ expresses this truth in speaking of the prodigal son's return: "And he arose, and came to his father. But when he was yet a great way off, his father saw him, and had compassion, and ran, and fell on his neck, and kissed him" (Luke 15:20).

This idea speaks to a teaching of the Christian tradition, both inner and outer, that is sometimes lost in current discourse: knowing God is ultimately a matter of cultivating a personal relationship. This contrasts with many Eastern teachings, which view the Absolute in essentially impersonal terms. Here one attains enlightenment simply through correct and assiduous practice, carried out, perhaps, over lifetimes.

In inner Christianity, spiritual practice is not solely a matter of technique, and it does not achieve its effects through individual effort alone. There is a subtle and profound dynamic between effort and grace, between activity that one performs and results that seem to come about on their own. This dynamic will always remain mysterious, because our conventional understanding of our own boundaries is essentially inadequate. We literally do not know what our own "I" is and consequently mistake its operations for exterior and seemingly coincidental events. The British esotericist Charles R. Tetworth refers to this factor as "the player on the other side"—the unseen force that constantly brings us up against exactly those situations we had dreaded and yet must face.

At the same time there is a rich heritage of spiritual techniques and practices in Christianity, though it has often been buried or hidden. During a visit to the Greek peninsula of Mount Athos, the center of Orthodox monasticism, Jacob Needleman had a monk say to him, "I could tell you of things a thousand times better than your yoga." But, Needleman adds, "he never said more, not even when pressed by the stunned interpreter." [2] While we will never know what the monk had in mind, some of the inner practices of Christianity have begun to come to the surface again. It makes most sense to discuss them in terms of the tripartite division of the human being into the body, soul, and spirit.

WORKING WITH THE BODY

The central maxim of the Benedictine Rule is *ora et labora*—"pray and work." The simplicity of this command conceals a profound esoteric teaching, expressed symbolically in Jacob's dream in Genesis 28:10–17. Fleeing his father's household in fear of the wrath of Esau, Jacob stops on the way "at a certain place" to sleep. Jacob puts down stones to serve as pillows, and he has a curious dream: "And behold a ladder set up on the earth and the top of it reached to heaven: and behold the angels of God ascending and descending on it."

Esoterically understood, the ladder is the celestial hierarchy—the cosmic system whereby God, the One and transcendent, manifests as the many and the immanent, and the many return to God again. This system involves a process of interchange, symbolized by the angels "ascending and descending." The transcendent and spiritual must have contact with the physical and transitory (symbolized by the stones Jacob used as pillows). It is taught that we as humans are the only beings—at least the only ones we know of—who have the possibility of linking all these dimensions.

Understood in this light, the Benedictine utterance takes on a new clarity. For the esoteric Christian, the path consists of a double process: the ascent toward God—"prayer"—and the descent toward materiality—"work." It is no coincidence that the Benedictine Rule alternates the day between devotion and physical work.

This teaching was known before Benedict, however, and has been practiced in other lines of the tradition as well. It was practiced by the Desert Fathers such as Anthony, and John Cassian said anyone who is not content to do some manual work every day will not be able to persevere on the path to the end. Gerard Zerbolt's *Spiritual Ascents* admonishes the Brethren of the Common Life, "Do not consider yourselves more fervent and more spiritual than was the great Antony, who, had he not learnt from the angel this kind of ascent and descent between manual and spiritual work, would have succumbed to tedium and returned to the world. . . . the work of the hands often subserves the spiritual ascent, inasmuch as it withdraws the obstacles to ascending."[3]

The records and journals of the Brethren show that they had a sophisticated and rigorous technology of practices for integrating the remembrance of Christ in their labors. Work was carried out in silence, and when speech was necessary, they would meditate for a moment or say *Ave Maria* silently before they spoke. Some Brethren made a practice of speaking only in Latin to one another as an aid to greater mindfulness. They also imitated the monastic practice of "ejaculatory" prayer—brief utterances such as "Blessed be the sweet name of our Lord Jesus Christ" or "Thanks be to God that I am alive now"—repeated, usually in silence, during the course of the day.[4] Similarly, Eastern Orthodox monks would repeat the Prayer of the Heart (which I will discuss in more detail below) as they went about their work.

Another key aspect of the Brethren's practice involved attention to the task at hand: "Do everything with attention and not habitually," urges Thomas à Kempis. Some of this had to do with an ancient teaching that mental distraction opens one up to negative influences: "If [a man] is idle, he is disquieted by truly innumerable demons," writes Zerbolt.[5] But a deeper meaning has to do with the dual process of ascent and descent symbolized by Jacob's ladder. We cannot serve as a link between heaven and earth if we are not conscious in the moment. Attention is not grounded; carried away by daydreams and fantasies, it is overwhelmed by the tides of the world. This truth helps explain the centrality of mindfulness practices, not only in inner Christianity, but in esoteric teachings all over the world.

Gurdjieff's teaching offers another perspective on the mastery of the body. Gurdjieff's central teaching was, as we have seen, the "sleep of man" and the fragmentation of the human psyche. The only way to begin the long and arduous task of unifying the psyche is to remember oneself. Casual readers of Gurdjieff may think he is talking about being self-conscious in the ordinary sense of the term: accompanying one's actions with a convoluted mental narrative. But of course this accomplishes nothing. Self-remembering in Gurdjieff's sense first has to do with conscious sensation of the body. As one contemporary Gurdjieffian puts it, "Someone who is in the Work is never far from the sensation of the body."

Although the theory behind this approach is extremely intricate and obscure, its central point is clear enough. The human being is fragmented because the mind, emotions, and the body are badly connected with each other. As a way of unifying them, practitioners of the Gurdjieff Work consciously direct the attention of the mind to immediate bodily sensation; mind and body thus draw closer together. Later, attention to the emotions is brought in as well.

While this integration is important, there is also another dimension to this type of work, which, in the terms I have been using in this book, has to do with the liberation of the "I" from the world. Ordinary consciousness is passive. If it is aware of the body, this is usually because the body has brought some item to its notice: a pain, an itch, a change in temperature. Once the problem is fixed, the mind moves along to something else, borne along on the stream of associations. Consciousness here has no volition, no power of its own. The "I" is passive, the world is active. This state is the bondage from which spiritual work attempts to liberate us.

To make a conscious effort to sense yourself, to do something even as simple as deliberately feeling your elbow on the chair while reading this book, introduces a powerful catalyst into the situation. The customary situation is reversed. The "I" consciously wills itself to experience the world in the form of the body. Now the "I" is active and the world is passive. Moreover, consciousness is not so intensely and immediately confused with its own contents, but is able to step back from them, even if only for an instant or two. This small but powerful polarization is the beginning of freedom.

In the Gurdjieff Work, the fundamental meditative practice is known as "sitting," and the basic directions are simple: to be aware of the sensations of the body while sitting upright. Anyone with even a little experience of this practice is likely to make a startling discovery: sensations begin to lose their solidity, their *thingness*, and become fluid and dynamic. Under certain circumstances one can even sense a circulation of subtle energy.

The question then arises of whether this circulation is going on all the time or the direction of attention has somehow brought about an inner transformation. Gurdjieff said, "Even a feeble light of consciousness is enough to change completely the character of a process, while it makes many of them altogether impossible. Our inner psychic processes (our inner alchemy) have much in common with those chemical processes in which light changes the character of the process and they are subject to analogous laws."[6]

With directed attention to the body, sensations seem to move from solid to liquid; what was seemingly hard and palpable suddenly turns out to be fluid and changing. One discovers the enormous difference between the body as physical object and the body as it is felt within. To have some familiarity with this experience gives a glimpse of what esoteric teachings mean when they speak of the "subtle body." While most systems say there are many such bodies (in Gurdjieff's there are four),[7] the most immediate and accessible is this subtle body to which we gain access through our own sensation.

WORKING WITH THE PSYCHE

Practices at the level of the soul or psyche sometimes involve taking inventory of the psyche's contents. One of the most common practices of this kind is found in various forms in the Gurdjieff Work, Steiner's Anthroposophy, Martinism, and the Kabbalah, as well as in other traditions: I have even heard it taught in Tibetan Buddhism. It is sometimes called "remembering the day" or "backward remembering." The basic practice simply involves remembering the events of the day backward, as if you are watching a film being played in reverse, while you are lying in bed and waiting to go to sleep. You may fall asleep before the day is finished, or you may not; it does not matter. If you practice this regularly, you may find that your dream life has greater depth and vividness: the mind in sleep is not so preoccupied with making sense of sorting through the events of the day and can penetrate to deeper levels. Backward remembering is sometimes said to aid in lucid dreaming. There are other variations on the practice; some, as in the Martinist tradition, focus more on taking a moral inventory of one's actions during the day in the fashion of the Catholic examination of conscience. Its chief purpose, however, may be to free the "I" from its involvement in the world so that it can enjoy some comparative liberty during the hours of sleep.

Other practices working with the psyche encompass those that people most often associate with the esoteric or the occult. This entails work with thought-forms. The esoteric tradition teaches that these are made of a subtle soul-stuff. As we have seen, this mental substance is sometimes known as the *astral light*; this is because its undulations have long been believed to be ruled by the movements of the planets. It is also symbolized as water, because of its fluid nature and because it takes the shape of the vessel that contains it. It can be shaped by thought.

The esoteric view has always held the opposite of conventional science: that it is mind and not matter that is fundamental to the universe and that a substratum of psychic imagery undergirds the whole physical world. On the most obvious level, this means that if, for example, you are going to create a meal, you have to begin with some idea of it—the dishes you will serve, the ingredients you will need, the time it will take. On a subtler plane, it means that a trained practitioner can alter reality by forming a mental picture and infusing it with vital energy. Most occult magic is centered around this process; so are popular adaptations such as creative visualization. This practice has enough power that instructions about it are usually hedged around with warnings. Used with malice or even clumsiness, it can harm the practitioner as well as those around him (this is one meaning of the tale of the sorcerer's apprentice). Thought-forms, known in the Orthodox tradition as *logismoi*, have a powerful and quasi-independent existence once they are generated. Under certain circumstances they can be felt or even seen by others; this is the source of certain types of psychic phenomena. A collectively generated thought-form, called an *egregore*, has even more power.

Like electricity or nuclear fission, thought power is in itself morally neutral; it does not and cannot dictate the ends toward which it works. Manipulating the astral light can do harm as well as good. Consequently, many esoteric Christians have avoided teaching it explicitly or have even warned against it. Nonetheless, it is part of the tradition and deserves some attention.

The late Stylianos Atteshlis, a magus who led an esoteric Christian community in Cyprus and was made famous by the works of Kyriakos Markides, used these mental images as part of his healing practice. Much of his work involved the generation of positive thought-forms (which he called *elementals*) and directing them to those who need help. This essentially involves vivid and concentrated visualizations of balls of light and mentally sending them to those who need healing.

While this is the basic practice, there are some intricacies to the task. In the first place, Atteshlis emphasizes that these should only be sent to those who have actually requested help. The color of the ball of light also needs to be keyed to the nature of the problem. Red light, directed to the person's heart center, will help someone whose strength is low; a rose-colored ball will benefit someone suffering from anger or low self-esteem, as rose is the color of love. When in doubt, white light is to be used; "it will enter through the head of the recipient where it will assume the shape of an egg expanding to engulf his entire body. The Archangels will assign the appropriate colours to the white light to address each individual problem."[8]

In his book *Experience of the Inner Worlds*, Gareth Knight, a Christian Kabbalist, gives a practice involving surrounding oneself with a sphere of light. "We should feel the reality of the symbol with our heart as well as picturing it in our imagination and speculating about it mentally. . . . Within this sphere it will be possible to penetrate both time and space, and the inner planes of Creation, as well as to approach the Creator." Knight goes on to say that "the regular performance of such an activity conforms the personal Will in freedom to the Will of God, which corrects and sanctifies the present moment." He recommends practicing it in the morning and the evening at first for ten minutes a day. Another practice involves a similar visualization of a fiery spear, "passing symbolically through the top of the head above, transfixing the spine and going deep into the heart of the earth."[9]

The fiery spear evokes the mystery of the crucifixion, because symbolically it is the spear that pierced the side of Christ upon the cross; "forthwith came there out blood and water" (John 19:34). It is also connected with the mystery of the Holy Grail, traditionally believed to be the cup Christ used at the Last Supper, because legend has it that Joseph of Arimathea caught some of this mixed blood and water in this cup and brought it with him to England. In medieval times there was a cycle of Grail romances written by Chrétien de Troyes, Robert de Borron, Wolfram von Eschenbach, and others, all of which focus on the search for this elusive cup by valiant knights. Only the pure of heart are allowed to see it.

In another exercise, Knight points toward the Grail's inner meaning: "Visualise, then, the Grail, before your heart. You may well find that it tends to coalesce with the physical heart inside your breast and that when it does, your heart burns inside you."[10] This in effect tells us what the true Grail is. Since it is a cup that holds blood, it is a symbol of the heart. And since it is found only by those who are pure of heart, it means that the Grail is itself the purified heart, awakened and vitalized to serve as a channel for higher energies.[11]

Seeing the Grail, however, is not enough. In the *Perceval* of Chrétien de Troyes, the young Perceval, traveling through a desolate land, comes to a castle of the maimed Fisher King, where he is received with great hospitality. During his meal he sees a mysterious procession, in which a maiden bearing the Grail passes through the hall, and he watches it in silence. The next day, after he leaves, he encounters a woman who talks to him about the experience. She asks if he inquired about the things he saw. He replies that he said nothing. "Ah, unfortunate Perceval!" she exclaims. "How unlucky it was that you did not ask all those things! For you would have cured the maimed King, so that he would have recovered the use of his limbs and would have ruled his lands and great good would have come of it! But now you must know that much misery will come upon you and others." [12]

In its dark, allusive way, this myth points to a major theme of esoteric Christianity, one that has often been lost or obscured in the tradition itself. An awakened heart is necessary but not sufficient. It must be accompanied by an awakened intelligence, one that is capable of inquiring into what it sees. Only then can the desolate land of the soul be healed and the true "I" liberated. As an apocryphal saying of Christ puts it, "Man, if indeed thou knowest what thou doest, thou art blessed: but if thou knowest not, thou art indeed cursed and a transgressor of the law." [13]

PRAYER OF THE HEART

This union between head and heart is the central objective of one of the most celebrated and important spiritual practices in the inner Christian tradition: the Prayer of the Heart. Here we move into the realm of the spirit proper, where in the silent depths of being the true "I" joins with the common Self of the Son and the transcendent, ineffable Father. This is effected by the practice of unceasing prayer, in obedience to Paul's command to "pray without ceasing" (1 Thess. 5:17).

We encounter the roots of this practice in the Desert Fathers. John Cassian, who brought their wisdom to Western Europe in the fifth century, tells of his encounter with a holy man called the Abbot Isaac. The abbot told Cassian of an ancient esoteric practice, which was to pray constantly using this formula, an adaptation of Psalm 70:1: "O God, make speed to save me; O Lord, make haste to help me." As the abbot said,

> It is not without good reason that this verse has been chosen from the whole of scripture as a device. It carries within it all the feelings of which human nature is capable. . . . It carries within it a cry

to God in the face of every danger. It expresses the humility of a pious confession. It conveys the watchfulness born out of unending worry and fear. It conveys a sense of our frailty, the assurance of being heard, the confidence in help that is always and everywhere present. . . . This is the voice filled with the ardor of love and charity. This is the terrified cry of someone who sees the snares of the enemy, the cry of someone besieged day and night and exclaiming that he cannot escape unless his protector comes to his rescue.[14]

This is not the only form this prayer has taken. The most familiar version invokes Jesus: "Lord Jesus Christ, Son of God, have mercy on me, a sinner." There are other versions as well: "Lord Jesus Christ, Son of God, have mercy on me"; "Lord Jesus, mercy"; or sometimes even simply the name of Jesus. Thus it is also known as the Jesus Prayer.

The masters who taught the Prayer of the Heart regarded it as a spiritual path that occupied a number of distinct though interrelated stages. At the outset, the practitioner repeats the prayer aloud, either in full voice or in a whisper. Posture and breath are important but must be adapted to the individual's needs: "One may pray standing, sitting, or lying," advises the nineteenth-century Russian bishop Ignatius Brianchaninov. "Those who are strong in health and physique pray standing and sitting. The weak can pray even lying, because in this prayer it is not the effort of the body that is paramount, but the effort of the spirit. The body should be given a position that allows the spirit full freedom to act properly."[15] Generally speaking, the breath should be slow but regular. Sometimes the recitations are accompanied by prostrations.

The prayer may be recited as little as a dozen times a day (for beginners) or as many as ten thousand times a day (for monks). What is essential is that the practitioner should direct the conscious attention to the meaning of the prayer.

This is a key issue. Throughout the centuries of Christian history, formulaic prayers like the Our Father or the Hail Mary have been repeated millions of times. The overwhelming majority of these utterances have been purely automatic: the believer learns the formula by heart and thereafter prays by running off a set number, perhaps using a rosary (a device originally imported from Asia, where its counterpart, the *mala*, a string of beads that helps practitioners count the number of mantras they have recited, serves exactly the same purpose). The sheer mechanical performance of these prayers is somehow supposed to confer grace or at any rate to add some extra points of merit to one's account.

Ironically, this is exactly the type of prayer that Christ denounced. "When ye pray, use not vain repetitions, as the heathen do: for they think that they shall be heard for their much speaking" (Matt. 6:7). A text known as *Unseen Warfare*, originally written by the seventeenth-century Italian priest Lorenzo Scupoli and later emended by Eastern Orthodox monks, addresses this issue:

> Owing to our negligence it sometimes happens that the tongue says the holy words of prayer, while the mind wanders away: or the mind understands the words of the prayer, but the heart does not respond to them with feeling. In the first case prayer is merely words, and is not prayer at all; in the second—prayer with words is connected with mental prayer, and this is imperfect, incomplete prayer. Full and real prayer is when praying words and praying thoughts are combined with praying feelings.[16]

But of course the mind is easily distracted and wanders ceaselessly toward thousands of distractions. Thus "full and real prayer" involves firm and often intense concentration, just as in yoga and other meditative practices.

The second phase of the Jesus Prayer is a more internal one. At this point the verse—still repeated with full consciousness and attention—is taken inward and begins to be repeated silently. It begins to have a momentum of its own, and while this has a certain automatic quality about it, the teachers of this method continually stress that the inward repetition of the prayer must never become a merely mechanical process. Instead, the consciousness, the mind, the emotions, and the body must slowly and patiently be unified and brought closer and closer together so that the soul may open to the presence of God.

Most important, however, the sensation of the prayer is rooted firmly in the physical heart, as *Unseen Warfare* indicates:

> Attention should be in the heart, or inside the breast, as some fathers say, namely a little above the left nipple—and there the Jesus prayer should be repeated. When the heart begins to ache with tension, follow the advice of Nicephore the monk, namely, leave that place and establish yourself with your attention and with the

words of the prayer where we usually converse with ourselves, namely under the Adam's apple in the upper part of the chest. Later again descend over the left nipple.—Do not disdain this remark, however simple and unspiritual it may seem to you.[17]

Eventually, a state of consciousness known as *hesychia* or "stillness" arises. When the turbulence of the mind and emotions has subsided, consciousness becomes still and clear, and the presence of God can be felt. Although, as we are constantly reminded, God is everywhere, we are rarely aware of this fact because our mental agitation makes it impossible to experience his presence. Practically all techniques of prayer and meditation are aimed at stilling the mind so that the Absolute can be made manifest in us.

This stillness is by necessity the absence of thoughts, feelings, and sensations. It is a blank spot in consciousness, and as such in the tradition it is often spoken of as "darkness." A common term applied to it, which has passed into the common parlance of modern spirituality, is "the dark night of the soul."

This phrase, though widely used, is not always clearly understood. In fact, it has two related but not identical meanings. The most common use of it today has to do with a sense of aridity, of dryness or darkness, that frequently arises as an intermediate result of spiritual practice. The seeker begins to see the preoccupations of the quotidian world in their proper perspective—as not all that important or interesting when viewed in the larger frame of things. The usual response to this realization is a sense of emptiness or depression. The Old Testament symbolizes this period by the Israelites' forty years of wandering in the wilderness. They are no longer in bondage to "Pharaoh in Egypt"—that is, to the ego preoccupied with the outward world—but have not yet arrived in the "Promised Land" of higher consciousness. Such a period can last for months or years until the practitioner begins to glimpse the "Promised Land" of peace and the presence of God.[18]

There is another sense to the "dark night of the soul" as well. Very often when someone starts a disciplined method of prayer or meditation, she experiences all sorts of sensational inner effects—flashing lights, sounds, brilliant insights, even what may appear to be divine apparitions. She becomes extremely excited and takes these effects to be the sign of great spiritual advancement on her part. She is usually disappointed when she tells her teacher about them and finds him to be singularly unimpressed. There is even a Zen story about a pupil who jumps up from his meditation mat and runs to his master exclaiming, "I just had a vision of a golden Buddha!" Unfazed, the master replies, "Just keep meditating, and it will go away."

Such manifestations do and should go away. However dazzling they may seem, they are almost always the simple result of opening the lid of the mind, like a Pandora's box, and allowing its contents to spill out. There is a point—and it comes reasonably soon—when these manifestations begin to cease; the practice becomes much more uneventful and, from an ordinary point of view, much less interesting. Even though the goal of the practice is mental stillness, the practitioner frequently takes the dawning of such stillness to be a sign that nothing is happening.

The source of the term "dark night of the soul" lies in the poem "Dark Night" by the sixteenth-century Spanish mystic John of the Cross, one of the most celebrated texts in the Christian contemplative tradition. The poet speaks of "a dark night" in which the soul finds "the One I knew so well, my delight, / In a place with no one in sight." He exclaims, "O night that joined / Lover with beloved, / Beloved in the lover transformed!" Like the biblical Song of Solomon, this poem uses the metaphor of lover and beloved to speak of the soul's union with God.

In his own commentary to the poem, John of the Cross indicates that the "dark night" refers not only to "purgation"—that is, a detachment from worldly interests—but also to "a dark night of the intellect." [19] This may be analogous to the *hesychia* of the Orthodox tradition. It is a kind of darkness in that the mind does not appear to perceive anything; it is a blankness, a state of consciousness without an object. Although some traditions regard this state as the final goal of meditation, the inner Christian tradition says it is only a preliminary, for at this stage the spirit becomes ready for direct contact with God—the union of the lover with the beloved. This stage is sometimes known as "infused prayer."

At this point, in the tradition of the Jesus Prayer, the heart will literally feel warm. One practitioner reported that eventually "a small sweet flame was lit in my heart. The sensation was like swallowing some delectable food. This little flame remained in the heart, and I felt as though someone was gripping my heart. From that time I prayed continuously, and kept my attention there, where this sensation was, my only care being to preserve it." [20] Here the seeker begins to sense directly the presence of God, penetrating even to the core of the physical body. Ordinary language and thought fail, or serve only as vague reflections of experience. Mystical writings, like those of John of the Cross, the Song of Songs, or the Sufi poet Rumi, frequently use the metaphor of lovers, who, though separate, are united, to express this elusive realm where the distinctions between God and the self, between "I" and "not-I," are blurred or obliterated.

CHRISTIAN MEDITATION AND CENTERING PRAYER

Most practitioners of the Jesus Prayer would probably balk at characterizing their discipline as a form of mantra meditation. (A mantra is a sacred word or syllable uttered as an aid in meditation; the term comes from the Sanskrit and has been imported to the West with Hindu and Buddhist teachings.) This is not only because of a reflexive antipathy to the religions of the East but also because many Christians see meditation not as a cognitive exercise but as a way of cultivating a relationship with God: the seeker in his personhood encounters God in *his* personhood. Even so, there are Christians who view their own prayer discipline in the light of mantra meditation. Among these is a movement known as Christian Meditation, started by the Benedictine monk John Main (1926–82). The word used is *maranatha*, an Aramaic expression meaning "Our Lord, come." It appears in 1 Corinthians 16:22 and is believed to have been widely used in ancient Christian liturgy. Here are Main's own directions for this practice:

> Sit down. Sit still and upright. Close your eyes lightly. Sit relaxed but alert. Silently, interiorly begin to say a single word. Recite the prayer-word *Maranatha*. Recite it as four syllables of equal length, *Ma-ra-na-tha*. Listen to it as you say it, gently but continuously. Do not think or imagine anything, spiritual or otherwise. If thoughts and images come, these are distractions at the time of meditation, so keep returning to simply saying the word. Meditate each morning and evening for between twenty and thirty minutes.[21]

This passage states the basic directions not only for this particular practice but for many other meditative techniques as well. The meditator is to sit still in an erect but comfortable position. (For most Westerners, this means sitting in a chair. Because we are not used to sitting cross-legged on the floor Asian style, this position tends to offer more obstacles than assistance for us.) The word is to be repeated silently, and the mind is to concentrate on the practice. As soon as the practitioner notices any distractions, she is to take them as a cue simply to return to the silent repetition of the mantra.

Despite or because of their simplicity, such practices hold great power. Eventually the mantra *maranatha*, like the Prayer of Jesus, begins to root itself in the heart, giving the meditator access to the deeper reaches of being in which the presence of God reveals itself. It is not a "vain repetition" but a means of freeing the mind from its customary shackles.

Thomas Keating, another contemporary Benedictine, has devised or resurrected a practice similar to Main's. Known as Centering Prayer, it is indebted to a mystical text called *The Cloud of Unknowing*, written by an anonymous Englishman probably late in the fourteenth century. The "cloud of unknowing" is the inner blankness, the dark silence in which God comes to the aspirant. "Beat away at this cloud of unknowing between you and God with that sharp dart of longing love," it exhorts.[22] This work also recommends using a meditation word:

> Take a short word, preferably of one syllable. . . . The shorter the word the better, being more like the working of the Spirit. A word like "GOD" or "LOVE." Choose which you like, so long as it is of one syllable. And fix this word fast to your heart, so that it is always there come what may. It will be your shield and spear in peace and war alike. With this word you will hammer the cloud and the darkness above you. With this word you will suppress all thought under the cloud of forgetting. So much so that if ever you are tempted to think what it is that you are seeking, this word will be sufficient answer.[23]

In Centering Prayer, the practitioner attempts simply to rest silently in the presence of God beyond thoughts or emotions. Although a meditation word is used, it is not repeated constantly, as in John Main's Christian Meditation or in the Prayer of the Heart. The meditator simply says it silently as a reminder to rest in God's presence when the mind becomes distracted.

And of course it *will* become distracted. The mere attempt to rest in inner silence is likely to bring long-hidden memories, desires, and urges to the surface. The old texts portrayed these experiences as demonic attacks, but more likely they are simply repressed elements of the mind unleashed by the meditator's attempt to rest in silence. As modern psychology teaches, the fact that these impulses can be glimpsed by the conscious mind, rather than lurking beneath the threshold of awareness, makes it possible to release and heal them. While this is not the ultimate goal of Centering Prayer, it is an important intermediary step. In many schools of Christian contemplation, ancient and modern, this process has been known as the phase of "purgation" or "purification."[24]

Although it would certainly be possible to begin meditation with the indications I have given in this chapter, many teachers stress the need for receiving instruction from someone with experience. This is not merely self-serving on their part. Meditation has to do with states of consciousness that are not necessarily difficult to achieve but may be far more readily attained if one is initiated into them by one who knows. Moreover, the mind can easily distort even the simplest directions, making the practice useless or even harmful. For this reason it is also recommended that the practitioner check back regularly with the instructor to ensure that the meditation is on course.

DIVINE READING

Another ancient practice—also kept alive by the Benedictines—relies on established texts, particularly the Bible. Known as *lectio divina* or "divine reading," it is essentially a slow and contemplative reading of Scripture. The practitioner takes a small passage, a page, a verse, or even a word or two, and dwells meditatively on it. Brother David Steindl-Rast elaborates:

> This reading sends you into—I would not say reflecting on what you have read, because that is too active—but into basking in it, savoring it, and that usually lasts for a little while, depending on your psychological state. Sooner or later you begin to daydream, and then you can come back to the next word or the next sentence or the next page, so that the reading is really like a landing strip from which to take off, and whenever you can't stay in the air anymore, you come back down to it, taxi, and take off again.[25]

This process has several levels. The first is known as *lectio* proper—the literal, physical reading of the text. As consciousness ascends, the reading passes into *meditatio*, or visualization, in which the mind interacts with the text through imagery. This is followed by *oratio*, or spontaneous prayer, which finally passes into *contemplatio*, where one simply rests silently in the presence of God.[26] These roughly correspond to the levels of body, soul, spirit, and the divine that we have seen in other contexts.

Lectio divina can use any passage of Scripture (or even other sacred writings), but the book of the Bible that has been by far the most central to Christian devotion is the Psalms. A cursory acquaintance with this work might lead one to suppose that it is little more than a collection of tepid praises to the Almighty like those in a church hymnal. But a closer examination reveals a strange, varied, and sublime series of texts, and the Psalms have long been regarded by Jews, Christians, and even Muslims as one of the pinnacles of sacred literature.

The Psalms consist of 150 poems of varying length. The shortest is the 117th, which consists of only two verses. The longest is the 119th, written in acrostic form in the original Hebrew and said to contain a summary of the esoteric path.[27] The rest include texts of praise, despair, repentance, and wrath. Frequently the poet cries out to God for protection from his enemies. Other Psalms express a serene confidence and faith in the Almighty, and the collection as a whole culminates with several songs of praise.

From this range it is clear that the Psalms have a use that is different from the way it is normally conceived. The ordinary view is that God is an omnipotent despot who, if he is not adequately appeased by supplications, will visit punishment on the believer. This is of course absurd, but even if it were true, the Psalms would not serve the purpose: there is too much excruciating honesty in them, as in the Twenty-second: "My God, my God, why hast thou forsaken me? why art thou so far from helping me, and from the words of my roaring?" (Ps. 22:1); or in the Forty-second: "I will say unto God my rock, Why hast thou forgotten me? why go I mourning because of the oppression of the enemy?" (Ps. 42:9).

The esoteric purpose of the Psalms goes beyond mere adoration. It is perhaps best understood in light of the need to unify the fragmented human character. In their range of expression, the Psalms touch upon the whole gamut of human experience. They also interweave a thread that ties together the multifold bundle of thoughts, hopes, and fears that make up our identity, and this thread is the remembrance of God. Someone who uses the Psalms for prayer does not put on a brave front before the divine presence, as we often have to do in front of other people, but rather turns all emotions toward God. This very act will serve to unify and integrate them at a higher level.

The ancient monks understood this fact, and they would recite the entire Psalter as a form of devotion. Benedict admonished his followers,

"We read that our holy Fathers strenuously performed this task in a single day. May we, lukewarm that we are, perform it at least in a whole week!"[28] The Benedictine Divine Office, with its seven daily services, is structured around the use of the Psalms in liturgy. Indeed, the whole tradition of Gregorian chant arises from the custom of intoning the Psalms in liturgy.

While the modern layperson may tend to regard chanting as something reserved to monks and nuns in choruses, this practice is not as difficult or arcane as it may seem. There are tapes available that teach chanting, but even without them one can develop a personal practice.[29] Simply take a Psalm in a translation that you like and begin to read it aloud. Once you are comfortable with the sound of your own voice, you can begin to intone the text, imitating the chants you have heard live or on recordings. You may even want to listen to some recordings to refresh your memory. The particular tune you use is not important; simply experiment with it until you hit upon a comfortable rhythm and pitch. After a certain point you will begin to feel an inner reverberation. The words will begin to resound in different parts of the body—the center of the head, perhaps, or the heart. If you continue, you may notice that it is possible to change the atmosphere of a room through this process. Chanting of this sort has no doubt fostered the air of serenity that abides in old cathedrals, monasteries, and other holy places.

Throughout this procedure, the key is to avoid inhibition or self-consciousness. Those who are shy may be afraid of what others may think of them; those who are more outgoing may begin, consciously or not, to make a performance of it. Thus it is best (at least at the outset) to do this practice when you are alone and no one else can hear you.

THE LORD'S PRAYER

Ultimately, however, prayer is done not out of self-interest but as a service, as a means of fulfilling the great purpose for which we were brought into being. Nowhere is this process more powerfully summarized than in the only prayer taught by Christ himself. Beginning with an invocation of God, it proceeds through the celestial realms and the "kingdom" of heaven into the human context of "debt" and "temptation," going so far as to touch upon the infernal dimension of "evil":

Our Father, who art in heaven,
Hallowed be thy name.
Thy kingdom come,

Thy will be done on earth as it is in heaven.
Give us this day our daily bread
And forgive us our debts as we forgive our debtors.
And lead us not into temptation,
But deliver us from evil,
For thine is the kingdom and the power and the glory forever.
Amen.

"The Lord's Prayer, the *Pater Noster*, is the core of the Doctrine" of inner Christianity, writes Boris Mouravieff. "It is no exaggeration to say that there never has been, never will be, on Earth, a prayer that surpasses it or even equals it."[30] He goes on to suggest that its different verses correlate to the Cosmic Octave I have set out in chapter 5.

Examined carefully, this prayer sets out the structure of a cosmic descent—the divine brought down to earth. The Lord is addressed in both his transcendent ("Our Father") and immanent aspects ("Who art in heaven"), and the first two elements of the prayer are for the fulfilling of God's will, in accordance with Christ's teaching "Seek ye first the kingdom of God . . . and all else shall be added unto you" (Matt. 6:33). The prayer is then brought down to the lower levels: "Thy will be done on earth as it is in heaven." This verse makes an often-overlooked point: although God's will is done automatically in heaven, on the higher planes of existence, it is not so on the level on which we live; effecting God's will requires conscious choice and action, of which prayer itself is a key feature.

Unlike the opening verses of the prayer, which use only the second person singular pronoun, the second half of the prayer has only the pronouns "we" and "us," indicating the interests of the one who is praying. Even so, the first person singular is never used. This is a way of bidding us to remember not the single isolated "I" of the individual, but the common "I" of the Sonship.

The verse "Give us this day our daily bread" would seem to contradict Christ's teaching "Take no thought, saying, What shall we eat?, or What shall we drink? or, Wherewithal shall we be clothed? . . . for your heavenly Father knoweth that ye have need of all these things" (Matt. 6:33–34). But as Mouravieff and other commentators point out, this is because the Greek word *epiousion* has been mistranslated as "daily."[31] While the meaning of this word is obscure, one thing it does *not* mean is "daily." Sometimes it is translated "for the morrow," as in a note to the Revised Standard Version; but the inner meaning is suggested by the Latin Vulgate as well as some of the older English translations, which render this word as "supersubstantial." A clumsy term, perhaps, but it points to the fact that the bread here is not physical but spiritual sustenance.

"Forgive us our debts as we forgive our debtors"—the Greek here does literally mean "debt" and not "trespass," as some versions have it— points to the centrality of forgiveness as a means of undoing the law of karma (a point I will address further in the next chapter), which is the linchpin of the structure of the world. And "deliver us from evil" refers to the lower dimensions of existence—those that are below the human plane per se but into which we are in danger of straying.

One point worth noting about the final doxology "for thine is the kingdom, and the power, and the glory" is that it correlates with three of the lowest *sefirot* or "principles" of the Kabbalistic Tree of Life: *Malkhut*, or "Kingdom"; *Netzach*, usually translated as "Eternity" but meaning something like the "power" of cyclical repetition; and *Hod*, or "Glory." [32] Although the Kabbalistic Tree is usually dated to thirteenth-century Spain, its striking resemblance to this formulation in the Lord's Prayer not only points to an older age for the Kabbalistic system but also suggests that its influence on and interpenetration with Christianity goes much further back than the Renaissance.

However this may be, it is clear even from this brief discussion that the Lord's Prayer is a deep and comprehensive formulation of esoteric ideas. And it points to the truth that prayer is a means not only of raising the state of consciousness of an individual and connecting with God, but also of helping divine energies make their cosmic descent to the world we know.

9

Love, Evil, and Forgiveness

SOME MAY FEEL DISSATISFIED with my discussion of evil in chapter 2. Even granting that the human condition is rooted in the "knowledge of good and evil," they may argue that this still fails to explain why evil exists in the first place. Is God responsible for evil? Did it arise from another source?

In a footnote to his book *People of the Lie*, M. Scott Peck deftly summarizes the main religious explanations for this problem. The first is a view found in Hinduism and Buddhism (as well as in Christian Science and *A Course in Miracles*) that evil is simply illusory; it is not real. The second, which Peck calls "integrated dualism," says that evil does exist but has been given to us by God so that we can have free will (a view that probably represents the beliefs of most Christians). The third, which Peck calls "diabolic dualism," holds that evil is a deliberate, willful rebellion against God—to use Peck's words, "a cancer in the universe beyond His control." [1]

Peck himself prefers the third option as the only one explaining his own experiences, which include an encounter with a grisly case of demonic possession like that in *The Exorcist*. But in fact, each of the other two explanations satisfy his criteria just as well: the Eastern religions constantly emphasize the compelling vividness of the power of illusion they call *maya*. On the other hand, if God permits evil to exist for the sake of our free will, there is no reason it should not manifest in the forms Peck describes, however gruesome.

On the other hand, none of these three explanations is totally satisfactory. While we may philosophically reflect on the unreality of evil in the comfort of an easy chair, it may be harder to do so in a torture chamber or while suffering from disease or privation. If the bad is illusory, it still *feels* real.

Nor does it make sense to say that God created evil to do us the favor of letting us have free will. A person given to disputing with the Deity, like Job, might well counter that in his unbounded creativity, the Almighty might have taught us free will by providing us with some less unpleasant options. As for the third view, even supposing the existence of a personal Devil whose will is in rebellion to God's, where did the Devil get such an idea to begin with? How did even the *possibility* of evil arise?

THE ORIGIN OF EVIL

The teaching about the origin of evil that is most prevalent in the esoteric tradition is perhaps one of its most vexing aspects, but it is also the only one that really makes sense. It is suggested by a verse in Isaiah: "I form the light, and create darkness; I make peace, and create evil; I the Lord do all these things" (Isa. 45:7). The Lord is God, and the Lord is One. All that exists, good and evil, justice and injustice, has its source in this fathomless and unutterable unity. All the powers of heaven and hell arise out of the One and serve it, each in its own way. We may not be able to understand how or why this should be, but so it is. As Jacob Boehme puts it, "In God there are two states, eternally and without end—namely the eternal light and eternal darkness."[2]

The supreme statement of this mystery appears in the Book of Job. This enigmatic work, one of the greatest and also one of the strangest in the Bible, tells a well-known story: God permits Satan to torment the righteous Job for reasons he does not understand. Most of the book alternates between Job's complaints and the stale rationalizations of his comforters. Finally, the Lord himself appears to Job "out of the whirlwind" and says, "Who is this that darkeneth counsel by words without knowledge? Gird up thy loins like a man: for I will demand of thee, and answer thou me. Where wast thou when I laid the foundations of the universe? declare, if thou hast understanding. Who hath laid the measures thereof, if thou knowest? or who hath stretched the line upon it?" (Job 38:2–5). The Lord proceeds to enumerate the wonders of the universe and to describe the primordial beasts Behemoth and Leviathan—which are too great for the mind of man to fathom.

In the end Job must bow in submission: "Therefore have I uttered that I understood not; things too wonderful for me, which I knew not" (Job 42:3). Some thinkers, like Jung in his *Answer to Job*, understand this passage to mean that Job has to yield to superior force. It is merely a face-off in power. But the answer to Job is not merely a show of force. It is a demonstration of the scale of the universe, reminding us that it is far higher and deeper than we can grasp. Our only recourse is Job's—to submit to the wonder of it all and to concede that our minds cannot comprehend it.

It is interesting to observe that the Lord's answer out of the whirlwind begins by speaking of "laying the foundations of the universe." What, esoterically speaking, could these foundations be? The *Sefer Yetzirah* ("Book of Formation"), the earliest Kabbalistic text, casts some light on this question:

> Ten Sefirot of Nothingness:
> > Their measure is ten
> > which have no beginning
> A depth of beginning
> > A depth of end
> A depth of good
> > A depth of evil
> A depth of above
> > A depth of below
> A depth of east
> > A depth of west
> A depth of north
> > A depth of south
> The singular Master
> > > God faithful King
> > dominates over them all
> > > from His holy dwelling
> > > until eternity of eternities.[3]

The concept of the *sefirot* is an elusive one. Although in chapter 1 I suggested that this word be translated as "principles"—and this is the best way to render it in most instances—here the *sefirot* are better understood as "dimensions." If we read the text in this way, suddenly we see the three familiar dimensions of space—above and below, east and west, north and south, or depth, breadth, and length. There is also the fourth dimension, time, which in our experience passes in a single direction, expressed here as "beginning" and "end." But there is also a fifth dimension to the universe: good and evil.

This text sets out the coordinates of the world as we know it: three dimensions of space, one of time, and a dimension of "good" and "evil." The Lord, in "laying the foundations of the universe," did so incorporating what is literally a moral dimension. Thus "I make peace and create evil."

Evil exists. If it lacks an *absolute* reality, if there is a realm where it does not hold sway—because God himself exists beyond and apart from the constraints of this universe—it has a *relative* reality. In our world it is neither more nor less real than the good.

What, then, *is* evil? Let us go back to the concept of the great cosmic spiral set out in chapter 3. Each plane in this infinite spiral represents one level of reality, of which our universe is only the thinnest slice. Above and below stretch dimensions of light and darkness inconceivably vast, expressing and exhausting all the possibilities of relative existence. Our world, it is said, is more or less in the center, neither particularly good nor particularly bad, in fact, a more or less equal admixture of the two. (The Germanic myths allude to this in calling our world Midgard, or the "middle realm"; similarly, Dante portrays hell as beneath the earth and heaven above.)

On this great cosmic spiral there are forces that move in both directions, like the angels ascending and descending Jacob's ladder (Gen. 28:12). These forces are necessary if all is not to freeze in a state of eternal stasis. The forces that incline upward, toward greater consciousness and freedom, we associate with the good; those inclined in the other direction are associated with evil. The realms of limitation, darkness, and severity are known esoterically as the "wrath" of God. From a human perspective, the level we inhabit, a lower one than we were created for, is part of this wrath: "For all our days are passed away in thy wrath" (Ps. 90:9).

Are these darker realms intrinsically wicked? The best answer may be suggested by looking in any nature magazine. There you will find photo after photo of strange, monstrous beasts with huge claws, jagged mouths, and bulging, sightless eyes. And then you learn that they are nothing more than the insects any backyard gardener may happen upon in the course of a dull afternoon. Or you discover a gloomy, Typhonic realm, which, like Milton's hell, has "no light, but rather darkness visible," and where thousands of pounds of pressure bear down on each square inch, and you then realize that it is the depths of our own oceans. The creatures who inhabit these spaces may look hideous, but there is nothing innately evil about them; we are no doubt as repellent to them as they are to us.

So it may be with the demonic realms. If these creatures seem ugly or threatening, it may be because they exist in niches of the cosmic ecosystem that are different from our own. Through the Fall, through our collective desire to "know good and evil," we chose to leave our native state and sink down to one that borders on the darker realms. So we feel ourselves in hostile territory, at the mercy of predators real and imaginary. We are, so to speak, on a plane where the gravity is heavier than we were created to bear, and we are constantly pulled down—a condition we experience as weakness, frailty, and proneness to temptation. Boris Mouravieff calls this the "General Law"—the state of affairs that characterizes the world, with its ups and downs, its luck and misfortune, its hates and loves and passions.

THE OPPOSITION

Is there a personal Devil? This is more or less the same question as whether there is a personal God. If God, being much greater than we can imagine, is not ultimately personal but is capable of relating to us as persons, something more or less similar is probably true of the great downward force portrayed as the unholy trinity of "the world, the flesh, and the Devil." Certainly the Devil is too real, too vividly experienced, to be completely impersonal. But to think of him just as a large, ugly character with horns who bothers us from time to time is far too simplistic. It ignores the fact that the Devil also personifies forces that constitute us, that are as fundamental to our being as gravity or electromagnetism. We may fear the Devil and struggle against him, but without him we would not be what we are.

The Devil makes a personal appearance in the Bible only three times. The first is in the prologue to Job, in which "the Satan" (the Hebrew word *satan* literally means "opponent") appears in the celestial court before the Lord and slyly requests permission to tempt Job's righteousness (Job 1:6–12). The second is in the Gospels, when Christ goes into the wilderness "to be tempted of the Devil": as we have already seen, the temptation is the object of his retreat. The third is in Revelation, where the Devil is allegorically portrayed as a red dragon, "that old serpent, the Devil" (Rev.

12:9). A fourth instance could arguably be added, the Genesis story of the Fall (as Revelation suggests in identifying the serpent with the Devil), but Genesis itself never mentions the Devil or Satan, simply speaking of the serpent as one of the "beasts of the field."

What is most striking about all these accounts (except perhaps Revelation) is that they portray the Devil not as an aberrant figure but as part of the natural order. Far from being a rebel against the will of God, Satan is part of the cosmic ecosystem, just as gravity is one of the forces that sustain the physical universe. His task is to serve as a kind of cosmic quality control officer, testing the will and integrity of those who would rise to a higher plane. We increase our spiritual strength by overcoming this resistance, just as a bodybuilder strengthens his muscles by lifting heavy weights. Thus the Devil is God's servant, not his enemy. Boris Mouravieff comments:

> Some people believe that Satan is God's adversary, a rival entity independent of God. This is an error, a sacrilege that amounts to blasphemy against the Holy Spirit. For *nothing* exists outside the Holy Trinity, which comprehends *everything* within itself, including Satan, with all the means allowed him for the accomplishment of his mission. Being engendered, he is a serving spirit. When [his] task . . . has been achieved, his mission will end. It was from these traditional notions that Origen taught the redemption of the Devil.[4]

None of this is to minimize the power of the opposition. It confronts us in different ways—in bodily appetites, in the irritations of life, in personal enemies, in the countless nagging voices that afflict our minds. To personify these as the Devil's handiwork can be helpful to the degree that it encourages us to see all obstacles as essentially the same obstacle—one that is both within us and outside of us—and to struggle against it. But this attitude can be unhelpful and even dangerous when it leads us to see the Devil everywhere and to project him onto those we dislike.

Even the notion of struggling against the Devil can be problematic. Few of us have such vivid imaginations as Luther, who once threw his inkpot at the Evil One, whom he saw lurking in the corner. Still fewer have the discrimination to see that struggling against one passion can create a susceptibility to another. The monk fighting his sexual urges often fails to see that in the process he has fallen prey to gluttony or hypocrisy; the puritan may vanquish sloth but is prone to avarice; and the one who picks a way through all these shoals usually crashes on the rocks of pride. The prince of this world is shrewder than we are. One way or another, he will exact his price from us.

ESCAPING KARMA

Perhaps the most fundamental law of the universe, more fundamental even than the boundless dimensions of the ten *sefirot*, is that everything that exists seeks to perpetuate itself. Life, we know, does so; an organism survives by defending itself and eating other things; it also seeks to reproduce so that it may live in its offspring. This principle applies to all things, inanimate as well as animate. A rock does not feed or reproduce, but at a more basic level it is sustained by the bonds of its molecules. The same is true of atoms and universes.

So too do good and evil seek to perpetuate themselves. As abstract as these entities may seem to us, they also in their way wish to live and grow and reproduce. In the moral dimension, this desire to continue expresses itself as the law of karma, which stipulates that good begets good and evil, evil.

Once the momentum of evil has been set upon its course, it gathers speed like a boulder down a mountainside, although it is not so easily evaded. The dynamics of karma—known to the Greeks as *nemesis*—serves as the mainspring for the great tragedies of Western literature. This law is so rigorously exact that those who have glimpsed its power have often been driven to fatalism and despair.

And who would not despair? Since none of us is perfect, we can expect to have to settle our accounts sooner or later. Even if our wrongs amount to no more than the petty slanders and spite of day-to-day life, the tally can still end up quite large. Yet by the law of karma, there is no escaping it. Even the salvific act of Christ does not acquit us from responsibility for our actions. No doubt it is this crushing realization that moves some criminals to confess even when they have no chance of being caught: like Raskolnikov in *Crime and Punishment*, by admitting what they have done and paying the price, they attempt to free their minds from the dread of retribution.

Nevertheless, Christianity does offer a way out of the inexorable chain of karma. It must be accounted as the unique contribution of Jesus

Christ to the spiritual life of humanity, since no teacher before him seems to have given this idea much attention. It is most succinctly expressed in the verse of the Lord's Prayer: "Forgive us our debts as we forgive our debtors" (Matt. 6:12).

While this is usually taken merely as a high-minded sentiment, closer examination reveals how it can turn the law of karma upon its head. We sow as we reap; thus if we forgive, we are entitled to forgiveness in turn. We will be acquitted of our shortcomings to the precise degree that we acquit others of theirs. Hence Christ instructs Peter to forgive not "until seven times, but until seventy times seven" (Matt. 18:22).

Of course, the whole point of this verse is that it is impossible for anyone to keep count to "seventy times seven." Forgiveness offers an escape from the monstrous quid pro quo that is the essence of the world. It not only turns the law of karma on its head but also frees us from the karmic ledger books entirely, since, if we extend forgiveness infinitely and unconditionally, we will receive it to the same degree. Forgiveness is a steadfast refusal to see wrongs, or, if seen, to remember them. It is the ultimate act of generosity, since it gives without keeping count, and it is the ultimate act of freedom, since it liberates those who practice it from bondage to harm or loss: by refusing to care about any supposed damage, we proclaim our immunity to it.

This is true forgiveness, and while often praised, in the world it is rarely practiced. What we generally experience in its place is the subtle hypocrisy that the *Course in Miracles* material calls "forgiveness-to-destroy."[5] In its most blatant form, an individual uses forgiveness to put himself on a morally higher plane; it is a gift condescendingly given by a superior to an inferior, much as the Pharisee in Christ's parable congratulates himself on not being "as other men are" (Luke 18:11). An even more sanctimonious version takes the form of "we are all to blame," in which culpability is not released but allocated to everyone equally. Still another offers forgiveness only as a way of meeting one's own unwholesome needs. Codependency is one instance of such transactions: someone "forgives" an abusive family member as a way of perpetuating her own self-image as a martyr or feeding an unconscious desire for mistreatment.

Possibly the principal reason forgiveness is felt to be difficult is that it is seen as unjustified. People often believe that in forgiving, they are overlooking genuine wrongs and sacrificing justice to mercy. But this is not really true. The human ego is not constructed so as to cast a fair light on a situation. The ego wishes to exonerate itself at all costs, frequently by casting blame upon someone else, and it minimizes its own shortcomings while exaggerating others'. As Christ says, "Why beholdest thou the mote that is in thy brother's eye, but considerest not the beam that is in thine own eye?" (Matt. 7:3). He makes a similar point in the parable about a wicked servant who is forgiven a debt of ten thousand talents by a king, only to turn around and have another servant, who owes him "a few pence," cast into debtor's prison (Matt. 18:23–35). Like the wicked servant, we tend to ask the widest latitude for ourselves while refusing to grant any to others. In this light, forgiveness is not so much an act of magnanimity as a way of compensating for our own distortions of reality.

Furthermore, exactly *whom* are we forgiving? Obviously, other people. But as we have seen, other people are in essence the same as ourselves. If we were to see truly, we would recognize our participation in the one, single, undivided Son of God; the chief consequence of the Fall is that the cosmic Adam perceives himself as fragmented into billions of separate and isolated specimens. To dwell upon the wrongs of others is to reinforce this fragmented state. Indeed, one could even insist that the refusal to forgive is the linchpin of the fallen state, perpetuating the human condition of conflict and suffering.

Although it may be easy to embrace forgiveness in the abstract, we often forget it at once if someone fails to return a greeting or cuts in front of us in line. At such moments the old defenses reassert themselves, and a minor slight suddenly takes the guise of an unpardonable crime. Or, with relationships that are overgrown with years of grief and vexation, we may be all too eager to forgive, but find that our deeper emotions will not go along, obstinately insisting on bearing a grudge even when we can see its complete futility.

Forgiveness is an art. Like all arts, it requires a subtle discrimination, a precise understanding of one's material, and a light touch that strikes a balance between inadequacy and excess. There will be times when forgiveness does not seem possible, when the pain felt exceeds the capacity to let it go, and our visceral impulses are all striving toward fury. This does not always happen in proportion to the offense. Sometimes we discover that a powerful blow glances easily off our backs, while some small and all but unnoticeable grievance nags at us without cease. The emotions have their reasons, which the conscious mind does not always see, and these reasons have to be respected—at least up to a point. Forgiveness often requires steering a narrow course between nursing a grudge and pretending we have pardoned someone when we have done nothing of the kind. The chief tool needed is a rigorous inner sincerity, since the grossest forms of hypocrisy are those we practice in front of ourselves.

In practical terms, this approach may involve fostering a small willingness to forgive while anger and rage burn themselves out inwardly for weeks and months. It may require drawing a line with someone—refusing to take abuse any longer while also refusing to nurture any hatred on account of it. Frequently it necessitates an inner detachment, a freedom from emotional dependence on others. In other instances it may entail looking at the situation from other people's viewpoint (which often leads to the conclusion that they could not have acted other than they did). Forgiveness takes forms as diverse and unpredictable as human beings themselves. For some, generous and high-minded, it comes naturally and spontaneously, while others may find that it has to be cultivated with effort in the hard soil of their natures. It is wise to be honest with oneself about such things, but it is also wise to remember that forgiveness is to be bestowed inwardly as well as outwardly and that a little mercy granted to ourselves sometimes makes it easier to extend this kindness to others.

THE UNJUST STEWARD

It may be all very well to speak of forgiveness of petty slights, and even of such personal damage as we may encounter in the course of life, but what about evil on a greater scale? What about the monsters of history—the tyrants and dictators who have butchered millions? Are we to forgive *them*?

A closer look at this question will reveal its essential pointlessness. To begin with, where are these monsters? Most are dead (generally as the result of their own enormities); even those who are alive are generally remote and are immune to anything we personally might do. Because we have no contact with them, our hatred only poisons ourselves. By contrast, many who have actually suffered at the hands of such tyrants appear to have found that the only sane recourse is to forgive, or at least to put bitterness aside and get on with their lives.

Seldom do we face evil directly. Far more often we contend with *imagined* evil: with anger against more or less distant figures, with lofty indignation over injustices half a world away that we cannot remedy and have no intention of remedying. While not all concern for large-scale issues can be dismissed in this way, usually the question of whether "we" can forgive the crimes of the past or present is rooted in the unconscious impulse to set oneself up as a moral authority in a way that is by no means justified. Anyone who has studied the atrocities of history can see that they are mass phenomena that engulf even supposedly decent people. In the same circumstances, would we act any better ourselves?

The Gospels themselves are free of such preoccupations. Christ does not launch into denunciations of wicked Roman emperors or ruminate about the evils of the past. Instead, he speaks about showing kindness and compassion to those one meets from day to day: "Thou shalt love thy neighbour as thyself" (Mark 12:31). Such concern lacks the grandiosity of slogans and lofty historical judgments, but human life would not be bearable without it.

Perhaps the ultimate issue of forgiveness is outlined in one of the most baffling passages of the New Testament: the parable of the unjust steward in Luke 16:1–9. I quote it in full:

> There was a certain rich man, which had a steward; and the same was accused unto him that he had wasted his goods.
>
> And he called him, and said unto him, How is it that I hear this of thee? give an account of thy stewardship; for thou mayest be no longer steward.
>
> Then the steward said within himself, What shall I do? for my lord taketh away from me the stewardship; I cannot dig; to beg I am ashamed.
>
> I am resolved what to do, that, when I am put out of the stewardship, they may receive me into their houses.
>
> So he called every one of his lord's debtors unto him, and said unto the first, How much owest thou unto my lord?
>
> And he said, An hundred measures of oil. And he said unto him, take thy bill, and sit down quickly, and write fifty.
>
> Then said he to another, And how much owest thou? And he said, An hundred measures of wheat. And he said unto him, Take thy bill, and write fourscore.
>
> And the lord commended the unjust steward, because he had done wisely: for the children of this world are in their generation wiser than the children of light.

Although Christ goes on to say, "Make to yourselves friends of the mammon of unrighteousness: that, when ye fail, they may receive you into everlasting habitations," this does not add much clarification. The parable is so obscure that even the reductionists of the Jesus Seminar are inclined to admit its authenticity, on the somewhat peculiar grounds that it does not seem to draw any obvious moral conclusion.[6]

To me the only explanation that makes sense has to do with forgiveness. Assume God is the master. Each of us then is in the position of the unjust steward. If we were called to make account of ourselves, we would no doubt be found to have wasted the master's goods. Our fellow humans are also in debt to the master, so the key to this parable has to do with forgiving the debts of others to God. (Recall the reference to forgiveness of our "debts" in the Lord's Prayer.)

What could these be? Here is where the power of the Devil—and the word "Devil" comes from the Greek *diabolos*, or "accuser"—works most insidiously. We may be willing to pardon personal offenses to ourselves, even to overlook the crimes of history, but it is very difficult to forgive sins against God. This issue has been the bane of Christianity from its inception. We see it in the New Testament, which begins with the Sermon on the Mount and ends with such writings as the Epistle of Jude, which rails against "murmurers, complainers, walking after their own lusts" (Jude 16). We see it in countless texts and treatises written by the devoutest of saints, who harp upon their own humility and meekness but rise in indignant accusation against the slightest hint of lèse-majesté against the Supreme Being. As the parable indicates, these "children of the light" are not even as wise as "the children of this world," who are willing to put aside their grievances for the sake of self-interest.

Put this way, the folly of such a stance is obvious. Does God have an ego to be offended by our petty failings? Obviously not. Can we really say what is in the hearts of others? We know we cannot. But Christians past and present persist in accusing others of heresy, blasphemy, and other such offenses in the pathetic belief that they are defending God. Of course, we can do no such thing. What we are defending here is the ego's last resort—itself reified into an image of God. And this is the last and perhaps most difficult lesson to learn in self-transcendence: the surrender of one's own cherished image of God, nurtured and fostered, perhaps, by years of religious education. This sacrifice is typified by the last words of Christ on the cross: "My God, my God, why hast thou forsaken me?" (Mark 15:34). The ultimate sacrifice we have to make is that of *my* God.

TWO LOVES

Having considered forgiveness in some detail, it now makes sense to ask what love is. For all that has been said about it in prose and verse, love is still an elusive entity. That certainly is part of its magic. It is somehow essential to the "I" that lies at the core of each of us, and yet goes beyond it. If this is disturbing, it is comforting as well, for there is nothing we long for so much as the assurance that there is something larger than ourselves.

Some of love's mystery, however, is no more than semantic confusion. English, a language with a stupefyingly rich vocabulary, is strangely impoverished in having only one word for love (perhaps two, if we include the verb *to like*). This word has to do service in referring to everything from the sublimest sentiments imaginable to plain old lust. Having to use this word to span such a range of experience, people are often genuinely confused and do not know what kind of love they are feeling.

Greek, including the Greek of the New Testament, has four words for love. The first is *eros*, or sexual desire. The second is *philia*, which is affection between friends. The third is *storge*, usually applied to the love parents and children have for one another. (The word also has the connotation of "putting up with," which casts an amusing light on the nature of family relations.) The fourth is *agape*, "implying regard rather than affection," as Liddell and Scott define it in their unabridged Greek lexicon.[7] This is the word used for the love between God and humanity, and it is also the word used in the most familiar New Testament passages about love, including the commandment "love thy neighbour" and Paul's paean to love in 1 Corinthians 13, one of the most commonly quoted parts of the Bible. (In this passage the King James Version translates this word as "charity.")

We can, however, reduce these four to two fundamental types. Augustine says, "Two cities make two Loves, Jerusalem and Babylon, the Love of God the one, and the Love of the world the other; of these two cities we are all Citizens, as by examination of ourselves we may soon find, and of which."[8] Here he echoes Plato, who distinguishes between "heavenly" and "earthly" love in his *Symposium*. We all know how Plato distinguishes the two: the heavenly, "Platonic" love is "innocent of any hint of lewdness."[9] The Christian tradition as a whole has echoed Plato's distinction, portraying carnal love as at best a necessary evil and agape as entirely free of fleshly impulses.

Unfortunately, this distinction is not entirely useful. Two thousand years after the founding of Christianity, we are in a position to see that the blanket demonization of sexuality has done more harm than good. Moreover, this distinction does not address the entire range of feelings between "pure" love and lust; where do the rest fit in?

It may be more helpful to define the two loves slightly differently. Agape is indeed the "love of God," expressed as a communication not only between the divine and us but also within human relations insofar as they replicate the love of God. It can also be regarded as unconditional love. This is the "charity" of which Paul speaks in 1 Corinthians: "Charity suffereth long, and is kind; charity envieth not; charity vaunteth not itself, is not puffed up. . . . [It] rejoiceth not in iniquity, but rejoiceth in the truth; beareth all things; believeth all things, hopeth all things, endureth all things" (1 Cor. 13:4, 6–7).

Contrasted to this conscious love is what Augustine calls "the love of the world." It comprises the other three types delineated in the Greek language: sexual love, friendship, and family love. Unlike agape, it is quite conditional. It has terms and stipulations, of which reciprocity and self-interest are by far the most powerful. Love in friendship involves a rough, half-conscious form of computation. In social relations, for example, it is generally expected that an invitation to dinner will be reciprocated in a reasonable measure of time; not to do so is an insult. Many is the person who has sadly decided to drop someone because that friend, after accepting several invitations, never invited her over in return. Only the most niggling of personalities keeps a rigorous count, but for practically everyone, if the balance of exchange goes too far out of whack, feelings are hurt and amity is destroyed.

Family love and sexual love do not adhere so rigidly to the terms of reciprocity, but even here they are at work. It is hard to repay completely the amount of care and attention that a parent expends on a child, but the child is expected to respond with some degree of gratitude and affection and to take care of the parents in their old age. Sexual passion often presents cases of unrequited love, yet only the most obstinate of fools will continue in his attentions after being repeatedly rebuffed. It is true, of course, that life presents many exceptions to this rule—instances of loyalty and sacrifice that surpass all considerations of repayment—but even here the admiration we feel for such acts bears witness to their rarity.

This, then, is the "love of the world," which resembles karma in its acute sensitivity to debits and credits. No one can live without this sort of love, just as no one can live without engaging in monetary exchange, but all the same there is something ultimately incomplete about it. We are not loved in or for our essence, for what we truly are, but for what we can supply, even if it is something as intangible as companionship.

Gurdjieff presents a series of enlightening aphorisms about love at its different levels:

Love of consciousness evokes the same in response
Love of feeling evokes the opposite
Love of body depends only on type and polarity.[10]

Clearly "love of feeling" and "love of body" constitute the "love of the world." Gurdjieff's remark about "love of body" is clear enough, since for everyone sexual attraction has to some degree to do with whether the other person is one's "type." His claim that "love of feeling evokes its opposite" is harder to grasp. Isn't it true that we tend to like those who like us? Up to a point, perhaps, but attention that is too intrusive can prove strangely annoying. Something deep inside us feels it is being grasped or clutched at and instinctively revolts.

And there *is* something grasping in "love of feeling." Underneath all the charms and blandishments lies an underlying emptiness, an unfulfilled need that reaches out to seek its satisfaction in another person. Perhaps the need is sexual, perhaps it is for social advancement, perhaps for mere companionship. Regardless: at its root this need is predatory. It seeks not so much to nourish and sustain another person as to feed on her. It lays claim to someone to fill its own emptiness.

"Love of feeling" does not, of course, always evoke its opposite. We are not the innocent victims of roving manipulators on the prowl. We too have our unmet needs, our inner sense of emptiness and grasping, and we respond to someone else with a complementary lack. Thus is born what *A Course in Miracles* calls "the special relationship."[11] It may be a romance, a friendship, a professional or even family relationship, but there is always an unwholesome bargain at the core: a sense of inner deficiency and a failure to see the other as she truly is. To use the terminology of Martin Buber, the other person is not a "thou" but an "it." Practically all relationships in the world fall into this category. This explains why they are so transitory and so prone to disruption. Frequently the wrongs and slights that are used as excuses for alienation merely mask the fact that the other person, for whatever reason, no longer serves the original purpose.

There is another kind of love: agape, unconditional or conscious love. While Christianity did not discover this type of love—which certainly has been known as long as there have been human beings—it is Christ's distinctive contribution to have articulated this principle and brought it to the forefront of human concern.

Agape has several characteristics. In the first place, it is *unconditional*. It is diametrically opposed to the "love of the world." Agape does not want anything, and it is not discriminating; in this it resembles the Creator, "who maketh his sun to rise on the evil and on the good, and sendeth rain on the just and the unjust" (Matt. 5:45). Agape does not reckon its own advantage; it does not do favors for the sake of having them returned. Nor does it engage in the elaborate social calculus of closeness and distance that is a key feature of the "love of the world." In the world, we have a hierarchy of obligations that we must honor. Charity begins at home, then extends to the wider circles of friends, community, nation; breaking this order incurs blame. In agape, it is not so: closeness confers no special status. This helps explain why Christ is so willfully oblivious to family concerns: "Whosoever shall do the will of God, the same is my brother, and my sister, and my mother" (Mark 3:35).

Unconditional love is possible only if the "I" is free from the world. If the "I" is not free, it is inevitably sucked back into the maelstrom of worries, fears, and calculations that are the mainspring of the world's mechanism. Inner Christianity would agree with the other great traditions in teaching that this freedom, sometimes called "liberation" or "enlightenment," is necessary. What is unique about the Christian path is that it suggests that the practice of this unconditional love is the best way to liberation. Bringing this inner knowledge to full awareness is ordinarily a matter of slow progress. At first you practice compassion more or less blindly. Later, as a result of your efforts, small changes begin to appear—not anything that has any value or consequence in the world's eyes, but a sense of greater space and freedom within. And such experience encourages you to persist despite whatever setbacks the world may present.

Agape is also *conscious*. This is not simply to say that it is self-aware: after all, the impassioned lover is all too sensible of his passions. Rather, agape possesses an innate wisdom and knowingness that lower forms of love lack. It is capable of taking in the whole situation and seeing the other person as she truly is, apart from one's own blind self-interest. Such knowingness naturally does what is right. This may or may not be expected or customary or even rational in any obvious way. But with an undeluded insight that is at the same time transcendently kind, agape is able to pierce through the surfaces of a situation and strike at the heart of the matter, giving exactly what that person in that situation requires. Christ in the Gospels exemplifies this quality. He is not a bland figure; often he is sharp and deliberately provocative. But the effects of his actions are profoundly beneficent.

This leads to the third, and perhaps least understood, characteristic of agape. The lexicographers hint at it by saying that it implies "regard rather than affection." Unlike the manifold forms of the love of the world, agape is not a sentiment. It does not necessarily imply a warm or loving feeling toward someone else. Conscious, dispassionate love is beyond all feelings of like and dislike, of love and hate. If agape is impartial, if we are to bestow it on the just and on the unjust, it must stand apart from our vacillating emotions and attitudes. It is shown forth most directly in its activities—in its works.

This is not to say that Christianity forbids us to have likes and dislikes. Inevitably we do; inevitably we play our part in the colossal game that is the "love of the world." Christ in the Gospels does as well: he has family relations; he has friends; he has enemies; perhaps, as some apocryphal texts suggest, he even had amorous relations with Mary Magdalene.[12] But the love that he exemplifies is not limited to these social contacts; it goes beyond to another dimension. "For if ye love them which love you, what reward have ye? do not even the publicans the same? And if ye salute your brethren only, what do ye more than others? do not even the publicans so?" (Matt. 5:46–47).

Even if the distinction between these two loves seems clear on the printed page, in life it almost always is not. One of the most frequent problems in the arena of love is when one kind is mistaken for the other—as, for example, when someone in love imagines that he desires nothing but the purest, highest good for his inamorata, only to change his tune the minute he is slighted.

This difficulty afflicts other forms of love as well, as is illustrated in an episode toward the end of the Gospel of John. Its point is weakened in the standard English versions by the fact that two different words—*philein* and *agapan*—are both translated as "love." Maurice Nicoll emends this passage as follows (using the term "mechanical love" for what I have been calling the "love of the world"):

Jesus saith to Simon Peter, Simon, son of John, lovest thou me (consciously) more than these? He saith unto him, Yea, Lord, thou knowest that I love thee (mechanically). He saith unto him, Feed my lambs. He saith unto him again a second time, Simon, son of John, lovest thou me (consciously)? He said unto him, Yea, Lord thou knowest that I love thee (mechanically). He saith unto him, Tend my sheep. He saith unto him the third time, Simon, son of John, lovest thou me (mechanically)? Peter was grieved because he said unto him the third time, Lovest thou me (mechanically)? And he said unto him, Lord, thou knowest all things, thou knowest that I love thee (mechanically). Jesus said unto him, Feed my sheep.[13]

Philia—the love of friends—is mechanical love; agape is conscious love. Here Peter simply does not understand what Jesus is asking him; he does not know the difference between conscious love and ordinary friendship; he even thinks Jesus has asked him the same question three times. And yet this difference is precisely what he must know if he is to assume a position of spiritual authority. The fact that Christ asks Peter three times and he never gets the point is a crucial one; finally Christ has to descend to his level and use the same word that Peter does.

As this episode suggests, the two forms of love are not so easily separated in practice. The old view was that the one somehow excluded the other, leading some to the odd conclusion that in order to practice perfect love, they had to withdraw from their fellow humans entirely. But the Gospels are set in the midst of the world, among the peasants, publicans, soldiers, and scribes of their time. Similarly, in our lives it is possible to display this kind of love in all our relations without having to cut ourselves off from them. To practice agape toward another person does not mean breaking off personal or even sexual ties with him or her. Rather, it means adding another, higher type of love that brings the relationship into the dimension of holiness.

SOUL MATES

What, then, of love in the most familiar sense of the term—the romantic, sexual love that occupies so much of our thoughts and hopes? The New Testament as we have it leaves only two choices: celibacy, as Paul ostensibly practiced, and marriage—a subject to which Christ returned on more than one occasion, insisting on the inviolability of the marital bond: "What . . . God hath joined together, let not man put asunder. . . . Whosoever shall put away his wife, except it be for fornication, and shall marry another, committeth adultery: and whoso marrieth her which is put away doth commit adultery" (Matt. 19:6, 9).

Certainly the conventional Christian insistence on the inviolability of marriage—a principle echoed by traditions around the world—is easy to understand on a purely sociological level. Childrearing is difficult and costly work, so in a couple, the man should have the right to know that the child he is bringing up is his own, while the woman should have some confidence that her husband's attentions will not be diverted to some other union. Moreover, promiscuity spreads diseases, and marital fidelity is a way of keeping these in check. These concerns were particularly acute in the days before birth control had been developed and the transmission of disease was adequately understood.

Yet there is a dark side to the sacrament of matrimony. Christ said, "What God hath joined together, let not man put asunder," but who, looking at the bitterness that has soaked into many marriages, can imagine that God has had any part in their union? I am reminded of Ambrose Bierce's acerbic definition of marriage as "the state or condition of a community consisting of a master, a mistress, and two slaves, making in all, two." It takes more than a few formulas uttered by a clergyman to bring down the influence of the divine. Moreover, if we are contrasting the "love of the world"—which must include marital love—with spiritual love, how do the two fit together?

Esoterically, those whom "God hath joined together" are what are usually known as "soul mates." This ancient and widespread idea appears in contexts as diverse as the Kabbalah and the novels of D. H. Lawrence. It makes its first appearance in Plato's *Symposium*, in which the comic dramatist Aristophanes says that there were originally three sexes: male, female, and hermaphroditic. These beings were not like ordinary humans but were "globular in shape, with rounded back and sides, four arms and four legs, and two faces, both the same, on a cylindrical neck, and one head, with one face one side and one the other, and four ears, and two lots of privates and all the other parts to match." Such was the power of these beings that they tried to storm heaven and throw down the gods.

To keep these creatures in their place, Zeus hit upon the expedient of dividing them in half, and "when the work of bisection was complete it left each half with a desperate yearning for the other." The male beings who seek to unite with their other halves are homosexuals; the females, lesbians; the hermaphroditic beings are heterosexuals. And so, Aristophanes goes on to say, "we are all like pieces of the coins children break in half for their keepsakes—making two out of one, like the flatfish—and each of us is forever seeking the half that will tally with himself."[14] This resembles the passage in Genesis that says God took a "rib" or "side" from Adam to create a "helpmeet" for him (Gen. 2:18–22).

It is hard to say exactly how seriously Plato meant this idea; after all, he puts it in the mouth of a comic. And yet the idea that each of us has some perfect counterpart in another human being is deeply felt. Boris Mouravieff makes this idea the centerpoint of the esoteric Christian path that he calls the "Fifth Way" (which, unlike Aristophanes, he characterizes in purely heterosexual terms). For Mouravieff, the true "I" of the human individual is bipolar—male and female—and it is because of this that each of us, in order to reach our fullest potential, must find and unite with our "polar opposite"—as Mouravieff puts it, the "Knight" must go in quest of "the Lady of his Dreams." He quotes from an otherwise unknown esoteric Christian text known as the *Golden Book*:

Every man is born bearing within him the image of his polar being.
As he grows, this image grows within him;
It takes form and is filled with life and colour.
Man is not conscious of it. Yet it is his *Alter Ego*,
The Lady of his dreams, his *Princess of the vision*.
In quest of her he must eternally go.
In Her alone, he will find a perfect echo of himself;
Of the most intimate, inexpressible movements of his soul,
For in their union, the limit between the *I* and the *Thou* is obliterated.
Since she is his *Singular*, his *legitimate Spouse*.
And *Silence* will then be the depositary of the fullness of his Love.[15]

When these two find each other—and Mouravieff says that polar beings are destined to meet at least once in their lifetimes—if they are sufficiently developed from an esoteric standpoint, they must achieve fusion through the "baptism of fire." To accomplish this, "the two lovers, conscious of their presumably integral polarity, are called upon to straightway renounce carnal love. They must do this consciously and of a common accord, at the same time cultivating the Sacred fire of their Love, which then takes the form of *courtly love*."[16]

This idea resembles teachings in many spiritual traditions that recommend transmuting sexual energy into a higher, spiritual energy. In certain oriental teachings, this is achieved by inner practices, such as bringing oneself to the point of orgasm (either through intercourse or masturbation) and then sending the energy up through the spine to the heart or head; much of what passes for Tantra in the West is some variant of this practice. On the other hand, Mouravieff's portrayal of this process of the "Fifth Way" is perplexing. He arrives at it by way of a complex system that has many affinities with Ouspensky's (not surprisingly, since he and Ouspensky were close friends), and I do not know of any counterpart to these exact ideas in other strains of esoteric Christianity. Yet his teaching has one strong point in its favor: if we accept it, suddenly much that was obscure in the Christian tradition becomes penetratingly clear. We see why the tradition has tended to denigrate carnal love in favor of a higher, spiritual love, and we also understand a number of otherwise inexplicable practices, ranging from the habit of early Christian married couples of lying together without intercourse to the "courtly love" of the medieval troubadours and even to the spiritual love Dante shows for Beatrice in the *Divine Comedy* and the *Vita nuova*.

One modern person who has dealt with this issue in a practical way is the Episcopal priest and contemplative Cynthia Bourgeault, who is familiar with Mouravieff's ideas and believes that they apply to her unconventional (though Platonic) relationship with a Trappist hermit monk named Brother Raphael Robin—a connection that only became stronger after his death. Bourgeault discusses her experiences in a profound and intimate book entitled *Love Is Stronger Than Death*.

No doubt there are those who, like Bourgeault, will find an intuitive truth in the idea of the "polar opposite" and will discover that their spiritual path will take them to it naturally. Others may never find the "Knight" or "Lady" of their dreams. Human life encompasses an enormous range of encounters and an equally enormous range of forms of love—passing affairs, deep friendships, and lifelong bonds—and there is no evidence that this will ever change. It is unlikely that in this dimension one size will fit all. The key, perhaps, is not to insist upon love in any rigid, preconceived form, but to gain access to the unconditional love that is at the center of Christianity and to allow it to touch all with whom we come in contact.

I O

Symbols and Sacraments

B Y NOW IT IS A TRUISM that there are layers of the mind deeper than those of the ordinary waking state. Psychological concepts such as the subconscious and the unconscious have made their way into everyday speech, and many people have tried to grapple with these parts of themselves through psychotherapy in its countless forms. We have also come to recognize that these parts of the mind are involved in religious experience, though there is little agreement on how. Nor is it entirely clear how these parts of our own natures can be addressed. If, as it seems, they are neither conscious nor verbally oriented, how does the conscious mind speak to them?

While there are as many models of the mind as there are people who have made them, I would like to look at this subject in terms of the ideas I have been trying to set out here. We have seen that inner Christianity views human nature as tripartite, consisting of the spirit, the soul or psyche, and the body. Of these the psyche is perhaps the most complex and bewildering. Nonetheless, because it serves as a middle term, a reconciling force between the pure awareness of the spirit and the solidity of the body, it is the linchpin of the human framework.

The psyche itself can be broken down into three parts or layers (see diagram 10-1). The central one is the best known and ostensibly the least problematic: the ego that we know from daily life and with which we tend to identify. Another part, which is below it, is called the "carnal mind" in esoteric Christianity. This is the dimension of the psyche that is closest to the body and governs and regulates it. The carnal mind is not conscious in the customary sense, although in another sense it is completely conscious—more so in some ways than the ego, since it has to direct the routine functions of the body such as the breath and heartbeat even in deep sleep. The carnal mind, as one might expect, thinks sensorily. It does not grasp words or concepts very well; what it understands best is physical actions.

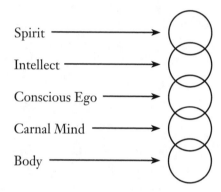

A schematic portrait of the human framework. At the top is the spirit; at the bottom the body. The three center circles represent the levels of the psyche: the intellect, the conscious ego, and the carnal mind. The circles interlock because a human being is not a layer cake; these levels interact and interpenetrate in manifold ways.

The third aspect of the psyche is the top story. It serves as a link between the lower parts of the psyche and the spirit. Of the three it is by far the least understood and has been more or less forgotten by modern humanity. Thus there is no name for it even in most modern psychological schools. But the ancient languages had words for it. In the Greek of Plato it was *episteme*, or "knowledge";[1] in the Hebrew of the Kabbalah it is *binah*, or "understanding"; in Sanskrit, *buddhi*; and in Latin, the *intellectus*, or "intellect." This third aspect is not, however, what we term the intellect in modern English; rather, it functions on a much higher level. René Guénon defines it as "that faculty which possesse[s] a direct knowledge of principles."[2] It thinks in terms of archetypal symbols and abstract figures, such as numbers and geometric shapes. To experience it nakedly is, from the point of view of ordinary cognition, an altered state of consciousness that is rarely reached today. Despite the inadequacy of the term, for lack of anything better I will refer to it here as the *intellect*.

To lead an individual toward inner integration under the direction of the true "I," Christianity must have some way of communicating with these three aspects of the psyche. The conscious ego understands verbally; it is addressed by such practices as hearing sermons and reading sacred texts. The carnal mind must learn through gestures and actions; for this aspect, ritual in all its forms has been designed. The intellect, on the other hand, is addressed by symbols. Because these faculties are innate in the human mind, rituals and symbols are found in all times and places.

SYMBOLS AND SACRED GEOMETRY

The influence of C. G. Jung and his school has led to a fairly widespread understanding of symbols as archetypes—deep structural patterns in the human mind that manifest unconsciously in dreams and art. The esoteric understanding of these archetypes resembles Jung's in many respects, though it is not identical. The greatest difference is that in the esoteric view, the level of the mind that thinks in symbols—which I am calling the intellect—is not, strictly speaking, unconscious but rather highly conscious; it is not unreasoning but a higher form of reason than we normally have access to. The modern mind is oblivious to this higher reasoning, however, and in most people today it remains as a more or less undeveloped faculty. This is why Jung can say it is "unconscious." In another sense, however, it is the ordinary ego that is unconscious of this higher faculty. There is no intrinsic reason that the intellect must remain unconscious; we simply have failed to develop it, like the athlete who neglects his mind or the thinker who ignores his body.

One of the most time-honored ways of cultivating the intellect is sacred geometry. The universe, insofar as we can comprehend it, is predicated on certain geometrical and mathematical principles. This can be seen most obviously in the natural world: a geranium blossom has a pattern of five petals, while certain lilies have six and irises three. We find the same in the animal world with creatures like the starfish, and as we can see from Leonardo da Vinci's famous drawing of a man with arms and legs spread out and measured according to geometric ratios, the human body is also based on a fivefold pattern. This is one meaning of Aleister Crowley's aphorism that "every human being is a star." The pentagram, contrary to the popular belief, is not a symbol of witchcraft or Satan but is the number of humanity on the natural level, as we can see not only from Leonardo's drawing but from the fact that we are usually said to have five senses. The five wounds of Christ are an esoteric allusion to this truth, the senses being the "wounds" by which the human being suffers and dies in the realm of materiality.

Someone who contemplates the geometric structure of the universe may eventually come to a strange though compelling conclusion: the numbers, notably the simple counting numbers from one to ten, are not only principles underlying the known universe from galaxies to subatomic particles, but are intelligences in their own right. They are living, dynamic creatures who exist, not so much in a remote and abstract world of ideas, but as the very framework and underpinning of our own life and consciousness. They are very much like the archetypes of Jung in this sense, and it is no coincidence that Jung wanted to devote his last work to numbers as archetypes. (His followers persuaded him instead to write the autobiographical *Memories, Dreams, Reflections*, so this book was never written.)

The idea that numbers possess this kind of living intelligence has an equally peculiar corollary. The esoteric view of symbols is the exact opposite of the conventional one. Usually, a symbol is believed to take its power from its meaning. In Christianity, the most obvious example is the cross. Almost any Christian would say that the reason the cross is a sacred symbol is that Jesus died on the cross, and the symbol recalls his redemptive act. But this is not so: the cross has always been a sacred symbol and will continue to be so long after Christianity has been forgotten.

A symbol like the cross has its own intrinsic power, which lies beyond meaning as we normally understand it; the same is true of other basic geometric shapes such as the six-pointed star and the crescent, today used as the defining symbols of Judaism and Islam respectively. These symbols will retain their living force and archetypal power for as long as the human mind is as it is now; meanings and movements will attach themselves to them and will attempt to draw power from them. (We can see this in the innumerable geometrical symbols that political movements, religions, and even corporations attempt to use to their own purposes.) Meanings come and go, but the symbol remains, with its archetypal power that attracts and inspires the intellect. One way of cultivating the intellect is by the active and conscious contemplation of geometric symbols, preferably by drawing them and gazing at them with an open attentiveness. Several recent books provide a good introduction to this discipline, notably Robert Lawlor's *Sacred Geometry* and Michael Schneider's *Beginner's Guide to Constructing the Universe*.

In its most sublime and sophisticated form, geometry provides the underpinning of sacred architecture. The great sacred buildings of the world, including the masterpieces of church architecture in Europe, are based on a complicated dynamic of sacred harmonies and proportions, of which the Golden Mean is the most famous. These are meant not only to illustrate certain esoteric principles but also, and just as important, to inspire certain emotions and insights in those who enter them. The proportions of a room or building can have in their own right a tremendous effect on the human organism; we know this even in daily life when we come into rooms that somehow create awkwardness and discomfort, while others by their very shape produce a sense of harmony and well-being. While the knowledge of sacred proportion and harmony has largely been ignored in modern architecture, it has not been entirely lost, and there are still practitioners of sacred architecture today. Among the best known is the Englishman Keith Critchlow, who has written several books on sacred geometry and its practical applications in addition to designing buildings on these principles.

All this is to say that a symbol cannot be approached entirely by way of its meaning, but at the same time its meaning is not to be ignored entirely. At this point it would be best to illustrate this point by means of an example. I will use one of the oldest—perhaps *the* oldest—symbol of Christianity, one that goes back to the first century and still adorns the car bumpers of many believing Christians in America today. It is the symbol of the fish, drawn in the following way:

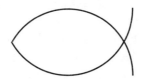

Before we go into a discussion of the meaning of this symbol, you may want to try to contemplate it directly with the intellect. This will work best if you make a photocopy of this page, cut out the illustration, and paste it on a blank sheet of paper. Or you may wish to trace the symbol or draw it freehand.

Sit quietly but attentively in a place where you will not be disturbed for ten minutes or so. You may find it easiest to fasten the page to the wall at eye level and sit fairly close to it—say two feet away—so you can gaze on it comfortably and without obstruction.

Relax and bring your attention to the breath for a minute or two. Now see if you can focus your complete attention on the symbol. Probably this will be difficult or even impossible. Your mind will stray; you will think of other things that have nothing to do with the matter at hand. Do not be disturbed by these distractions; they are one layer of the psyche—associations. When your thoughts wander, gently bring them back to simple contemplation of the object.

As you focus on the symbol, you will probably also notice that it has certain meanings for you, which will chiefly have to do with how you have interpreted it in the past. You may have read of what it means; you may have seen it in other contexts, which has created a meaning for you. Note this level of experience but again do not confine yourself to it. Instead, return your attention again to the simple contemplation of the object.

Eventually you may find that both the associations and the meanings that arise from them fall away, and you are left nakedly confronting the symbol. Everything has passed away but you and the symbol. At this point you may find it helpful to close your eyes and visualize it in your mind's eye or even gaze at the afterimage until it fades away. If you do this exercise properly, you may have a subtle sense of being *penetrated* by knowledge. The knowledge that is embedded in this symbol has somehow entered and made its home inside you. Do not preoccupy yourself with trying to analyze it or put your finger on it. The knowledge itself knows where in you it will lodge.

It is possible, of course, to do this exercise with any sacred symbol or image you choose, including the icon cross that I will discuss later in this chapter. But in general this practice will work the best with extremely simple and basic geometric shapes. Embellishments add meanings and associations, and these tend to get in the way of the naked experience of the intellect.

Now to the meaning of the fish symbol. A comparatively well informed Christian will say it originally derived from an acronym in Greek: ᾿Ιησοῦς Χριστός, Θεοῦ ῾Υιός, Σωτήρ: *Iēsous Christos, Theou Huios, Sotēr*: "Jesus Christ, Son of God, Savior." The first letter of each word of this phrase spells out the word ΙΧΘΥΣ, *ichthys*, or "fish"; hence the fish symbol. It was a secret password by which Christians could identify each other in the persecutions of the early days.

This explanation is not wrong, but it gives only one level of meaning. Another, deeper level has to do with how this symbol is constructed. It is made by drawing two circles in this fashion, so that the center of one is on the circumference of the other. They intersect in this way:

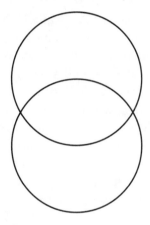

This symbol is known as the *vesica piscis* (or "bladder of the fish," in reference to its shape—a bladder that, when inflated, looks like a fish).[3] It is also known as a *mandorla*, which means "almond," again in reference to its shape. This symbol is found in many forms of Christian sacred art, for example, in the tympanum of Chartres Cathedral, which has a bas-relief of Christ enthroned in a vertical mandorla.

One key meaning of the *vesica piscis* has to do with the fact that it is created by two interpenetrating circles. One circle symbolizes the "I," the spirit; the other, the world. The mandorla is the place where these two interconnect and interpenetrate; it is the world of human life and intelligence, which is capable of relating to both spirit and matter. This figure also represents Christ, who is said theologically to have two natures, fully human and fully divine. (From an esoteric point of view this not only is a theological statement about one man named Jesus Christ but also indicates the destiny to which each human being is called.)

The cross is of course the symbol of Christianity par excellence, and I have already discussed some of its fundamental meanings. Again, the crucifixion of the man Jesus is only one of these; far more immediate is the fact that the cross represents the dimensions of time and space on which each of us is crucified. Time, which we experience in a linear, one-dimensional fashion, can be seen as the horizontal line, while the vertical line signifies the exact point in space in which we happen to find ourselves.[4] Others say the vertical line represents the dimension of the sacred, which elevates us above the horizontal perspective of the world.

As we saw in chapter 3, a third perspective, given by René Guénon, holds that the fullest version of this symbol is a three-dimensional cross, of which the Chi-Rho figure is a two-dimensional depiction. Here each of the six arms corresponds to one of the dimensions: the "boundless north," the "boundless south," the "boundless east," the "boundless west, "the "boundless depth," and the "boundless height," as described in the *Sefer Yetzirah*. In contemplating these different perspectives, the object is not so much to rifle through them and pick one that is supposedly right, but rather to let the intellect be informed and inspired by all of them together.

The cross represents materiality in another way. The equal-armed cross is known iconographically as the Greek cross, while the Latin cross, more familiar in the West, takes this form:

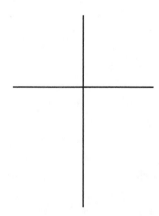

Its proportions can be seen as a collection of six squares:

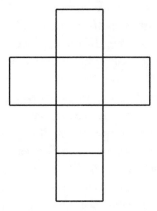

Viewed in this way, the Latin cross looks like a cube that has been opened up and laid out flat, and indeed one can make a Latin cross to these proportions and fold its six sides to make a cube. The cube is one of the primordial symbols of materiality. Many Western churches are built on the plan of a Latin cross, indicating that on their precincts the sacred is embodied in materiality.

THE BESTIARY OF CHRIST

Other primordial symbols such as the crescent, pentagram, and six-pointed star of David could yield similar insights if approached in the same way. But since these are not normally associated with Christianity, it would perhaps be better to move on to symbols of other types. An exhaustive list would include objects and creatures from the entire world known to us: plants, stones, metals, numbers, artifacts. Some of the most powerful are taken from the animal kingdom. There is an esoteric teaching that the cosmic Adam extends far wider than humanity as we know it: the animals and birds are also parts of this primordial being, representing faculties of his that have been sheared off by the Fall and now are forced to live in mutual isolation and hostility until the restoration of all things.

However literally we take this idea, it is inescapably true that animals have long been seen as representations of certain sides of the human character. We see this in everyday language, for example, when we consider what it means to call someone a cat or an ape or a bitch.

This idea permeates the language of sacred symbols as well: one instance I have already discussed is the meaning of the four holy living creatures of Ezekiel, which are correlated to the four Evangelists. Others are more or less obvious from their constant use in sacred art, the lamb symbolizing innocence; the dove, peace; the lion, strength; and the dog, fidelity. But the iconographic treasury of the Christian tradition is far richer than this. The French esotericist Louis Charbonneau-Lassay, in his *Bestiary of Christ*, lists creatures as diverse as the vulture (symbolizing the vice of gluttony, or Satan as predator), the bee (suggesting social order and harmony; sometimes the sign of a beehive denotes the presence of an esoteric school), and even the sea urchin (a representation of the World Egg that gives life to all).[5]

Listing all the symbolic attributes of the world's animals would be an encyclopedic task, but one facet of the subject that might be interesting to consider here is the category of mythical beasts. Many of these are not quite as mythical as they may seem; some, like the unicorn, may have come from travelers' tales of animals such as the rhinoceros, while others—the dragons and monsters of universal lore—may have been inspired by the unearthed bones of dinosaurs. Some ancient Greek vases even depict monsters with heads identical to those of dinosaur skulls.

Other mythical creatures are clearly composite figures. In *Beelzebub's Tales* Gurdjieff has his hero give a long description of a statue in the capital city of Atlantis, which, Beelzebub says, resembled the Great Sphinx of Egypt. The statue in Atlantis was called "Conscience," and it had the body of a bull, the legs of a lion, and the wings of an eagle. In place of the head, however, it had "two breasts representing in themselves what are called 'Breasts of a virgin.'" Beelzebub explains that each of these features is designed to represent a feature necessary for self-perfection. The bull's body symbolizes the "indefatigable labors" needed for this work; the lion's legs mean that "the said labors should be performed with that cognizance and feeling of courage and faith in one's own 'might,'" while the wings of the eagle serve as a reminder that one must meditate constantly on things that are not of this world. As for the detail of the virgin's breasts, "this expresses that Love that should predominate always and in everything."[6]

As with most of *Beelzebub*, it is not clear how literally Gurdjieff wants us to take his depiction of Atlantis; it is, after all, a work of allegorical fiction. But the iconography has considerable validity to it, and most composite creatures are meant to represent some admixture of the primary virtues. It is no coincidence that in this figure, as in the Sphinx itself, we see representations of the four living creatures of Ezekiel and the Evangelists: the ox, lion, eagle, and human. Here too they portray the different functions of the psyche and the need to integrate them into a higher whole.

Another curious case of a composite creature, this one of a negative variety, is discussed by Boris Mouravieff, who speaks of the chimera—a fantastic creature whose very name has become synonymous with illusion.[7] It traditionally has the body of a goat and the head of a lion. What does this signify? In the first place, as the ox and lamb are images of a submissive "carnal mind" (which is why these animals are shown at the manger near the newborn Jesus), the goat represents a rebellious and contrary aspect of the same nature: goats in the Gospels symbolize the wicked, and the goat has long been associated with the Devil. In the second place, as Gurdjieff suggests, the lion, noted for its courage, represents the emotional nature. But here the creature has a lion's *head*, indicating that it is letting the emotions do the thinking. This combination—an unbridled carnal mind and a mind dominated by the emotions—are a fitting symbol for man in his unredeemed state, prey to the forces of illusion. Hence the chimera is the illusory creature par excellence.

The horse has an iconographic role somewhat similar to the lion's: it represents the emotions, again usually (though not always) in submission to the higher force of reason. So it appears as early as the *Phaedrus* of Plato, which portrays human nature as a chariot drawn by two horses, "one of these horses fine and good and of noble stock, and the other the opposite in every way." These horses symbolizes the better and baser aspects of our nature. The task of the charioteer—the reason—in governing them is, Plato adds, "a difficult and unpleasant business."[8] The Chariot card in the Tarot alludes to this truth.

Usually when the horse is shown with a rider, it indicates an emotional life that is under the guidance of consciousness. This gives a key to one of the best-known icons in the Orthodox tradition, which shows Saint George mounted on his horse thrusting a spear into a dragon. Thus there are four key elements. The dragon or serpent is the force of illusion, the downward pull of the world embedded in the reptile brain. The horse is the emotions. The knight represents the Christian wearing "the whole armour of God" (Eph. 6:13), while the spear may be equated with what *The Cloud of Unknowing* calls "the dart of longing love" that pierces illusion and enables the spirit to reach God.

But this image can be taken one step further and correlated to the human structure. As we know from Hindu esotericism, the serpent force of illusion resides at the base of the spine. The emotional life, the horse, is usually conceived as residing in the torso (and in fact scientists have found a large nexus of nerve cells in the digestive tract that give new and literal force to the term "gut feelings"). That which is distinctively human, the reason, is put in the head. The spinal cord, the spear, is what links all these things. Thus this image is attempting in another way to tell us something about the proper relationship between the different and often conflicting parts of ourselves.

But, one may ask, how are we expected to know all this? How are we expected to look at sacred images and be able to see these ideas in them?

To begin with, most of these images were conceived in a time and place very different from the modern world. Most people could not read and relied far more heavily on pictorial representations than we do today. Peasants used shepherd's almanacs, which had no writing but were set out entirely in pictures. In his work *The Dwellings of the Philosophers*, the twentieth-century alchemist Fulcanelli discusses how this symbolic language was worked into sculpture as a way of encoding sacred knowledge. To take a simple example, he discusses a tympanum from a twelfth-century French house. At the top is a scholar teaching a student out of a book. Below, on the left, is a man strangling a dragon; on the right are a pair of lovers. This arrangement indicates that knowledge is superior to both strength and love.[9]

Many aspects of this symbolic language have been forgotten. On the one hand, to grasp it fully would be a matter for exhaustive scholarship. On the other hand, there is an aspect of this art that does *not* rely on scholarship or understanding the picture language of five hundred or seven hundred years ago. Many of these symbols are universal and, as Jung so famously emphasized, are embedded in the human mind at a collective level. Thus they should speak to us in much the same way as they did in times past. Moreover, there are other dimensions to sacred art in addition to visual symbolism. Sacred images in both West and East often conformed to a rigorous canon of harmony and proportion, and as in architecture, these very proportions were designed to transmit certain states of consciousness and even knowledge, which are still available to those who approach them with the right frame of mind.

THE OCTAVE OF THE ICON CROSS

Another aspect of the imagery of icons is worth mentioning here. In chapter 5 I set out a view of the universe as a cosmic octave. Many icons portray this octave symbolically, such as a Russian icon cross in my possession (see page 208). It has seven levels, which correspond exactly with the levels of the octave:[10]

God the Father	Do	*Dominus*	The Lord
The angels	Si	*Sidereus Orbis*	The Starry World
The saints (portrayed by Mary and John)	La	*Lactea Via*	The Milky Way
The crucified Christ	Sol	*Sol*	The Sun
A city	Fa	*Fatum*	The Realm of the Planets
The natural world	Mi	*Mixtus Orbis*	The Mixed World of Good and Evil
A cave with a skull	Re	*Regina Astrorum*	The Moon, "Queen of the Stars"

Most of the correspondences between the figures on the icon cross and this octave should be reasonably clear: the starry and galactic realms correspond to the level of the spirit, portrayed by angels and saints; the crucified Christ (often connected with solar imagery) is at the level of the sun; while the human city is correlated with the planetary realms, which govern fate, including the rise and fall of civilization. The earth is the realm of nature, while the cave is the "outer darkness," connected with the moon.[11]

The image of the skull in the cave is of particular interest. Christ was crucified on Golgotha, the "place of the skull" ("Calvary," the Latin equivalent, has exactly the same meaning). Christian lore says that this place was so named because it was the exact spot where Adam's skull was buried, suggesting that the redemptive act of Christ entails the healing of the brokenness and death engendered by the Fall. To put it more concretely, Christ's work begins where Adam's left off.

Many, if not most, icons depict these levels in some way or another.

This eighteenth-century icon cross shows the levels of the cosmic octave in pictorial form. It also casts an interesting light on the structure and dynamics of the three-armed cross widely used in Russian Orthodoxy.

The art of making icons is a rigorous one, requiring painters to grasp a hidden language of symbols and proportions to which the images must conform. Indeed, in Orthodoxy those who make icons are known as "iconographers," which literally means "writers of icons": creating these images is envisaged as an act of communicating sacred knowledge.

Many other rules stipulate how icons must be made. They must, for example, be clearly two-dimensional: they cannot take the form of plastic sculpture, and they are not to obey the laws of perspective, which would give them a more three-dimensional appearance. This is not an accident or the result of limited artistic ability. It partly reflects the idea that icons are regarded as "windows into heaven"—as points at which the believer can have some glimpse into higher worlds. The requirement of two-dimensionality reflects a lengthy dispute in the Eastern Orthodox tradition about the use of sacred images, which are, after all, forbidden by the Second Commandment: "Thou shalt not make unto thee any graven image, nor any likeness of any thing that is in heaven above, or that is in the earth beneath, or that is in the water under the earth" (Exod. 20:4). In the eighth century this controversy led to an open conflict between the "iconodules," who venerated the icons, and the "iconoclasts," who reviled them as transgressing the divine command. The struggle between these two parties threatened to split not only the Eastern Church but the Byzantine Empire itself. It was finally resolved in the Eighth Ecumenical Council of 787, which represented a triumph for the iconodules and which set down the guidelines for iconography that the Eastern Church follows to this day.[12]

Although the Catholic Church in the West was bound by the same ruling (the Catholic and Orthodox churches did not split finally until 1054), these guidelines have not been observed in the Western church, where religious themes have inspired much of the greatest sculpture and perspective painting of our civilization. The Orthodox Church has always looked askance at this trend on the grounds that too graphic a presentation of the human body, even in ostensibly sacred art, leads to unwholesome carnal thoughts. A modern person may be tempted to laugh at this overconscientious puritanism, but it is not entirely mistaken. Western Christian art, particularly from the sixteenth century on, has often shown a unwholesome fascination with sanguinary themes— blood, wounds, implements of torture. This in turn has reinforced a certain sadomasochistic quality that is one of the least appetizing aspects of Catholicism in recent centuries.

RITUALS AND "BROTHER ASS"

"The way up and the way down are one and the same," said the Greek philosopher Heraclitus. This dark utterance may mean in part that spiritual growth is not possible in an "upward" direction—toward the level of the spirit—unless the lower aspects of our nature are involved as well.

If, as I have suggested, symbolism is designed to appeal to the higher intellect, then there must also be a part of the Christian tradition that appeals to the carnal mind. While this part of the human makeup has often been regarded with contempt—Francis of Assisi famously called it "Brother Ass"—it cannot be ignored. It is the keeper of the animal vitality, without which no action on this earth is possible. Yet its understanding of words and intellectual concepts is extremely primitive. To engage the help of the carnal mind on behalf of spiritual growth, sacred rituals of all kinds have been invented.[13]

Rituals of all sorts—and they exist in secular as well as sacred contexts—have two key characteristics: they engage the body through actions and gestures, and they have a more or less fixed form. Both of these facts say a great deal about the nature of the carnal mind. In the first place, it likes movement, activity, and sensory stimulation. Anyone who goes to one of the more elaborate Catholic or Orthodox services will observe that all the senses are involved: the sight, through the decor of the church and through visual observation of the rite; the hearing, through words and music; the smell, through incense; the taste, through eating the Eucharist; and the sense of touch, through the rhythmic alternation of sitting, standing, and kneeling in which all participate. Together all these components create a sensory context for evoking the sacred.

The fixed form of the ritual is a key component of its appeal. Anyone with experience of small children or pets knows that they are extremely fond of predictable patterns of activity. A child may want to have a bedtime story read each night, while a dog may count on receiving a treat at exactly the same hour of each day. Adult humans are much the same. People become irritable if they miss their morning coffee or shower; they also find comfort and relaxation in familiar social rituals like a dinner party, which, however informal it may be, is actually a carefully scripted enaction. In fact, the familiar pattern of such occasions is one of the chief sources of their appeal. Conversely, if the ritual is violated by the omission or transposition of some key detail, the gathering will seem odd and irritating—as would happen at a dinner if, say, drinks were not provided or dessert were served before the main course. This fact is no doubt the cause of superstition: the carnal mind becomes anxious if some prescribed part of a familiar ritual is left out or if it ends up doing something it has been led to believe is unlucky. Often such fears prove to be warranted, not because these actions are bad in their own right, but because an apprehensive carnal mind will tend to fulfill its own worst fears.

The principal rituals of Christianity are the sacraments. Catholicism has seven: baptism, the Eucharist, confession, confirmation, matrimony, holy orders, and extreme unction or the last rites. Orthodoxy has rites corresponding to most of these, although the number is not so fixed; moreover, it does not administer confirmation separately but gives it to the infant immediately after baptism in the form of "chrismation," or anointing. (In Orthodoxy, the sacraments are known as "mysteries.") Most Protestant denominations have some versions of baptism and the Eucharist (the only sacraments that can be traced back to Christ himself), though there are wide differences in how these are practiced. Protestant churches also perform matrimony and some form of clerical ordination, though these are generally not regarded as sacramental in the sense understood by Catholics, for whom sacraments are instruments of grace administered by the church. Protestants, by contrast, tend to regard these rites as outward confirmations of an individual's inner commitment.

BAPTISM

The first sacrament a Christian traditionally receives is baptism, either directly after birth or upon reaching a stage of commitment to Christ. In the New Testament, adult baptism seems to have been the only form practiced. Infant baptism came later, although the sources are unclear about when and scholars do not agree on how old this practice actually is.[14]

Baptism as we know it is older than Christianity, having been originally instituted not by Christ but by John the Baptist, known in the tradition as the Precursor. The Gospels indicate that John's rite was slightly different in intent from what it later became: it was "the baptism of repentance for the remission of sins" (Luke 3:3). Many scholars believe that John was connected with the community of Essenes at Qumran on the Dead Sea, which produced the series of texts today known as the Dead Sea

Scrolls. From these writings it is clear that one of the chief impulses behind the creation of this community was a conviction that the Temple priesthood in Jerusalem was defiled and illegitimate. If John studied with the Essenes, he may have begun to practice baptism as an alternative to the traditional rites of purification centered around the Temple: a corrupt priesthood could hardly be expected to cleanse others of their sins.

Thus John may have provided the initial impulse behind the Christian tradition as a whole. One of the chief differences between Christianity and Judaism is that the latter is at its core the religion of a *people*: the spiritual life of the individual is centered around participation in the heritage and history of the Jewish nation. Christianity, despite the strong collectivity present in the church, is fundamentally a religion of the *individual*: it is a person's commitment to a new life that marks him or her as a Christian. John may have been the first figure to begin to draw this distinction: if the collective rite of the Jewish people was no longer capable of bestowing purification, it would have to be done individually.

One can take this idea further and say that this new impulse was not merely a response to the misdeeds of the Jerusalem hierarchs but also a new phase in human self-consciousness, the full development of individual awareness apart from the tribe or nation. While we see this impulse arising before Christianity (for example, in the *Antigone* of Sophocles, where individual conscience is pitted against political authority), it is in Christian civilization that individual consciousness reaches its fullest flower. Eventually this awareness must lead back to the realization that what is most truly "I" is exactly what one shares with the rest of humanity and indeed with the rest of the universe; but the phase of individuality is an essential one on this path and cannot be skipped.

The forgiveness of sins is certainly a vital element in the Christian sacrament of baptism, but it is far from the only one. Another component is exorcism. The early Christians regarded the gods of classical antiquity not as figments of the imagination but as evil spirits; those who had worshiped them were seen as being at least potentially possessed by the powers of "spiritual wickedness in high places." In the elaborate rites for adult baptism of the fourth and fifth centuries, exorcisms might take place over several days in a process that included fasting and other types of purification. Today baptism still entails the renunciation of "Satan and all his works and all his pomps."

From an esoteric point of view, this renunciation is a reversal of direction. The individual has been subject to the downward pull of the world.

Repudiating "Satan and all his works" symbolically changes his orientation from the world to the spirit. In the old rites, the candidate had to face west when renouncing Satan, the west being the direction of sunset and hence symbolically of darkness. Some rites even required the candidate to spit in the Devil's face. Then, as the fifth-century bishop Ambrose of Milan says, "after you enter to behold your adversary, whom . . . you had to renounce to his face, you turn to the east," which, as the direction of sunrise, is equated with illumination.[15]

The central aspect of baptism, however, has to do with what Christ describes to Nicodemus as a rebirth "of water and the spirit." The symbol of water is a manifold one. Most obviously it is used to clean. For this purpose it should ideally be "living water," which is not just a poetic term but has a specific meaning. The Jewish tradition holds that "living water" is the only kind suitable for purification. This is water connected to a larger source, such as a stream or the ocean; to this day Jewish *mikvehs*, ritual baths, must adhere to rigorous specifications in this regard (hence perhaps John's baptizing in the river). On a physical level, water of this kind is believed to have certain energetic properties that stagnant water lacks.[16] On a symbolic level, it indicates that the psyche is dead unless it maintains a constant connection with the deeper streams of universal life. Christ alludes to this truth in promising the Samaritan woman "living water," which will be "a well of water springing up into everlasting life" (John 4:14).

In addition, to immerse someone in water is symbolically to drown him, so immersion in the waters of baptism is a kind of death, as Paul indicates: "Know ye not, that so many of us as were baptized into Jesus Christ were baptized into his death? Therefore we are buried with him by baptism into death: that like as Christ was raised up from the dead by the glory of the Father, even so we also should walk in newness of life" (Rom. 6:3–4).

Like most rituals of the highest order, this symbolic death and rebirth has many meanings. To die and to be raised up from the waters of baptism evoke the death and resurrection of Christ, as Paul indicates. Moreover, to emerge from waters indicates a new birth, as one emerges from the waters of the womb at the time of physical birth. But there is another meaning as well. Since the waters symbolize mind-stuff, the astral light that is the ground of materiality, immersion in and rising from them also signify the journey of the soul. Each of us is immersed into the waters of becoming, into the undulating tides of good and evil that are the world. From a spiritual point of view, this is death, because we are no longer aware of our connection to the whole that gives us life. This is why God tells Adam in Genesis that on the day he eats of the fruit of the tree of knowledge, "thou shalt surely die." Life in this world is death to the higher world; conversely, death to this world, symbolized by rising from the waters of baptism, constitutes a new life in the spirit. In its deepest essence, then, baptism is the birth of the true "I." It marks the stage at which the spirit decisively detaches itself from immersion in the world.

These considerations, paradoxical and enigmatic as they are, suggest why the sacraments are known as "mysteries" in Eastern Orthodoxy. This is part of the process of a sacrament such as baptism. It not only involves the carnal mind through the physical acts of the rite, but also gives the conscious mind different layers of meaning that it must struggle to interpret. This does not take away from the beauty and profundity of the experience, but enhances it. The conscious mind senses that there are dimensions of experience that it does not really understand. If approached in the right way, it will bow down before these mysteries and honor them as Christopher did Christ.

Another key aspect of baptism, both in ancient times and in the present, is anointing: the ritual application of holy oil to certain parts of the body, such as the forehead, which is marked with the sign of the cross. In ancient times the oil (usually olive oil mixed with balsam, a substance known as *myron*) was applied all over the candidate's body before the service, as explained by Ambrose: "You were rubbed with oil like an athlete, Christ's athlete, as though in preparation for an earthly wrestling-match, and you agreed to take on your opponent," the Devil.[17] Sometimes oil was poured over the candidate's head in accordance with the verse that speaks of "the precious ointment upon the head, that ran down upon the beard, even Aaron's beard: that went down to the skirts of his garments" (Ps. 133:2).

On the simplest level, anointing is cosmetic. It was part of the ancient ritual of washing: people would take a bath and then apply scented oils to themselves after they were clean. Doing so in the context of baptism reinforces the sense that the newly initiated Christian is washed clean and purified. Anointing is also used to consecrate priests and kings, as Samuel does when he acknowledges David as the rightful king of Israel (1 Sam. 16:13); this aspect of the rite indicates that a Christian is a king and a priest in his own right.

Furthermore, esoteric teachings hold that there are higher centers of perception and awareness. Today these are most commonly associated with the chakras, as known in New Age teachings (taken over from Hinduism), but they have always been known under different names. The forehead, the top of the head, the mouth, the throat, the heart, and the palms of the hands are among the most important of these centers. Anointing opens these centers and stimulates them to work on their own. Oil is used partly because these centers, when they are active, can feel as if oil is being poured on them; when they are fully awake, it can even feel as if oil is flowing over the entire body, as Psalm 133 suggests.

Scented oil is also meant to bestow protection. Tradition holds that beneficent spirits are drawn to pleasant scents and hostile spirits to unwholesome ones; the Tibetan Buddhists even have an entire category of helpful spirits known as *gandharvas*, or "scent eaters." Anointing the candidate with pleasant scents is thus a means of protecting him or her from diabolical influences.

These considerations help explain why baptism began to be practiced on infants. C. W. Leadbeater discusses this issue in one of the most fascinating and unusual studies of the Christian rites ever written: *The Science of the Sacraments*, published in 1920. Leadbeater was one of the early leaders of the Liberal Catholic Church, a small denomination founded in 1916 that seeks to harmonize Theosophy with esoteric Christianity. Leadbeater was a clairvoyant and wrote several books on his perceptions of realms that are unseen to most of us, including *Man, Visible and Invisible*, *The Chakras*, and *Thought Forms*. Practically all of the countless New Age books on chakras, auras, and extrasensory perception are indebted directly or indirectly to him.

Leadbeater observes that in the ancient rite of the church, the priest made the sign of the cross over the baby's forehead, throat, heart, and solar plexus, an arrangement restored in the Liberal Catholic Church. He comments:

> These are four of the special force-centres in the human body, and the effect of the sign, and of the intelligent exercise of the will, is to set these centres in motion.
>
> If a clairvoyant looks at a new-born baby he will see these centres marked; but they are tiny little circles like a threepenny piece—little hard discs scarcely moving at all, and only faintly glowing. The particular power which the Priest exercises in Baptism opens up these centres and sets them moving much more

rapidly, so that a clairvoyant will see them growing before his eyes to the size, perhaps of a crown-piece, and beginning to sparkle and whirl, as they do in grown-up people.[18]

Leadbeater goes on to say that infant baptism is meant not only to awaken these centers but also to offer a stimulus to the infant, so that the good impulses that it brings into incarnation are fostered and the evil impulses aborted. He adds:

A Sacrament is not a magical nostrum. It cannot alter the disposition of a man, but it can help to make his vehicles a little easier to manage. It does not suddenly make a devil into an angel, or a wicked man into a good one, but it certainly gives the man a better chance. That is precisely what Baptism is intended to do, and that is the limit of its power.[19]

Even granted that the spirit of the newborn child marks the awakening of these subtle centers on some level, there is still a world of difference between the rites of infant baptism and the rebirth of water and the spirit of which Christ speaks. To some degree this is the consequence of that which was formerly esoteric devolving into an outer rite, granted either to purge the baby of original sin (a doctrine that was not fully formulated in the West till the fifth century, and which has never been accepted in Eastern Orthodoxy) or to protect it from diabolical forces. But infant baptism, whatever advantages it may confer in leaving an indelible mark of grace on the child's soul (to use the terms of Catholic theology) or to awaken its subtle centers (to use Leadbeater's), will remain fruitless unless at some point the individual comes to a conscious awareness and choice of this rebirth. Some Protestant denominations, such as the Baptists, try to forestall this difficulty by refusing to baptize candidates before they have consciously accepted Jesus Christ into their hearts; thus they must be of an age to do so. The Catholic Church deals with this issue through the sacrament of confirmation, in which the candidate is anointed as a soldier of Christ and given a symbolic blow on the cheek as a recognition of the martyrdom that he must be willing to face for the sake of the faith. This is never administered until a child has reached the age of reason (twelve is the traditional age, though many today are confirmed earlier).

THE MASS OF THE CATECHUMENS

If baptism at its core has to do with awakening the true "I," what of that other great Christian rite, known as the Eucharist? In essence the Eucharist has to do with the transformation of the spirit into the divine, of the true "I" into the "I" that is "we." To understand why, it would be helpful to examine this rite more closely.

The mass or Eucharist is divided into two portions: the Mass of the Catechumens and the Mass of the Faithful, which, as we have seen, correspond to the exoteric and the esoteric levels of the Christian tradition.[20] In the early years of the church, the Mass of the Catechumens was open to those who had not yet undergone the baptismal initiation, while the Mass of the Faithful was open only to those who had. Later, when Christianity became universal and baptism was practiced upon all at birth, the second half of the mass lost its hidden character.

The Mass of the Catechumens comprises two chief features: invocation of the deity and the proclamation of the Word. Because the Eucharist is intended to draw the divine presence down to the congregation, it must begin with an address to God. The opening invocations are meant to elevate the participants' consciousness to a level higher than that of ordinary life and to ask God to show mercy by making his presence felt. Hence the prayer known as the "Kyrie," which is said almost at the outset of the mass. *Kyrie eleison*, which means "Lord, have mercy," is repeated three times, followed by a threefold *Christe eleison*, "Christ, have mercy," followed by *Kyrie eleison* three more times, the tripartite nature of the prayer echoing the three persons of the Trinity.

The Kyrie and other prayers are followed by readings from the Scriptures, first usually from the Epistles, though passages from the Old Testament may also be used, and then from the Gospels. Then follows a brief sermon by the priest. Together these represent the two chief means of transmission of the teaching: through the written text of the Bible and through oral interpretation. Furthermore, the twin reading of texts contains its own symbolism: The Old Testament and the New represent the two dispensations of divine revelation. Alternatively, the Epistles can be seen as commentaries on the primary text of the Gospels. In many traditions text and commentaries are the two main forms of sacred literature. In Hinduism these are called *shruti* and *smriti* respectively.[21] In Chinese the word for a sacred text is *ching* (as in the *I Ching,* or "Book of Changes"), where *ching* means "book" or "classic" but also literally "warp." The sacred text is the warp of a fabric upon which the weft of the commentaries are woven; the latter are thus understood to have somewhat less authority than the primary texts.[22] This symbolism is implicit in Christianity—there being a "Gospel side" and an "Epistle side" of the altar, for example—although it is rarely spelled out, and the Scriptures are usually seen as a single authoritative whole.

THE MASS OF THE FAITHFUL

The Mass of the Faithful begins with the recitation of the Christian creed, usually the Nicene Creed, attributed to the ecumenical Council of Nicea, which met in 325 A.D. A careful examination of the creed indicates that it serves as a kind of touchstone for winnowing out unbelievers and heretics; each phrase implicitly repudiates some alleged heresy. The opening sentence, for example, "I believe in God, the Father Almighty, maker of heaven and earth," is a repudiation of Gnosticism, which in some of its forms held that the world was not created by the true, good God but by the inferior Demiurge. Similarly, saying that Jesus Christ "suffered under Pontius Pilate" counters the heresy of Docetism, which held that Jesus was a divine being who did not really suffer on the cross but created a phantom that appeared to suffer in his place.

One could thus create a kind of heresiology of the Christian church by going through the entire creed in this fashion. To be able to say it is a kind of passkey to Christian orthodoxy, and in fact the original name for the creed was the *symbolon,* the word from which "symbol" is derived. It comes from the Greek *symballein,* which means "to put together," and it refers to the original use of a symbol. An object, say a bone or a shard of pottery, might be broken in half and given to two people. If they met later and their fragments fit together, this was a verification of their identity. In the same way, the *symbolon* of the creed served to guarantee that the participants were all Christians in good standing and neither heretics nor impostors.[23] In their early forms the creeds were only taught to those initiated into the faith. So was the Lord's Prayer, which is also recited in this portion of the Eucharist, after the consecration of the host.

The creed as a "symbol" of faith can be perplexing for many who are drawn to inner Christianity but have difficulty with orthodox dogmas. How you reconcile these conflicts in yourself will ultimately remain a personal matter. But one way of dealing with the creeds is to step back from the rational mind, with its automatic mechanism that sorts everything into the pigeonholes of "yes" and "no," and simply contemplate the words attentively and with an open mind. "I believe in God, the Father Almighty." Who or what is God in us? What is the Father? Where can he be experienced in yourself? "And in our Lord, Jesus Christ, his only-begotten Son." Who is the "Lord" in us? What does he have to do with the historical Jesus? How does his Sonship relate to ours? If you reflect on these and other parts of the creeds thoughtfully, you may find new insights and inspirations that were hidden to you when you viewed them only as a kind of party platform.

THE TRANSFORMATION OF THE EUCHARIST

The central element of the rite of the mass is the consecration of the bread and wine and its transformation (literal or symbolic, depending on one's theology) into the body and blood of Christ. This begins with the Offertory, in which the gifts are presented to God. It is both a relic and a transformation of the ancient mode of worship, in which animals were sacrificed to gods. In the case of the Offertory, the bread and wine are meant to commemorate Christ's sacrifice of his body and blood on behalf of the human race. As the Epistle to the Hebrews indicates, Christ is in this sense "an high priest for ever after the order of Melchisedec" (Heb. 6:20). Melchisedec, or Melchizedek, is a mysterious priest-king who appears briefly in an encounter with Abraham in Genesis 14, where he brings bread and wine and blesses the patriarch. In the Kabbalah, Melchizedek is sometimes regarded as the bearer of the hidden tradition, which he passed on to Abraham at this juncture. It is possible that this episode points to a secret lineage of initiates whose rites employed bread and wine, and in which Christ was initiated. But like all truly secret orders (of which there is likely to be little or no evidence precisely because of their secrecy), its existence must remain a matter of speculation.

The Offertory is followed by the Consecration, in which these gifts are mystically transformed into the body and blood of Christ, and by Communion, in which they are shared among all the participants. The symbolism of bread and wine and its transformation into flesh and blood is not only the central mystery of the Christian religion but provides a key to the esoteric symbolism of much of the Bible, and even to a certain degree of other traditions such as Sufism. It can be best understood by relating two sets of symbols to the four levels known to esoteric Christianity:[24]

Physical	Ground	Stone
Psychological	Wheat	Water
Spiritual	Bread	Wine
Divine	Flesh	Blood

The physical level is represented by inert mineral elements: the ground and stone or rock. This is the literal, external level of life and of spiritual teaching: Moses gave the Law to the Israelites on tablets of stone. The second level is that of the "natural" or psychological. It is represented by natural organic substances: wheat is a living thing, and so, we have seen, is water from an esoteric point of view. The third level is that of the spiritual, symbolized by substances that are both themselves alive and yet have required human ingenuity to fashion: bread and wine. Spiritual development is a combination of natural growth and a person's own effort. Moreover, bread and wine both require yeast or leaven, which is the symbol of an esoteric tradition, a subtle, mysterious substance that infuses the soul and transforms it into something new.

Finally, there is the level of the divine, symbolized by flesh and blood. They are the essence of a living thing, as the divine is in the world. For this reason blood was forbidden as a food to the Jews: "Therefore I said unto the children of Israel, Ye shall eat the blood of no manner of flesh: for the life of all flesh is the blood thereof: whosoever eateth it shall be cut off" (Lev. 17:14). To this day the elaborate provisions for koshering meat are intended to carry out this commandment in the strictest possible manner.

The schema of four symbolic levels makes an extraordinary amount of the Bible much clearer. It is perhaps most apparent in the Gospels, where it casts light on such parables as those of the sower and the seed and the workers of the vineyard (the vineyard being a symbol for an esoteric school, where the wine of spirit is produced). But this symbolism appears in the Old Testament as well, for example, in the story of Moses' crucial disobedience of God's command as described in Num. 20:7–12. Throughout the years in the wilderness, Moses has provided the children of Israel with water by striking a rock. But at a certain point God commands him to bring forth water by *speaking* to the rock. Vexed at the rebellious Israelites, Moses strikes it nonetheless, perhaps momentarily forgetting God's command and resorting to his habitual approach. The rock still gives forth water "abundantly," but because of this transgression Moses is barred from the Promised Land.

While this episode is often written off as another instance of the cruel whimsy of the Old Testament God, the symbolism above suggests another way of seeing it. The four levels also correspond to the levels of meaning of sacred teaching. In this instance Moses could be said to have failed to discern the appropriate psychological meaning in the "rock" or "stone" of the literal Law. Instead of finding a fresh meaning, as the situation required, he relied on his usual approach, and for this failure he was barred from entering into Canaan. This story suggests that the lawgiver in the human psyche, however necessary, is not the true "I." It can set rules and interpret them according to its custom, but it is constitutionally unable to enter the Promised Land of the spirit. To put it more concisely, habits, even good habits, are not the same thing as consciousness. They are incapable of seeing beyond the "stone" of the literal level.

The symbolism of stone and water also appears in a famous Talmudic story about four rabbis who, through mystical practices, enter into Paradise. Three of them fail to assimilate this revelation: one dies on the spot, one goes mad, and one becomes a heretic. Only the fourth, the great sage Rabbi Akiva, "departed unhurt." In advance he had warned the others, "When you arrive at the slabs of pure transparent marble, do not say: Water, Water! For it is said, 'He that speaketh falsehood shall not be established before Mine eyes' (Ps. 101:7)."[25] This cryptic utterance, coupled with the fate of the other three mystics, suggests that mystical insight can even be fatal for those who mistake the "transparent slabs" of the literal meaning for higher insight.

Like the stories of Moses and Akiva, the admonitions on this score in the Gospels tend to warn against confusing levels (which is "adultery" in an esoteric sense) or trying to pass over one or more of them. Thus it is significant that Satan in the wilderness tempts Jesus by suggesting that he turn stones into bread; this is an inadmissible skipping from the physical to the spiritual levels, omitting the psyche. Thus Jesus refuses, although he is later quite willing to break bread to feed the multitude (suggesting the infinite richness of the spirit) and later still to transform bread into flesh at the Last Supper (which does not entail a skipping of levels). On another occasion he says, "What man is there of you, whom if his son ask bread, will he give him a stone?" (Matt. 7:9), indicating that spiritual needs cannot be filled by material substances.

It is perhaps in John's Gospel that this symbolism reaches its fullest flower. Here Christ begins his public career by changing water to wine at the wedding of Cana. The account of this miracle is structured on the three lower levels of symbols as described above. We learn that "there are six waterpots of stone, after the manner of the purifying of the Jews" (John 2:6). Two details are noteworthy. First, the pots are of stone, suggesting the physical level. Second, the water has to do with "the manner of the purifying of the Jews." As we have already seen, this purification requires living water. Jesus commands the servants to draw forth this water, and it becomes wine.

In its elliptical fashion, this brief story suggests how the life of the spirit arises from the life of the psyche. It takes place at a wedding, which in terms of spiritual development indicates a marriage of higher and lower levels. There is a "governor of the feast," who is in charge of the proceedings but who does not know how the water becomes wine. This indicates the "faithful and wise servant" that is a well-disposed ego, which can set the stage for spiritual awakening but cannot direct it. Only the true "I," represented in this parable by Christ, can transform the living water of the psyche into the wine of the spirit. Moreover, this can happen only after a certain stage of preparation, as is suggested by the governor's remark that "every man at the beginning doth set forth good wine; and when men have well drunk, then that which is worse: but thou hast kept the good wine until now" (John 2:10).

In John's Gospel, just as Jesus' public career commences with his transformation of water into wine, so it ends with the transformation of wine into blood at the Last Supper. Thus his work (particularly as described in John's Gospel) can be seen as operative at the level of the spirit. It begins at the point where the true "I" is awakened in baptism (it is significant that the discussion of baptism with Nicodemus comes very soon after the wedding at Cana) and ends at the point where it joins with the greater, collective "I" at the level of the divine. This is what the Catholic Church calls the Mystical Body of Christ; admission to it is conferred and commemorated by the Eucharist. In ancient times, the newly baptized candidate was admitted to the Eucharistic feast for the first time directly after baptism.

The Eucharist is a collective ceremony. Though a priest may perform it alone, it is ideally a rite in which many participate. In this it differs from baptism, which, even though it may be administered to many on the same occasion, remains a profoundly individual event. The reason for this should now be clear: baptism has to do with the awakening of true individuality, while the Eucharist is a sign and seal of the fact that this individuality reaches its ultimate fulfillment only in union with others. Hence the command constantly emphasized in John's Gospel "that ye love one another as I have loved you" (John 13:34). At its best, this rite thus takes the individual from the level of the spirit to the level of the divine Son.

ESOTERIC SACRAMENTALISM TODAY

At this point some may ask where they can go today to find an esoteric understanding of the sacraments. The very nature of this question makes it hard to answer, since what is at issue is not the outward form of the rites but the spirit behind it. A mass performed in one church may be full of sacred power, while the same rite conducted down the street may be empty and tedious. It is not a matter of sincerity or even enthusiasm—many Pentecostal revivals are full of an enthusiasm that signifies not the presence of the Holy Spirit but ordinary emotional excitement. It is the presence of the leavening of gnosis that gives a rite its true power—even if only one or two people present has contact with this level of consciousness.

This much said, there *are* corners of Christianity where there is more interest in the esoteric dimension of the sacraments than others. For the most part they tend to be on the fringes of Christian denominationalism, such as the "independent sacramental" movement, which is part of a larger group of denominations known as the Old Catholics. These trace their origins to Roman Catholic bishops who have, for various reasons, split from the church over the centuries without losing their right to consecrate their successors. (Catholic doctrine, articulated by Augustine, holds that a bishop may still hold valid apostolic succession even if he disagrees with the papacy on doctrinal matters.) One of many such branches traces its origins to the Dutch Old Catholics, founded in the seventeenth century; an older branch, in southern India, claims to go back to the Apostle Thomas, who is said to have settled in that region. Around the turn of the twentieth century, two bishops in these lines began to consecrate a number of men in the same lineage, giving rise to many tiny independent sacramental movements. Some of these have laid claim to a Gnostic heritage, including the French Église Gnostique Universelle, led by Papus, and in contemporary America, the Ecclesia Gnostica in Hollywood, California, led by Stephan A. Hoeller, an independent bishop whose teachings combine the insights of C. G. Jung with those of the ancient Gnostics. Hoeller's monograph *The Mystery and Magic of the Eucharist* explains the esoteric underpinnings of his own Gnostic version of the mass.[26]

Another movement that has an esoteric approach to the sacraments is the Christian Community, also known as the Movement for Religious Renewal, inspired by the work of Rudolf Steiner. One of the main themes of Steiner's intricate and voluminous teachings is that humanity has evolved in recent times, so that individual consciousness is not what it was two thousand or even one thousand years ago: our sense of self has grown and developed since then. Consequently, religious rites must be updated to reflect these changes. The Community's version of the Eucharist is known as "The Act of Consecration of Man." As its name suggests, its emphasis is not so much on a divinely oriented act of thanksgiving but on an inward-oriented blessing of humanity. Eight times in the course of the service, the priest turns to the congregation and utters the doxology "Christ in you." Moreover, the priest's movements around the altar are orchestrated to create a form in the astral light—specifically, a lemniscate or figure eight, which, Steiner believed, is an archetypal representation of humanity. (Steiner, like Leadbeater, was highly clairvoyant and claimed to be able to see astral forms.)[27]

Some may be tempted to explain away these approaches to the sacraments as eccentric innovations for novelty's sake. But such an attitude presupposes that there is some predetermined form of a rite that is forever fixed in stone. And there is not. The Roman Catholic mass is the result of a long evolution that, as the reforms of Vatican II have proved, is not yet complete. The Orthodox Church is more resistant to change, priding itself on the purity and antiquity of its customs, but it too has accepted changes over the centuries, however grudgingly. In the seventeenth century, for example, the Russian Orthodox Church suffered a major schism as a result of such apparently trivial innovations as requiring believers to join three fingers when crossing themselves (in honor of the Trinity) instead of the older practice of joining two fingers (in honor of the dual nature of Christ). Those who refused to accept the new forms split off from the main church and became known as Old Believers.[28]

The truth is that ritual can and must change. Although Christ may have instituted the Eucharist, no one can pretend that the current forms of the rite bear any but the most skeletal resemblance to what he did on the night of the Last Supper. Many of the details of any ritual are not essential but peripheral and may need to be cleared away if too many of them accumulate. On the other hand, the current resistance to the post–Vatican II mass among certain traditionalist Catholics may not be entirely due to sentimental attachment to the past. It may also indicate that such changes cannot be made willy-nilly, even with the best intentions. A certain knowledge is required that grasps the subtle form of the ritual and can modify it while retaining its essence. Not many people know how to do this, and it is far from clear that the current Christian establishment has preserved this knowledge or managed to integrate it into practice.

The *truths* to which Christianity points—the nature of the spirit and its unity with the spirit of all beings—are immutable. They have always been true and will always remain true, just as they were before Christianity was ever dreamt of. This is why Augustine could write, "That which is now called the Christian religion existed among the ancients, and never did not exist, from the planting of the human race until Christ came in the flesh, at which time the true religion which already existed came to be called Christianity."[29]

The *forms* in which these truth are expressed, however, are impermanent and dispensable. Once the human spirit, in its relentless striving toward its great final destiny, loses contact with them, they are thrown away and new forms take their place. This is not a criticism of these forms, any more than it is a criticism of an eighty-year-old man to say he is not as strong as he used to be. On the other hand, it would be a mistake to cling to them either out of superstitious dread or out of a pining for the imagined glories of the past. Today the rites and symbols of Christianity hold tremendous meaning for some and seem empty observances to others. It is only through their usefulness in pointing toward inner knowledge that each seeker can decide upon their value in his or her own life.

I I

The Secret Church

You know without doubt, dear Unknown Friend, that many . . . in France, Germany, England, and elsewhere, promulgate the doctrine of the so-called "two churches": the church of Peter and the church of John, or of "two epochs"—the epoch of Peter and the epoch of John. You know also that this doctrine teaches the end—more or less at hand—of the church of Peter, or above all the papacy which is its visible symbol, and that the spirit of John, disciple loved by the Master, he who leaned on his breast and heard the beating of his heart, will replace it. In this way it teaches that the "exoteric" church of Peter will make way for the "esoteric" church of John, which will be that of perfect freedom.[1]

IN THIS WAY VALENTIN TOMBERG, the author of *Meditations on the Tarot*, introduces the concept of a secret church, associated with John, that has existed within and alongside the familiar outer institutions. Some authors, including Éliphas Lévi, say there was even a secret Johannine doctrine carried on first by John's circle of disciples and later in secret societies such as the Templars.[2]

Although the notion of a secret church of John is not to be taken literally as a conspiracy theorist might, it does have some truth to it. To understand it, we might return to a small detail mentioned in chapter 6. John Scotus Eriugena tells us that of the two disciples who rushed to the empty tomb of Christ, Peter symbolizes faith and John, knowledge. The church of Peter is the outer church. Faith holds the keys to this kingdom. But there is another dimension of Christianity as well, for an era to come. The risen Christ says to Peter of the beloved disciple (John), "If I will that he tarry till I come, what is that to thee?" (John 21:22). The Gospel seems to be suggesting that in an era long after its own time, the stream of knowledge associated with John will come into its own.

That this church is connected with John is not without import. Curiously, it has been connected with *both* the Johns, the Precursor as well as the beloved disciple. These figures in a sense serve to bracket Christ: John the Baptist coming before and John the Evangelist coming after. The coincidence of their names has led them to be linked in other ways as well. The liturgical calendar puts the feast of John the Baptist on June 24, close to the summer solstice, while that of John the Evangelist is on December 27, at the opposite end of the year. Even more interesting is the fact that these two solstices mark transition points in the journey of the spirit into and out of physical life. The tradition says that at the summer solstice all who are to be incarnated in the coming year enter the solar system from the realms beyond; at the winter solstice, all those who have died during the year are gathered up to leave. The two Johns serve as guardians of the gates.[3]

These are the gates of birth and death, which are also the gates of knowledge. Initiates are those who have gone past the borders of life and death to the consciousness of the eternity beyond. To make this journey is to know experientially that the death of the body does not mean the death of consciousness, that the true "I" is indestructible precisely because of its essential unity with the "I" of all other beings, the Son of God or the Christ within. Such initiation involves the death of the "old man," the lower self or the ego.

Those who have attained this realization, whether through spiritual discipline or through spontaneous insight, constitute the secret church of John. As A. E. Waite comments, "The Secret Church is . . . a state of attainment. . . . It is a brotherhood established under a common realisation in consciousness. Unless the members are brought together in the flesh, it is not suggested that they know one another, otherwise than in a mystic state of co-consciousness. . . . They are otherwise friends in God and when they meet in the flesh, it is said that they recognise one another, as Englishman recognizes Englishman, all the world over."[4]

The classic account of this interior church is a treatise entitled *The*

Cloud upon the Sanctuary, written by a Bavarian esotericist named Karl von Eckhartshausen around 1795. In it he writes:

> The interior Church was formed immediately after the fall of man, and received from God at first-hand the revelation of the means by which fallen humanity could be again raised to its rights and delivered from its misery. It received the primitive charge of all revelation and mystery; it received the key of true science, both divine and natural.
>
> But when men multiplied, the frailty of man and his weakness necessitated an exterior society which veiled the interior one, and concealed the spirit and the truth in the letter. Because many people were not capable of comprehending great interior truth, and the danger would have been too great in confiding the most Holy to incapable people [*sic*]. Therefore, interior truths were wrapped in exterior and perceptible ceremonies so that men, by the perception of the outer, which is the symbol of the interior, might by degrees be enabled safely to approach the interior spiritual truths.[5]

Much of this book has been concerned with looking at some of the "interior spiritual truths" of the Bible and the rites and symbols of Christianity. Ultimately, grasping these truths requires a thirst for cultivating inner experience; those who have this thirst and act upon it constitute the "inner church." But as Eckhartshausen says, many people have little interest in such experience. They constitute the "outer church," and the exterior forms of religion are designed for them. But even here there will always be a small minority who suspect there is something more. By penetrating deeper into the meaning of the "exterior and perceptible ceremonies," they move toward the inner circle "by degrees."

THE TEMPLE AND THE CHURCH

Although the idea of an inner church has often been ignored or forgotten, it is expressed in many forms of Christian symbolism. One of the most visible of these is the layout of a traditional church building, which has four levels, in imitation of the Temple of Jerusalem, with its outer court, inner court, holy place, and Holy of Holies.

The outermost is the foot of the church, the point at which one enters. Here is the *porch*, or *narthex*, an anteroom to the church proper. Here you will find a small font of holy water, "blessed for the special purpose of defeating the arts of the Devil," as Alan Watts comments in his *Myth and Ritual in Christianity*.[6] This is the outermost, physical level, where the sacred meets the secular. I. V. Lopukhin, a Russian esotericist of the eighteenth century, observes:

> In the Porch of the Temple are those who have a vivid feeling of the need for salvation, whose minds are earnestly employed in searching for the truth, and who begin to feel all the vanity of this world. The more a man is penetrated with this feeling the nearer he is to the gates of the Temple, which open only to repentant souls that have a horror of self-love and walk sincerely and with all their might towards the good.[7]

To reach the *nave*, the second level, one passes the baptismal font. This, the beginning of the church proper, serves as a reminder that the church is entered by baptism. The nave contains the pews for the laity; Lopukhin says it is "filled with those who have been attracted by the Father. Inasmuch as they have faith in the revealed truths of the Gospel, they walk in the way of regeneration, and labour diligently to fulfil the law of grace."[8] But their understanding remains primarily external. They participate in the sacred rite of inner transformation only secondarily, and they watch its enactment on the altar from the pews.

The third level, that of the spirit, contains the *altar*, the holy place. Traditionally it is separated from the rest of the church by a choir screen (in the West) or an iconostasis (in the East). This screen represents what is sometimes called the "dweller on the threshold," the "veil" that separates higher from lower consciousness. The altar is where the bread and wine are consecrated and become the body and blood of Christ; it is the place of transformation, just as the true "I" is the place in each of us where the divine meets the earth.

The fourth level is the *sanctuary*, the area behind the altar. It is the Holy of Holies, corresponding to the fourth level, the Son, that "I that is we." Here, says Lopukhin, "sit the priests of the universal redemption, surrounded by happiness and crowned with the gifts of grace and nature, who shine with all the fulness of the light which radiates truth and life."[9] This condition is symbolized by the *cathedra*, or bishop's seat, which is located here in cathedral churches—that is, churches that have bishops associated with them.

In sum, then, as Alan Watts points out, "the path from the Font to the Altar represents the whole course of the spirit's ascent into liberation—from the material waters into which it descended at Creation and Incarnation."[10]

The corporate structure of the church reflects the same four levels. Outside is the world—the unbelievers. Then there is the laity, those who have progressed to some degree on the spiritual journey. The clergy symbolize those who have a strong and more or less permanent connection with the true "I." The bishops correspond to the level of the Son, to those who realize their unity with the common Self that dwells in the center of us all.

Of course, this corporate structure is merely symbolic. In practice those who are awake at the level of the spirit are not always among the clergy or bishops. Many people of high spiritual development have no institutional status whatsoever, whereas a large number of those who have advanced far in the hierarchy have done so through the worldly routes of cleverness and ambition. The discrepancy between institutional status and real attainment has clearly been a problem in Christianity back to the earliest times, but the church has always acknowledged the difference. Few saints have been bishops, and few bishops have been saints.

THE MYSTICAL BODY OF CHRIST

Another equally ancient image gives a slightly different perspective on the secret church. Here it is likened to a human body as a whole; each individual is a cell or "member" of this body. The idea goes back to Paul: "For as we have many members in one body, and all members have not the same office; so we being many, are one body in Christ, and every one members of one another" (Rom. 12:4–5). Paul was very likely influenced by Jewish esoteric thought, which envisages the whole human race as Adam Kadmon, the primordial man.[11] In Christianity, this idea evolved into the image of the church as the Mystical Body of Christ. To quote Lopukhin again:

> The mystical body of Jesus Christ is brought forth and grows without ceasing, and its members are quickened in various degrees and measures by the spirit of his love who has given the new

law of love. To each member of this mystical body of Jesus Christ there is given a different gift: to one the manifestation of the spirit for the service of the faithful; to another the word of wisdom; to this the word of knowledge; to that faith . . . [The] spirit directs and regenerates them, filling them with its unction, in proportion as it finds them divested of the old man.

In this way is established and extended the holy invisible church, the domain of the heavenly king, where he shall reign till he has put his enemies under his feet.[12]

The inner church is a living, organic body. As this passage indicates, evoking Paul, who speaks of the "diversities of gifts, but the same Spirit" (1 Cor. 12:4), each "member" of this body has a different function, like the body's own organs. In this macrocosmic human, the Christ consciousness is the animating principle, the life force that unites and coordinates the individual "members," just as a hidden but omnipresent intelligence in ourselves keeps all our cells working in harmony. "There are diversities of operations, but it is the same God which worketh all in all. . . . For as the body is one, and hath many members, and all the members of that one body, being many: so also is Christ" (1 Cor. 12:6, 12–13).

This idea can be found in many corners of the Christian tradition— for example, in Renaissance Kabbalists such as Pico della Mirandola and Cornelius Agrippa—but the Christian esotericist who takes this idea the furthest is Emanuel Swedenborg, who says, "Heaven in its totality reflects a single person, and . . . it is a person in image and is therefore called the universal human. . . . For this reason, the heavenly communities that make up heaven are arranged like the members, organs, and viscera in a human being."[13]

Swedenborg takes up another ancient thread of the tradition, beginning with Paul (1 Cor. 12:21–31) and echoed, for example, in the Lopukhin passage just cited: that each cell or "member" in this body is differentiated in function. The angels in heaven (all of whom, Swedenborg says, once lived as humans on earth) take their places in this organism on the basis of their dispositions and capacities. Those who are in the head "are supremely involved in everything good." Those in the chest are "involved in the qualities of thoughtfulness and faith"; "people who are in the eyes are in understanding." Those in the ears excel in "attentiveness and obedience," while those in the kidneys, liver, and spleen are occupied with discrimination and purification.[14]

This relentless anthropomorphism may seem quaint, but similar correspondences could be drawn between the body and human society. Each has sectors devoted to producing and circulating nourishment; to protecting from outside attack; to healing and recuperation from damage; to thought and creativity; and to governing and regulating the entity as a whole. Traditional societies often assigned roles in this social organism by heredity or caste, as in the ancient Hindu *Laws of Manu*. In a freer society it becomes the individual's task to find his own place and serve in the way best suited to his abilities.

With esoteric development, a growth in maturity produces a corresponding growth in responsibility, which makes one aware of having a certain role to fill in the human collectivity. Nearly everyone feels it at some point or another: each of us has the sense, however faint, that there is some unique purpose for which we have been called into being and which no one else can fill. A few know what this is from their earliest moments of awareness; for most of us, there is a long and often painful process of sorting out this essential purpose from whatever the world may try to force upon us.

A Course in Miracles characterizes this unique role as the "special function": "To each [the Holy Spirit] gives a special function in salvation he alone can fill; a part for only him. Nor is the plan complete until he finds his special function, and fulfills the part assigned to him. . . . The Holy Spirit needs your special function, that His may be fulfilled. Think not you lack a special value here. You wanted it, and it is given you."

The *Course* does not, and of course cannot, say what this special function is for any individual, except to stress that "the form is suited to your special needs, and to the special time and place in which you think you find yourself." [15] Nor can anyone else tell us what this is. Some may dream of finding a guru who will be able to see clairvoyantly one's special function and offer it up on a platter. Not only is this unrealistic, but it also defeats the purpose. The "special function" is integrally connected to the nature of the true "I" in each of us, so that finding this function is a way of discovering who we are in our most intimate reaches. Other people can give helpful advice or point the way, but no one will be able to see our function for us. We ourselves will see it to the extent that we can penetrate to the realm of pure awareness that is the Self.

TEAMS AND SCHOOLS

According to Boris Mouravieff, esoteric development requires involvement with a "team." This is a group of individuals whose functions are linked and who embark upon a task of greater or lesser size depending upon their capacities. "The more evolved the *team*, the more important the task entrusted to it," Mouravieff writes. "History provides examples of the work of *teams* in all fields: legislative, military, political, and religious." Examples he cites from secular history include the team surrounding Alexander the Great, which created the Hellenistic world as a cradle for Christianity, and the one centered around Peter the Great, aimed at freeing Russia from "the consequences of two and a half centuries of the Mongol yoke." [16] Teams he mentions from the Bible are those surrounding Noah, Moses, David, and Christ. To these we might add such esoteric Christian movements as the Desert Fathers, the Brethren of the Common Life, and the Rosicrucians of the seventeenth century.

One of the Rosicrucian tracts, the *Fama fraternitatis*, summarizes some principal aspects of a team. This pamphlet tells of the journeys of a man named Christian Rosenkreutz in search of knowledge. He goes to the East, to Damascus, Egypt, and Morocco, and returns with a system of hidden teachings that he eventually establishes in Germany. He collects a small number of associates and starts the Fraternity of the Rosy Cross:

> Their agreement was this: First, That none of them should profess any other thing than to cure the sick, and that *gratis*. 2. None of the posterity should be constrained to wear one certain kind of habit, but therein to follow the custom of the country. 3. That every year upon the day C. they should meet together in the house *S. Spiritus*, or write the cause of his absence. 4. Every brother should look about for a worthy person, who, after his decease, might succeed him. 5. The word C.R. should be their seal, mark, and character. 6. The Fraternity should remain secret for one hundred years. [17]

Much, if not all, of this story is allegorical. Today it is generally acknowledged that no such individual as Christian Rosenkreutz ("Christian

Rose Cross") probably ever lived. Even the fraternity he is said to have founded may well be fictitious, despite the claims of many groups to be its successor. Nevertheless, this passage says a great deal about esoteric work in the modern era.

In the first place, the brothers will heal the sick without charge. This alludes not only to physical healing but to the sickness of the soul, for which spiritual work is the sovereign remedy. They are to provide this service for free, meaning that it is not to be a source of income. One does not charge for spiritual teaching. "Freely ye have received, freely give" (Matt. 10:8).

Next, they are not to wear any special kind of clothing, but should blend in with the customs of the country they are in. On the simplest level, this means avoiding distinctive or archaic modes of dress meant to set a person off from ordinary mortals. On another level, it could also refer to a mandate for clothing the inner teaching in the predominant religious "garb" of the surroundings. An esotericist may be a Christian in a Christian country, a Muslim in a Muslim country, a Hindu in India. The members of this team are to avoid anything that will make them seem better or different from those around them, whether in dress or doctrine.

Third, they are to assemble together in the house of the Holy Spirit ("*Sanctus Spiritus*") once a year. In all likelihood this does not refer to a meeting in the flesh, but to maintaining a spiritual connection: the house of the Holy Spirit is not built with hands. Some esoteric societies keep in contact through a group meditation at a prearranged time, in which all participants, however far apart they may be on earth, "gather" on the inner planes.

Fourth, every brother is to find someone to succeed him. This refers to the necessity of continuing the tradition by training new members. Probably for many esoteric teams throughout the centuries, it was, as this passage suggests, a matter of one-on-one transmission. In certain eras, depending on need and resources, more people might be taken in and trained. In any case, the successor has to be "worthy": quality is more important than quantity, and no esoteric team has ever succeeded by the weight of numbers alone.

The word "C.R." is to be their seal. The most obvious interpretation for this is "Christian Rosenkreutz," the name of their putative founder, but it could mean any number of other things as well: *crux rosea*, "rosy cross," or even *crux roris* or "cross of dew"—referring to the drops of subtle blessings from heaven. We will never really know. This too is characteristic of an esoteric team: it provides the full meaning of its signs and symbols only to initiates.

Finally, the society's existence is to be kept secret for a hundred years. In the Rosicrucian pamphlets, this has a literal force. These documents say that Christian Rosenkreutz was born in 1378 and lived for 106 years. His fraternity kept his "tomb" secret for 120 years, bringing us to 1604, which is around the time these tracts were written. Thus his teaching was hidden for over a century. But this rule has another meaning as well. Esoteric work generally goes on under cover. It does not seek immediate public attention but operates on a larger scale, which may bear fruit only decades or even centuries later—which, as we saw in chapter 1, was true of the work of the Rosicrucians themselves.

Gurdjieff speaks not of teams but of *schools*. He identifies his teaching with what he calls the "Fourth Way," which, unlike the ways of the fakir, the monk, and the yogi (whom Gurdjieff characterizes as those who limit their development to their bodies, emotions, and minds, respectively), integrates these three facets of the human character. Also unlike the other three ways, the Fourth Way does not require seclusion but is pursued in the course of everyday life. As Gurdjieff explains,

> The fourth way differs from the old and the new ways by the fact that it is never a permanent way. It has no definite forms and there are no institutions connected with it. It appears and disappears governed by some particular laws of its own.
>
> The fourth way is never without some work of a definite significance, is never without some *undertaking* around which and in connection with which it can alone exist. When this work is finished, that is to say, when the aim set before it has been accomplished, the fourth way disappears, that is, it disappears from the given place, disappears in its given form, continuing perhaps in another place in another form. Schools of the fourth way exist for the needs of the work which is being carried out in connection with the proposed undertaking. They never exist by themselves for the purpose of education and instruction.[18]

If we accept that many of the esoteric Christian schools we have observed may have been working on similar principles, we can understand why so many came and went—why, for example, the Brethren of the

Common Life flourished for a few generations before disappearing, why the Rosicrucians of the seventeenth century took a brief stroll across the public stage before resuming their invisibility. Conventional thinking could see these movements only as failures. Understood as "schools" in Gurdjieff's sense, they start to look much more like undertakings to achieve certain definite purposes that then disappeared in their given forms.

When such tasks have been completed, Gurdjieff goes on to say, the school shuts its doors, and those of its members who have reached a certain level move on to work independently. But sometimes the school continues in the hands of those who viewed the school only in an outward sense, seeing only the forms, not the inner meaning. They carry on the teaching as they can. "All this naturally can only be outward imitation. But when we look back on history it is almost impossible for us to distinguish where the real ends and the imitation begins." [19]

Elsewhere Gurdjieff suggests that this sort of imitation is exactly what we know as conventional Christianity. "The Christian church is—a school concerning which people have forgotten that it is a school. Imagine a school where the teacher gives lectures and performs explanatory demonstrations without knowing that these are lectures and demonstrations; and where the pupils or simply the people who come to the school take these lectures and demonstrations for ceremonies, or rites, or 'sacraments,' or magic. This would approximate to the Christian church of our times." [20] Although this assessment may sound harsh, it does help explain the pervasive sense that something is missing in the Christian church—and that what is missing is not faith or devotion but knowledge.

Gurdjieff's portrait of a school also says something important about the path for individuals. A school teaches knowledge only as a means of accomplishing its task: "Mechanical man cannot give conscious work so that the first task of the people who begin such a work is to create conscious assistants." [21] Consequently, the best way to progress is to make yourself useful to the work. This is not an eagerness to run and fetch at a master's whim, but a deeper, quieter willingness to serve in a greater sense. As Gurdjieff points out, a crucial dynamic operates between *work for oneself*, *work for the sake of the group*, and *work for the work's sake*. [22] These three levels run on parallel lines; keeping them all going at once prevents inner stagnation. This is partly because, as spiritual awareness deepens, it becomes increasingly clear that progress is impossible unless you are working for others and for humanity as a whole. We cannot develop alone because we do not exist alone.

THE TASK TODAY

It remains to ask what work presents itself to esoteric teams at the beginning of the twenty-first century. Some teachers have been guarded about addressing this issue in all but the most general terms: Gurdjieff, for example, said only that schools undertake work of a "cosmic character" and even avoided explaining his own aims to his pupils. Others have addressed the issue more specifically.

Prime among these was Boris Mouravieff, who devoted a great deal of *Gnosis*, his magnum opus, to this question. He says the present era is at a crossroads: "If the already precarious equilibrium between the divergent tendencies of the past century is accentuated, life tomorrow will either be placed entirely under *diabolical* influence, to be annihilated in a cataclysm foreseen by the Apostle St. Peter, or will then be *sanctified* so that, in accordance with the Apostle's words, there will be established '*new heavens and a new earth wherein dwelleth truth*.'" The cataclysm foreseen by Peter is "the day of the Lord," in which "the elements shall melt with fervent heat, the earth also and the works that are therein shall be burned up" (2 Peter 3:12). Writing in the early 1960s, at the height of the Cold War, Mouravieff was obviously alluding to the possibility of nuclear holocaust—a danger that has by no means disappeared since then.

To avert this disaster, Mouravieff could see only one option: the formation of a spiritual elite that is capable of distinguishing "the true from the false," and the ultimate investment of power in such an elite. Such a program is perhaps less reactionary than it sounds. Even in the freest and most democratic of nations, real power rests in the hands of a small nexus of political and economic leaders; this has not changed since Mouravieff's time and shows no signs of changing. Mouravieff is simply saying that if we are to avert disaster, these leaders will need to be spiritually awake in a way they have not been in the past. If all goes well, he writes, "tomorrow's elite will all be *twice born*, in accordance with the famous word of Jesus to Nicodemus."[3]

Whether any real progress has come about in this direction in the forty years since Mouravieff was writing is highly debatable. Nor is it clear how Mouravieff himself saw his own role in bringing this about. Although he taught his version of esoteric Christianity at Switzerland's University of Geneva in the last years of his life, he did not establish any team that endured; only a few scattered pupils of his remain. Most likely, he saw his writings as his chief contribution to this task. As we have seen, esoteric work usually does not have immediately apparent results; in fact, a standard instruction to those undertaking it is to avoid looking for results. This is partly to teach members of a team not to become attached to external appearances (a lesson that nearly everyone has to learn many times over before it sinks in), partly to reflect the fact that the results of such work do not always accord with the laws of ordinary causation. In this dimension one is working with the unseen, and unseen causes produce results in a unseen fashion. The British magician Charles R. Tetworth gives an example of how this may feel in practice:

> The most effective magic that I have observed was performed by a group of people who were sitting around in an ordinary room, in an odd assortment of chairs, wearing ordinary clothes and chattering as usual. Then they just stopped smoking, drinking tea, and chatting. The leader reminded them why they were there, checked the roles each was to fulfill, and then, without apparent evocation or invocation, proceeded with the matter. To me, as an observer, the atmosphere in the room became electric. It felt as though danger was present. In the course of time, I happened to attend a seminar on a comparatively abstruse branch of morphology and—whether or not this was a coincidence—one of the speakers talked about the very matter that the magical group had attempted to bring into general consciousness.[24]

As this story suggests, one never can really see a linear, causal connection between one's work and results, even when they appear.

THE ROSE OF THE WORLD

Daniel Andreev, one of the greatest Christian visionaries of the twentieth century, gives his perspective on the direction of esoteric work in our time. He himself felt he was taking part in this task by writing his *Rose of the World*.

The "Rose of the World," whose name, *Roza Mira*, is far more euphonious in Russian than in its English equivalent, is a higher integration of the spiritual vision of all the world religions. It is not a mere synthesis of previous traditions, nor is it some new megareligion that will sweep away all the others. Rather, it will encompass and embrace all the religions and spiritualities that we know today without depriving them of their distinctive features. Andreev writes:

> It will be an interreligion or pan-religion, in that it will be a teaching that views all religions that appeared earlier as reflections of different visions of spiritual reality. . . . If the older religions are petals, then the Rose of the World will be a flower: with roots, stem, head, and the commonwealth of its petals. . . .
>
> The Rose of the World sees its surreligiosity and interreligiosity in the reunification of the Christian faiths and in the further amalgamation of all religions of Light in order to focus their combined energies on fostering humanity's spiritual growth and on spiritualizing nature. Religious exclusivity will not only be foreign to its followers, it will be impossible. Co-belief with all peoples in their highest ideals—that is what its wisdom will teach.
>
> The structure of the Rose of the World will therefore suggest a series of concentric circles. No followers of any right-hand religion should be considered outside the global church. Those who have not yet reached an awareness of surreligious unity will occupy the outer circles; the middle circles will be composed of the less active and creative of the Rose of the World's followers; the inner circles will be for those who have equated the meaning of their life with conscious and free divine creative work.[25]

Here again we encounter the idea of inner and outer circles; here too is a sense of higher, organic unity in which each individual, knowingly or not, takes part. As Andreev goes on to say, the manifestation of this cosmic Rose is the task that will occupy humanity in the centuries to come.

Some evidence does suggest that we are moving in this direction. We can see it not only in the numerous ecumenical and interfaith movements but also in the rising number of people who respect the essential truth and unity of all religions, and who understand that their manifold forms are merely different forms of the same truth. We see it in the dissemination of religious faiths throughout the world—of the coming of Christianity to Africa and Asia in the last two centuries, and of the counterflow of Eastern and indigenous teachings to the West over the past two generations—as well as in the spread of globalization, which throws people of many faiths together who had little or no interaction before.

There are, of course, forces that oppose this work; like the individual seeker, this blossoming Rose of the World will have to be "tempted of the Devil" to ensure its soundness and solidity. In the darker sides of his vision Andreev claims that Hitler and Stalin will reincarnate to this end in coming centuries. But, he says, there is reason to believe that the Rose of the World will eventually triumph, bringing about a "new heaven and a new earth." Such a transformation will not entail a literal return of Christ to earth, but rather the conscious manifestation of Christ's Mystical Body in a united and harmonious humanity.

Is this vision true? Many times in this book we have seen how faith is "the evidence of things unseen," so there is no way of proving it to those who limit their understanding to the material plane. One has to approach it with the inner eye of discrimination and to take measure of it with the knowledge of the heart. But whatever one may conclude in the end, such a prophecy has a rare and sublime beauty about it; and even in the world of appearances, there is enough to remind us that beauty is truth and truth, beauty.

AFTERWORD

Continuing the Journey

A N ACUTE PARADOX CONFRONTS anyone who dips into today's spiritual literature. Currently it is *de rigueur* to stuff books with elaborate promises about how a spiritual path will lead you to enlightenment while showing you how to get along with your family, enhance your sexual performance, and become a hard-charging executive to boot. Yet if we turn to much of the traditional literature, we find it devoid of such promises. It insists on the opposite: the spiritual way demands great personal sacrifices and promises no visible rewards.

This is certainly true of inner Christianity, going back to Christ himself: "Foxes have holes, and birds of the air have nests; but the Son of man hath not where to lay his head" (Luke 9:58). "He that loveth his life shall lose it; and he that hateth his life in this world shall keep it unto life eternal" (John 12:25). "He that loveth father or mother more than me is not worthy of me: and he that loveth son or daughter more than me is not worthy of me" (Matt. 10:37).

The same message echoes throughout the literature from the earliest days to modern times. To take some examples culled at random: "When we not only refrain from worldly actions, but no longer call them to mind, we have reached true tranquillity," writes the fifth-century Desert Father Neilos the Ascetic.[1] "The more man progresses on the *Way*, the more his feeling of being a stranger intensifies," observes Boris Mouravieff. "Soon he will become boring; later still he will become unbearable, and finally, odious."[2] "The world I see holds nothing that I want," says a lesson in *A Course in Miracles*.[3]

What, then, can you expect to get out of inner Christianity?

The tradition is practically unanimous: From the point of view of ordinary reality, nothing. Inner Christianity will *not* help you advance in the world; it will not improve your sex life or show you how to win friends and influence people. Nor is it meant to. Indeed, the spiritual journey frequently begins with a sense that things are being taken away: jobs, relationships, prestige, money. Inner awakening seems to be met initially by outer deprivation.

When this happens, says *A Course in Miracles*, "it is rarely understood initially that their lack of value is merely being recognized." That is to say, we are losing these things because unconsciously we ourselves realize their emptiness and have decided to rid ourselves of them. Work that was once fulfilling now becomes dreary; friends that used to be fascinating now seem dull or repellent. Although you will not lose everything, you *will* lose everything that is false. Often this is heartbreaking. The *Course* calls this the stage of "undoing." We recognize that what we ordinarily trust in is not trustworthy; it is the sand on which the foolish man in the parable has built his house. Even in ordinary life we know this deep inside, and yet we fight with all our strength *not* to know it. If there is anything that is fundamentally tragic in the human condition, it is this: life in illusion is not worth living, yet the road to illumination can be so painful.

If this were all, the story would be a gloomy one indeed. Some have gone this far and no further: they are the nihilists and cynics of our era and of all eras. Staring into the emptiness of conventional reality, they have stopped there. But they have seen only a partial truth. They do not recognize that there is something beyond that will more than make up for these losses. It is the only thing in the world worth having, the "pearl of great price," for which a man sells all he has. It is *yourself*. It is the dawning of the true "I," the recognition that that in you which *sees*, which peers out at the world through the telescope that is your soul and body, is deathless and impervious to pain. All the great religious teachings point to this truth.

To the extent that you possess this realization, you know you need nothing else. At first it will come and go, sometimes manifesting brightly and clearly, sometimes obscured by worries and cares. But if you persist, eventually you will begin to notice and trust in it more. Out of this feeling will arise a subtle but imperturbable joy.

Even so, the way is not one of ceaseless sacrifice. Around the "I" a fresher, more vital world begins to constellate—new relationships, new forms of work, that are more in harmony with one's inner nature. This new life may well have nothing to do with success as usually understood—but it is likely to prove far more satisfying.

Some may ask where they can find inner Christianity. This is not an easy question to answer. In the first place, inner Christianity is precisely that. The turning of the personality to the higher "I" of the true Self has to be an internal process. It cannot be made into a mere list of things to do, particularly since the crucial moments of this internal turning are often unconscious or unnoticed. The will makes its decisions in the silence of the heart, where the mind cannot interfere. In the second place, not every spiritual teaching is suited to everyone; the curriculum is highly individualized. Christianity itself is not for everyone. Perhaps in the future people will be drawn to religions not by cultural or family background but as a result of personal need and inclination. In multicultural America, we already see some signs that this is happening.

What strengths and qualities will one need to start on the path? The hallmark of the spiritual search is responsibility—the willingness to be accountable to and for oneself. This is the first prerequisite for making contact with the true "I." Taking responsibility means being free from the impulses of the world at least to the extent that you act from inner initiative rather than waiting around for someone to tell you what to do. Responsibility also entails active investigation—an interest in pushing past the surfaces and finding the deeper truth in a situation or in yourself.

This heightened sense of responsibility extends to daily life. One does not turn into a tramp or lunatic incapable of working and paying the bills. As Rudolf Steiner observes, "No higher duty should force us to neglect even one of our duties in the ordinary world. If we are parents, we shall continue to fulfill our responsibilities just as well as we did before entering upon the path to higher knowledge. Whatever our job may be, whether government official or soldier, following the path to higher knowledge should not keep us from doing our job. On the contrary, esoteric training enhances, to a degree inconceivable to the uninitiated, the very qualities that make us competent in life."[4]

The increased competence of which Steiner speaks, the fruit of a more disciplined and integrated psyche, is real enough. This fact does not contradict what was said above. Spiritual development usually does not produce success in the conventional arenas of wealth and power, because it shifts one's priorities as well. One becomes less driven by worldly goals and hence takes them less seriously. "Ye cannot serve God and mammon" (Matt. 6:24).

In fact, real commitment to the path in terms of time and energy is necessary. If you feel you are already overworked and overextended in your present life, you will probably not have the time for spiritual work. You may as well be realistic with yourself on this score. On the other hand, it can be helpful to remember that time is flexible and will usually accommodate itself to a firm decision to devote some effort to inner work. The world, which we normally see as hard-edged and inflexible, is far more pliant than we believe, and many obstacles that seem insurmountable melt away when confronted directly.

Having made some sort of commitment—which is far less likely to be a sort of New Year's resolution than an ineradicable wish in the heart—you will begin to come into contact with what Gurdjieff and Mouravieff call "magnetic center."[5] As its name suggests, this is an internal faculty that is drawn like a magnet toward inner truth. If it is powerful enough—and if the circumstances of outward life resist it—it can produce major tensions and upheavals in the soul. The real "I" wants to break out of its constraints and is quite capable of upsetting life if its needs are not acknowledged.

In a positive form, the influence of "magnetic center" can take the form of uncanny synchronicities and meetings with mysterious helpers at just the right time. It may be something as simple as having the right book fall into your hands at a crucial moment, overhearing an idle remark that answers a deep question, or making a chance acquaintance who happens to tell you about a group that is exploring exactly what you want to do. Like attracts like: a burgeoning higher consciousness in yourself is drawn to something similar outside.

Usually a genuine esoteric contact will not take the form you would have expected. Spiritual truth has no regard for the surfaces of life. "Magnetic center" has to see past appearances. Besides, our expectations of reality are usually appallingly banal: we think a spiritual teacher will take the form of some monk with a long beard or a man from the East with a shaven head, so we do not notice true worth hidden behind the exterior of someone far less exotic. Certain teachers even make use of this fact as a means of testing discernment. They will pretend not to know anything and will even try to push a seeker away as a means of finding out whether he or she can see through appearances. On the other hand, this principle cannot be taken too far: gurus who act manipulatively and abusively are almost always merely showing their true colors and are best avoided.

In the end, the curriculum is shaped to our own ends. It will take different forms for everyone, and even the same person may be led down different paths at different times in some kind of invisible accordance with his own needs. Even the grossest errors may have their value (though of course they are best avoided): I have known more than one person who has emerged from dangerous cults with more knowledge and depth. As you progress, it becomes harder and harder to look back and say what was a mistake and what was not. The greatest risk is in allowing yourself to be imprisoned by your own fears.

Today there are places in which the teachings of inner Christianity, long hidden and disguised, are beginning to poke their head out again. No single denomination can be equated with esoteric Christianity as such, but there are many individual churches of all stripes that are vitally concerned with this approach. You may find an Episcopal church that sponsors a small contemplative group; an Orthodox or Catholic congregation cultivating the Prayer of the Heart; a New Age church that works with *A Course in Miracles*; or small groups that practice the magical side of the tradition. You will have to let your "magnetic center" take the lead.

One way of finding direction is from books. I have tried to document the ideas in this book, partly to stress that these ideas have always been present in the Christian tradition, partly to give leads to people who may want to pursue certain ideas further. You may find some threads and teachings more inspiring than others; these will probably provide you with a good place to start your inquiries.

Of the books currently available on esoteric Christianity, there are three I have found particularly helpful; I have quoted them often. They are *A Course in Miracles*; Boris Mouravieff's *Gnosis*; and Valentin Tomberg's *Meditations on the Tarot*. They do not always agree with each other; in fact they differ on many points. Overall, though, all three are unusually penetrating and profound, and it would be hard to read them sincerely and attentively without undergoing a major change in inner direction. None is easy or light reading, but they will abundantly repay any effort they receive.

Below are some other works, ancient and modern, that I have found helpful and inspiring. Books go in and out of print astonishingly quickly these days, but as of this writing in the spring of 2001 most of the following are comparatively easy to find, either new or used. Full titles and publication information for all of them can be found in the bibliography.

The Cloud upon the Sanctuary by Karl von Eckartshausen. A short but extremely powerful and influential treatise on the meaning of the inner church.

A Different Christianity by Robin Amis. Amis is an Englishman who has spent many years exploring the esoteric heritage of Orthodox Christianity. He is the man responsible for publishing Mouravieff's works in English. In *A Different Christianity* he relates his own insights, gleaned from his explorations of the hesychast tradition preserved on Mount Athos.

The *Fama fraternitatis*, or "Rumor of the Brotherhood." An anonymous pamphlet, written around 1615, discussing the true meaning of the inner circle of humanity. It can be found as an appendix to Frances Yates's *Rosicrucian Enlightenment*.

Icons and the Mystical Origins of Christianity by Richard Temple. This book gives a brief overview of esoteric Christian cosmology, tracing it back to its Greek roots as well as showing how it is incorporated into the symbolism of icons.

Letters of the Scattered Brotherhood by Mary Strong. A collection of anonymous letters on the spiritual path, written around the time of World War II. Powerful and inspiring.

Myth and Ritual in Christianity by Alan Watts. Watts is chiefly known as a popularizer of Eastern religions, but he was an Anglican priest, and his discussion of the sacred year in liturgy and ritual casts a great deal of light on these aspects of the Christian tradition.

The Nag Hammadi Library in English, edited by James M. Robinson. The one-volume collection of the celebrated cache of Gnostic scriptures discovered in 1945. It contains the *Gospel of Thomas* and many other eye-opening texts of early Christian esotericism.

The New Man by Maurice Nicoll. Nicoll, a British psychiatrist who studied with both Jung and Gurdjieff, gives a lucid exposition of some of the key symbolic meanings of the Gospels.

The Philokalia. Translated by G. E. H. Palmer, Philip Sherrard, and Kallistos Ware. This five-volume edition puts this key work of Orthodox mysticism into the hands of the English-speaking reader. The texts are very rich, but because they are principally written for monks it is not always easy for the layperson to see how to incorporate their wisdom into daily life.

The Rose of the World by Daniel Andreev. Andreev's book is fascinating, unusual, and in many instances simply weird. But there is something powerful and, one senses, profoundly true in his vision of the inner planes and of the Rose of the World.

NOTES

INTRODUCTION

1. The term "inner Christianity" is not my invention. The first reference to it that I know of appears in some texts published by Robin Amis's Praxis Institute Press; the Episcopal priest Cynthia Bourgeault has also used it in some contexts.

2. Biblical quotations in this book are from the King James Version unless otherwise noted.

3. See, for example, René Guénon, *Aperçus sur l'ésotérisme islamique et le Taoïsme* (Paris: Gallimard, 1973), pp. 21–22. Many writers do not make this distinction and use the terms "mystical" and "esoteric" more or less interchangeably.

4. From *The Philokalia of Origen*, trans. George Lewis, quoted in Richard Temple, *Icons and the Mystical Origins of Christianity* (Shaftesbury, Dorset, England: Element Books, 1990), p. 34. Cf. Origen, *On First Principles*, book 4, chapters 2 and 3.

5. [Christopher Walton], *An Introduction to Theosophy, or The Science of the Mystery of Christ* (London: John Kendrick, n.d.), p. 57. The book is anonymous; for the identity of the author, I am indebted to Arthur Versluis, *Wisdom's Children: A Christian Esoteric Tradition* (Albany: State University of New York Press, 2000), pp. 113–25.

6. A version of this diagram appears in Boris Mouravieff, *Gnosis: Study and Commentary on the Esoteric Tradition of Eastern Orthodoxy*, vol. 1, trans. S. A. Wissa and Robin Amis (Newburyport, Mass.: Praxis Publishing Co., 1990), p. 149.

7. See Arthur Versluis, *Theosophia: Hidden Dimensions of Christianity* (Hudson, N.Y.: Lindisfarne, 1994), p. 37.

CHAPTER 1

THREADS OF A HIDDEN TEACHING

1. Morton Smith, *The Secret Gospel: The Discovery and Interpretation of the Secret Gospel according to Mark* (New York: Harper & Row, 1973), pp. 14–17. Additions in square brackets are Smith's. For an update on the authenticity of this text, see Charles W. Hedrick and Nikolaos Olympiou, "Secret Mark," *The Fourth R* 13, no. 5 (September–October 2000): 3ff.

2. On Q, see Burton L. Mack, *The Lost Gospel* (San Francisco: Harper San Francisco, 1993); James M. Robinson, Paul Hoffman, and John S. Kloppenborg, eds., *The Critical Edition of Q*, *Hermeneia* (Minneapolis: Fortress; Leuven: Peeters, 2000).

3. *Gospel of Thomas* 1, trans. Thomas O. Lambdin, in James M. Robinson, ed., *The Nag Hammadi Library in English* (San Francisco: Harper & Row, 1977), p. 119. Further references to *Thomas* will be to this version, following the standard enumeration for the *logia*.

4. See Gregory J. Riley, *One Jesus, Many Christs* (San Francisco: HarperSanFrancisco, 1997), pp. 10–14, for a brief overview of these communities.

5. Clement of Alexandria, *Stromata* (or *Stromateis*), book 7, chapter 17.

6. For a discussion of how the Gnostics used these passages and others like them, see Elaine Pagels, *The Gnostic Paul* (Philadelphia: Trinity Press International, 1975), pp. 4–7.

7. Elaine Pagels, *The Gnostic Gospels* (New York: Vintage Books, 1981), p. 32.

8. Kurt Rudolph, *Gnosis: The Nature and History of Gnosticism*, trans. Robert MacLachlan Wilson (San Francisco: HarperSanFrancisco, 1987), p. 367.

9. Clement of Alexandria, *Stromata*, book 4, chapter 22; in *The Ante-Nicene Fathers*, ed. Alexander Roberts and James Donaldson, vol. 2 (reprint, Grand Rapids, Mich.: Eerdmans, 1994), p. 434.

10. Didymus of Alexandria, quoted in Jerome, *Praef. in Hom. Orig. in Ezechiel* and in G. W. Butterworth, ed., *Origen: On First Principles* (New York: Harper & Row, 1966), p. xxiii.

11. This system is set out in Origen, *On First Principles*, book 1.

12. Ibid., book 4, chapter 2, in Butterworth, pp. 275–76.

13. Sandra M. Schneiders, "Scripture and Spirituality," in Bernard McGinn et al., eds., *Christian Spirituality: Origins to the Twelfth Century* (New York: Crossroad, 1997), pp. 12–13.

14. See Jean Gribomont, "Monasticism and Asceticism," in McGinn et al., *Christian Spirituality*, esp. pp. 92–93.

15. Paul Johnson, *A History of Christianity* (New York: Atheneum, 1987), p. 149.

16. Franz Josef Molitor, *Philosophie der Geschichte, oder Über die Tradition*, 4.11, quoted in Versluis, *Theosophia*, p. 43.

17. René Guénon, *The Esoterism of Dante*, trans. C. B. Bethell (Ghent, N.Y.: Sophia Perennis et Universalis, 1996), p. 23.

18. See Dante Alighieri, *The Divine Comedy*, ed. and trans. Charles S. Singleton, *Inferno 2: Commentary* (Princeton, N.J.: Princeton University Press, 1970), pp. 34, 43. Because it is seen as moving through the sky, the sun was traditionally regarded as a "planet," which comes from the Greek word meaning "wanderer," though today we know it is a star.

19. Dante's system also reflects the influence of Ibn 'Arabi, a major figure in the Islamic esoteric tradition known as Sufism. See Guénon, *The Esoterism of Dante*, pp. 31, 35–38.

20. Johnson, *A History of Christianity* pp. 191–92.

21. Meister Eckhart, Sermon 18, "Justice Is Even," trans. Raymond B. Blakney, in Blakney, ed., *Meister Eckhart* (New York: Harper & Row, 1941), p. 181.

22. Blakney, *Meister Eckhart*, pp. xxii–xxiv.

23. For the English version, see *The Philokalia: The Complete Text*, trans. G. E. H. Palmer et al., 5 vols. (London: Faber & Faber, 1979–).

24. For the following account I am chiefly indebted to John van Engen's introduction to his edition of *Devotio Moderna: Basic Writings* (Mahwah, N.J.: Paulist Press, 1988). See also Otto Gründler, "Devotio Moderna," in Jill Raitt et al., eds., *Christian Spirituality: High Middle Ages and Reformation* (New York: Crossroad, 1987), pp. 176–93, and Ross Fuller, *The Brotherhood of the Common Life and Its Influence* (Albany: State University of New York Press, 1995).

25. Robin Waterfield, "The Quiet Revolution," *Gnosis* 25 (fall 1992): 24.

26. Van Engen, ed., *Devotio Moderna*, p. 27.

27. See Peter Kingsley, "Poimandres: The Etymology of the Name and the Origins of the *Hermetica*," *Journal of the Warburg and Courtauld Institutes* 56 (1993): 1–24.

28. Gershom Scholem, *Major Trends in Jewish Mysticism* (New York: Schocken Books, 1941), p. 35.

29. Gershom Scholem, *Kabbalah* (Jerusalem: Keter, 1974), p. 173.

30. Chaim Wirszubski, *Pico della Mirandola's Encounter with Jewish Mysticism* (Cambridge, Mass: Harvard University Press, 1989).

31. Pico della Mirandola, *Heptaplus, or Discourse on the Seven Days of Creation*, trans. Jessie Brewer McGaw (New York: Philosophical Library, 1977), pp. 17, 18.

32. For more information on the diagram of the Kabbalistic Tree, see Richard Smoley and Jay Kinney, *Hidden Wisdom: A Guide to the Western Inner Traditions* (New York: Penguin Arkana, 1999), pp. 78–83.

33. *Confessio Fraternitatis*, in Frances A. Yates, *The Rosicrucian Enlightenment*

(1972; reprint, London: Ark, 1986), p. 259. Yates's account of the Rosicrucians is the best and most scholarly, and I follow it here. The Rosicrucian tracts are generally thought to be the work of a Lutheran divine named Johann Valentin Andreae.

34. *Fama fraternitatis*, in ibid., p. 238.

35. See ibid., pp. 206–19.

36. Ibid., pp. 171–92.

37. Brian Riggs, "The Pope and the Pornographer: The Long Quarrel between Freemasonry and Catholicism," *Gnosis* 44 (summer 1997): 46–50.

38. Saint Teresa of Avila, *Interior Castle*, trans. E. Alison Peers (New York: Doubleday/Image, 1961), p. 36.

39. Pier Luigi Zocatelli, *Le lièvre qui rumine: Autour de René Guénon, Louis Charbonneau-Lassay et la fraternité du Paraclet* (Milan: Archè, 1999), esp. pp. 119–25. The translation of the excerpt from Clavelle is mine.

40. Mike Restivo, "Martinez de Pasquales and the Élus Cohen," http://www.patcom.com/~mtronics/rcmo/marhis1.htm. "Pasquales" is a common variant of "Pasqually."

41. Mike Restivo, "Papus and L'Ordre Martiniste," http://www.icbl.hw.ac.uk/~bill/paom.htm.

42. Éliphas Lévi, *Transcendental Magic*, trans. A. E. Waite (London: Bracken Books, 1997), p. 141. This work is a translation of *Dogme et rituel de la haute magie*.

43. Ibid., p. 480.

44. [Valentin Tomberg], *Meditations on the Tarot*, trans. Robert A. Powell (Warwick, N.Y.: Amity House, 1985).

45. Jean-Pierre Laurant, "The Primitive Characteristics of Nineteenth-Century Esotericism," in Antoine Faivre and Jacob Needleman, eds., *Modern Esoteric Spirituality* (New York: Crossroad, 1995), p. 285.

46. Cris Monnastre and David Griffin, "Israel Regardie, the Golden Dawn, and Psychotherapy," *Gnosis* 37 (fall 1995): 36–42.

47. These have been collected in René Guénon, *Fundamental Symbols: The Universal Language of Sacred Science*, trans. Alvin Moore Jr. (Bartlow, Cambridge, U.K.: Quinta Essentia, 1995).

48. For an overview of Steiner's life and work, see Robert A. McDermott, "Rudolf Steiner and Anthroposophy," in Faivre and Needleman, eds., *Modern Esoteric Spirituality*, pp. 288–310.

49. Sara Draper, "A New Order of Priests," *Gnosis* 45 (fall 1997): 55–59. The best book-length introduction to the Christian Community is James H. Hindes, *Renewing Christianity* (Hudson, N.Y.: Anthroposophic Press, 1996), which also contains a good overview of Steiner's teachings.

50. C. G. Jung, *Memories, Dreams, Reflections*, trans. Richard and Clara Winston (New York: Random House, 1961), pp. 189–91. *Seven Sermons to the Dead* appear in an appendix to this work.

51. C. G. Jung, *Aion: Researches into the Phenomenology of the Self*. trans. R. F. C. Hull (Princeton, N.J.: Princeton University Press/Bollingen, 1959), p. 37.

52. G. I. Gurdjieff, *Views from the Real World: Early Talks of G. I. Gurdjieff* (New York: Dutton, 1973), p. 152. See also P. D. Ouspensky, *In Search of the Miraculous: Fragments of a Forgotten Teaching* (New York: Harcourt, Brace, 1949), p. 102.

53. Gurdjieff, *Views from the Real World*, p. 154.

54. See Robin Amis, *A Different Christianity* (Albany: State University of New York Press, 1995), pp. 347–48.

55. For further discussion of the New Age, see Smoley and Kinney, *Hidden Wisdom*, chapter 12.

56. See Peter Caddy et al., *In Perfect Timing: Memoirs of a Man for the New Millennium* (Findhorn, Scotland: Findhorn Press, 1996).

57. Pensatia [Helen Merrick Bond], *The Master H* (New York: Euclid Books, 1961), p. 30.

58. See D. Patrick Miller, *The Complete Story of the Course* (Berkeley, Calif.: Fearless Books, 1997).

59. *A Course in Miracles*, workbook (Tiburon, Calif.: Foundation for Inner Peace, 1975), pp. 18, 34.

60. Ibid., workbook, p. 103.

61. Ibid., teacher's manual, p. 39.

62. Siobhán Houston, "Turning to Orthodoxy," *Gnosis* 31 (spring 1994): 39–42.

CHAPTER 2

THE WORLD AND THE FALL

1. See, for example, Margaret Talbot, "A Mighty Fortress," *New York Times Magazine*, 27 February 2000, 34ff.

2. Rudolf Steiner, *Theosophy*, trans. Catherine E. Creeger (Hudson, N.Y.: Anthroposophic Press, 1994) p. 48.

3. Mouravieff, *Gnosis* 1:14–15.

4. Hans Jonas, *The Gnostic Religion* (Boston: Beacon Press, 1958), pp. 112–29.

5. *The Theologia Germanica of Martin Luther*, ed. and trans. Bengt Hoffman (Mahwah, N.J.: Paulist Press, 1980), p. 106. Contrary to what the title of this edition may suggest, this work was not written by Luther but simply edited by him.

6. Ibid., p. 79.

7. Quoted in John Shelby Spong, *A New Christianity for a New World* (San Francisco: HarperSanFrancisco, 2001), p. 76.

8. Thomas Merton, *New Seeds of Contemplation* (New York: New Directions, 1962), p. 7.

9. Quoted in Amis, *A Different Christianity*, p. 49.

10. For a discussion of the primordial human state, see Mouravieff, *Gnosis* 3:113–15, and Z'ev ben Shimon Halevi, *A Kabbalistic Universe* (London: Rider, 1977), pp. 99–103.

11. Papus, "Fall and Rise," in *Martinist Digest* 3 (n.d., n.p.), pp. 24–25.

12. John Bunyan, *The Pilgrim's Progress* (1678; New York: Washington Square Press, 1957), pp. 67–68.

13. Walter Hilton, *The Scale of Perfection*, ed. Evelyn Underhill (London: Watkins, 1948), p. 191. The reference to the "prophet" is to Jer. 9:21.

14. Nicolas [Nikolai] Berdyaev, *Freedom and the Spirit*, trans. Oliver Fielding Clarke (London: Bles, 1935), p. 22.

15. Emanuel Swedenborg, *Heaven and Hell*, trans. George F. Dole (New York: Swedenborg Foundation, 1976), pp. 129, 132. "Time in Heaven," the chapter from which these quotes are taken, is of great interest in elucidating the difference between time in heaven and time in the world.

16. Quoted in Temple, *Icons and the Mystical Origins of Christianity*, p. 62.

17. In St. Nikodimos of Corinth and St. Makarios of the Holy Mountain, ed., *The Philokalia: The Complete Text*, trans. G. E. H. Palmer, Philip Sherrard, Kallistos Ware, et al., vol. 1 (London: Faber & Faber, 1979), p. 24.

18. Cf. Mouravieff, *Gnosis* 1:142.

19. Plato, *Meno*, 85c–e.

CHAPTER 3

SALVATION AND GNOSIS

1. For this diagram and its implications, see René Guénon, *The Symbolism of the Cross*, trans. Angus MacNab (London: Luzac, 1958), which discusses it in detail.

2. Guénon, *Fundamental Symbols*, p. 276.

3. W. G. Davies, *The Phoenician Letters* (Manchester, U.K.: Mowat, 1979), p. 45.

4. Swedenborg, *Heaven and Hell*, p. 380.

5. Ibid., pp. 489–90.

6. *Gospel of Philip*, 66, in Robinson, ed., *The Nag Hammadi Library in English*, p. 140. Bracketed material is the translator's.

7. C. S. Lewis, *The Great Divorce* (New York: Macmillan, 1946), p. 72.

8. Origen, *On First Principles* 3.2.1, p. 81; on Clement's views, see p. 82n.

9. Swedenborg, *Heaven and Hell*, pp. 312–13.

10. Daniel Andreev, *The Rose of the World*, trans. Jordan Roberts (Hudson: N.Y.: Lindisfarne Books, 1996), pp. 156–57.

11. Gurdjieff alludes to this possibility in *Beelzebub's Tales to His Grandson* (New York: Dutton, 1950), pp. 212–20.

12. See Tomberg, *Meditations on the Tarot*, pp. 243ff.

13. There is, of course, a masculine bias implicit in referring to God as "he" or "him." I have chosen to do so throughout this book not because God is innately masculine, but because it is the most common—indeed nearly universal—approach in the Christian tradition. To refer to God as "she" or "it" would create at least as many conceptual problems, so I beg the reader's indulgence on this score.

14. For an engaging account of Elvis as a religious figure, see John Strausbaugh, *E: Reflections on the Birth of the Elvis Faith* (New York: Blast Books, 1995).

15. Helen Waddell, *The Desert Fathers* (1936; reprint, Ann Arbor, Mich.: University of Michigan Press, 1957), p. 16.

16. Ouspensky, *In Search of the Miraculous*, pp. 161–65.

17. T. S. Eliot, *Four Quartets*: "Burnt Norton," in *Collected Poems: 1909–62* (New York: Harcourt, Brace, & World, 1963), p. 177.

18. Guénon relates this image of the eye of the needle to the Chi-Rho monogram, and even suggests that the *P* symbol resembles needles as they were made in antiquity; *Fundamental Symbols*, p. 276.

19. Francis de Sales, *Introduction to the Devout Life*, trans. John K. Ryan (New York: Image Books, 1972), pp. 161–62.

20. *Theologia Germanica*, p. 71.

21. Waddell, *The Desert Fathers*, p. 112.

CHAPTER 4

THE SECOND BIRTH

1. Thornton Wilder, *Our Town* (1938; reprint, New York: Harper Perennial, 1985), pp. 87–88.

2. Pagels, *The Gnostic Paul*, passim.

3. Quoted in *The Philokalia* 1:73–74.

4. *The Rule of St. Benedict*, chapters 8 and 9.

5. Morton Smith, *The Secret Gospel: The Discovery and Interpretation of the Secret Gospel According to Mark* (New York: Harper & Row, 1973), pp. 121ff.

6. For the most detailed discussion, see Mouravieff, *Gnosis* 2:195–207.

7. Ouspensky, *In Search of the Miraculous*, p. 59.

8. *Philokalia* 1:363–64.

9. Ibid. 1:367.

10. *Writings from the Philokalia on Prayer of the Heart*, trans. E. Kadloubovsky and G. E. H. Palmer (London: Faber & Faber, 1951), p. 22.

11. *A Course in Miracles*, workbook, p. 30.

12. Ibid., text, p. 25.

13. De Sales, *Introduction to the Devout Life*, p. 246.

14. Siobhán Houston, "Spiritual Directors: An Alternative to Gurus," *Gnosis* 51 (spring 1999): 7–10.

15. *The Life of St. Paul the First Hermit*, in Waddell, *The Desert Fathers*, p. 38.

16. *A Course in Miracles*, text, p. 29. Emphasis here and in other quotes in the original unless otherwise noted.

17. George Fox, *The Journal of George Fox* (New York: Capricorn Books, 1968), p. 88.

CHAPTER 5

COSMOLOGY

1. *Philokalia* 2:332.

2. Gurdjieff, *Beelzebub's Tales to His Grandson*, pp. 751–52.

3. Papus, *The Tarot of the Bohemians*, trans. A. P. Morton (London: Chapman & Hall, 1892), p. 21.

4. Johannes Reuchlin, *De Arte cabbalistica*, book 3; quoted in P. G. Maxwell-Stuart, ed., *The Occult in Early Modern Europe: A Documentary History* (New York: St. Martin's Press, 1999), p. 39.

5. Rudolf Steiner, *The Mysteries of the East and of Christianity* (Blauvelt, N.Y.: Spiritual Science Library, 1989), p. 71.

6. Matthew Fox and Rupert Sheldrake, *The Physics of Angels* (San Francisco: HarperSanFrancisco, 1996), p. 74.

7. This is almost certainly not the author's real name. It is an allusion to a figure mentioned in Acts 17:34, who was converted by Paul during his stay in Athens and about whom we otherwise know nothing. But the language and thought of these works attributed to Dionysius (of which there are several) suggest that their author lived in the sixth century, not the first. For this reason he is sometimes known as "pseudo-Dionysius." Since we have no other name for him, however, I shall simply call him Dionysius.

8. Bonaventure, *De Triplici via*, 3.14; quoted in Tomberg, *Meditations on the Tarot*, pp. 136–37.

9. Fox and Sheldrake, *The Physics of Angels*, p. 117.

10. Swedenborg, *Heaven and Hell*, pp. 72–73.

11. Fox and Sheldrake, *The Physics of Angels*, p. 1.

12. Dionysius the Areopagite, *Mystical Theology*, chapter 1 (http://www.esoteric.msu.edu).

13. *Corpus Hermeticum* 1:25–26, in Brian P. Copenhaver, ed. and trans., *Hermetica: The Greek Corpus Hermeticum and the Latin Asclepius in a New English Translation* (Cambridge: Cambridge University Press, 1992), p. 6.

14. *Philokalia* 2:25.

15. Charles Baudelaire, "Les Correspondances," in *Oeuvres complètes*, ed. Y.-G. Le Dantec and Claude Pichon (Paris: Gallimard, 1961), p. 11; my translation.

16. Enid Starkie, *Baudelaire* (Norfolk, Conn.: New Directions, 1958), pp. 225–33.

17. Faivre and Needleman, eds., *Modern Esoteric Spirituality*, pp. xvi–xvii.

18. Mouravieff, *Gnosis* 1:91. A similar system appears in Ouspensky, *In Search of the Miraculous*, p. 94.

19. Ouspensky, *In Search of the Miraculous*, p. 57.

20. Elisabeth Vreede, *Anthroposophy and Astrology*, trans. Ronald Koetzsch and Anne Riegel (Great Barrington, Mass.: Anthroposophic Press, 2001), p. 298.

CHAPTER 6

THE GOSPELS AND THE WORK OF CHRIST

1. Mouravieff, *Gnosis* 2:186.

2. Isaac Myer, *Qabbalah: The Philosophical Writings of Avicebron* (1888; reprint, New York: Weiser, 1970), pp. 228, 259.

3. Mouravieff, *Gnosis* 1:179–80.

4. *Oxford Classical Dictionary*, s.v. "Quirinius," "Herod the Great."

5. Versluis, *Theosophia*, p. 20.

6. Ibid., p. 20.

7. Christopher Bamford, ed. and trans., *The Voice of the Eagle: John Scotus Eriugena's Homily on the Prologue to the Gospel of St. John*, rev. ed. (Great Barrington, Mass.: Lindisfarne, 2000), pp. 69–70.

8. Ibid., p. 73. Eriugena uses the term "intellect" not in the modern sense but to denote a state of higher cognition; cf. p. 145, as well as chapter 10, below.

9. Maurice Nicoll, *The Mark* (1953; reprint, Boston: Shambhala Publications, 1985), p. 130.

10. Philo, *On the Migration of Abraham*, 1.1–2.

11. Tomberg, *Meditations on the Tarot*, p. 150.

12. For an esoteric understanding of Christ's passion and resurrection, see

Annie Besant, *Esoteric Christianity, or The Lesser Mysteries* (London: Theosophical Publishing House, 1918), esp. chapters 5–8.

13. Rudolf Steiner, *Christianity As Mystical Fact*, trans. Andrew Welburn (Hudson, N.Y.: Anthroposophic Press, 1997), p. 139.

14. Besant, *Esoteric Christianity*, p. 195.

15. Not all of Paul's letters are accepted today as genuine. Those that are, are Romans, 1 and 2 Corinthians, Galatians, Philippians, 1 Thessalonians, and Philemon. Most scholars regard the others essentially as pious frauds—written later and attributed to him so as to have greater authority in the church.

16. Ioan P. Couliano, *The Tree of Gnosis: Gnostic Mythology from Early Christianity to Modern Nihilism* (New York: HarperCollins, 1992).

17. *A Course in Miracles*, teacher's manual, p. 83, text, p. 6; emphasis in the original.

18. Ibid., text, p. 5.

19. Ibid., teacher's manual, p. 83.

CHAPTER 7

THE FEMININE FACE OF GOD

1. Davies, *The Phoenician Letters*, p. 74.

2. Martin Heidegger, *Early Greek Thinking*, trans. David Farrell Krell and Frank A. Capuzzi (New York: Harper & Row, 1975), pp. 59–66.

3. Kathleen M. O'Connor, *The Wisdom Literature* (Collegeville, Minn.: Liturgical Press, 1988), pp. 187–88.

4. Eusebius, *The History of the Church*, trans. G. A. Williamson (London: Penguin, 1965), p. 6 (book 1, part 2).

5. For this summary I am relying on Rudolph, *Gnosis: The Nature and History of Gnosticism*, pp. 76–80.

6. Jonas, *The Gnostic Religion*, p. 176.

7. Jonas himself equates them with Heidegger's concept of "existentials," which are similar, though not identical, to Kant's categories; ibid., p. 335.

8. *The Thunder: Perfect Mind*, 26, in *The Nag Hammadi Library in English*, p. 272.

9. Vladimir Solovyov, *Lectures on Divine Humanity*, trans. Boris Jakim (Hudson, N.Y.: Lindisfarne, 1995), p. 130. For a brief introduction to Solovyov, see Stephan A. Hoeller, "Vladimir Soloviev: Russian Orthodox Apostle of Gnosis and Sophia," *Gnosis* 16 (summer 1990): 29–33. The introductions both to *Lectures on Divine Humanity* and to Sergei Bulgakov's *Sophia: The Wisdom of God*, trans. Patrick Thompson et al. (Hudson, N.Y.:

Lindisfarne, 1994), contain brief accounts of the main trends and teachings in Sophiology.

10. Andreev, *The Rose of the World*, pp. 342–58.

11. Lévi, *La Clef des grands mystères*, quoted in a translator's footnote to Lévi's *Transcendental Magic*, p. 15.

12. C. G. Jung, *Mysterium Coniunctionis*, trans. R. F. C. Hull, 2d ed. (Princeton, N.J.: Princeton University Press/Bollingen, 1970), p. 21.

13. Ean Begg, *The Cult of the Black Virgin* (London: Arkana, 1985), p. 3.

14. See ibid., pp. 6–8, for a discussion of these theories.

15. Temple, *Icons and the Mystical Origins of Christianity*, pp. 159–67.

16. Jung, *Mysterium Coniuncitionis*, p. 466.

17. R. E. Witt, *Isis in the Greco-Roman World* (Ithaca, N.Y.: Cornell University Press, 1971), pp. 272–76.

18. On the history of this doctrine, see J. N. D. Kelly, *Early Christian Doctrines*, rev. ed. (New York: Harper & Row, 1976), pp. 310–29.

19. Temple, *Icons and the Mystical Origins of Christianity*, p. 166.

20. Information taken from the web site "Marian Apparitions of the Twentieth Century," www.udayton.edu/mary/resources/aprtable.html.

21. Reported in the *Detroit News*, 14 January 2000: http://detnews.com-/2000/religion/0001/21/01150013.htm.

CHAPTER 8

SPIRITUAL PRACTICES

1. Quoted in J. P. Ross, *A Recapitulation of the Lord's Prayer* (n.p.: self-published, 1985).

2. Jacob Needleman, *Lost Christianity* (1980; reprint, Boston: Element, 1993), p. 36.

3. Quoted in Fuller, *The Brotherhood of the Common Life*, p. 282.

4. Ibid., pp. 135–42.

5. Quoted in ibid., p. 136.

6. Ouspensky, *In Search of the Miraculous*, p. 146.

7. Gurdjieff did not believe that everyone possesses these bodies as a matter of course. Rather, he said that they only exist in those who have consciously developed them. See ibid., pp. 32, 54, et passim.

8. Stylianos Atteshlis, *The Esoteric Practices* (Strovolos, Cyprus: Stoa Series, 1994), p. 89. Full directions for this practice can be found on pp. 83–84, 87–89.

9. Gareth Knight, *Experience of the Inner Worlds: A Course in Christian Qabalistic Magic* (Cheltenham, Gloucestershire, U.K.: Helios, 1975), pp. 17–18, 42.

10. Ibid., p. 99.

11. For further discussion of this topic, see my article "The Illumined Heart," *Gnosis* 51 (spring 1999): 12–15.

12. Chrétien de Troyes, *Perceval*, in John Matthews, ed., *Sources of the Grail* (Hudson, N.Y.: Lindisfarne, 1997), p. 158.

13. *The Apocryphal New Testament*, trans. M. R. James (Oxford: Clarendon Press, 1924), p. 33.

14. John Cassian, *Conferences*, trans. Colin Luibheid (Mahwah, N.J.: Paulist Press, 1985), p. 133.

15. Ignatius Brianchaninov, *On the Prayer of Jesus*, trans. Father Lazarus (London: Watkins, 1965), p. 71.

16. *Unseen Warfare: Being the Spiritual Combat and Path to Paradise of Lorenzo Scupoli As Edited by Nicodemus of the Holy Mountain and Revised by Theophan the Recluse*, trans. E. Kadloubovsky and G. E. H. Palmer (London: Faber & Faber, 1952), p. 205.

17. Ibid., p. 217.

18. Z'ev ben Shimon Halevi, *Kabbalah and Exodus* (London: Rider, 1980).

19. *St. John of the Cross, Alchemist of the Soul: His Life, His Poetry (Bilingual), His Prose*, ed. and trans. Antonio T. de Nicolás (York Beach, Maine: Weiser, 1996), pp. 103, 165–67.

20. *Unseen Warfare*, p. 219.

21. From John Main, *The Way of Unknowing*, quoted in Paul T. Harris, ed., *The Heart of Silence: Contemplative Prayer by Those Who Practise It* (Ottawa, Canada: Novalis, 1999), p. 15.

22. *The Cloud of Unknowing and Other Works*, trans. Clifton Wolters (Harmondsworth, Middlesex, U.K.: Penguin, 1978), p. 76.

23. Ibid., pp. 69–70.

24. Cynthia Bourgeault, "From Woundedness to Union," *Gnosis* 34 (winter 1995): 41–45.

25. Richard Smoley, "Heroic Virtue: The *Gnosis* Interview with Brother David Steindl-Rast," *Gnosis* 24 (summer 1992): 40. See also M. Basil Pennington, *Lectio Divina: Renewing the Ancient Practice of Praying the Scriptures* (New York: Crossroad, 1998).

26. Cynthia Bourgeault, "The Hidden Wisdom of Psalmody," *Gnosis* 37 (fall 1995): 27.

27. Amis, *A Different Christianity*, p. 303.

28. *The Rule of St. Benedict* (Collegeville, Minn.: Liturgical Press, 1980), p. 215.

29. See, for example, Cynthia Bourgeault, *Chanting the Psalms: How to Chant in the Christian Contemplative Tradition*, 3 cassettes (Boulder, Colo.: Sounds True, 1997).

30. Mouravieff, *Gnosis* 3:163–64. Mouravieff has altered the conventional translation on some points; for the purposes of simplicity I am staying with the more familiar form here.

31. See also Maurice Nicoll, *The Mark* (1951; reprint, Boston: Shambhala Publications, 1985), p. 207.

32. Dion Fortune, *The Mystical Qabalah* (London: Benn, 1935), p. 4.

CHAPTER 9: LOVE, EVIL, AND FORGIVENESS

1. M. Scott Peck, *People of the Lie: The Hope for Healing Human Evil* (New York: Simon & Schuster, 1983), p. 46.

2. Jacob Boehme, *The Three Principles of Divine Being* 9.30, quoted in Franz Hartmann, *The Life and Doctrines of Jacob Boehme* (London: Kegan Paul, Trench, and Trübner, 1891), p. 68.

3. *Sefer Yetzirah: The Book of Creation in Theory and Practice*, trans. Aryeh Kaplan (York Beach, Maine: Weiser, 1990) 1:5, p. 44.

4. Mouravieff, *Gnosis* 2:109–10; emphasis in the original.

5. See *The Song of Prayer: Prayer, Forgiveness, and Healing* ([Tiburon, Calif.]: Foundation for Inner Peace, 1978). This booklet, though not published as a part of *A Course in Miracles*, is regarded as coming from the same source and is more or less identical to the *Course* in language and thought.

6. Robert W. Funk et al., *The Acts of Jesus: The Search for the Authentic Deeds of Jesus* (San Francisco: HarperSanFrancisco, 1998), pp. 357–58.

7. See Henry George Liddell and Robert Scott, *A Greek-English Lexicon*, ed. Henry Stuart Jones et al. (Oxford: Clarendon Press, 1968), s.v. "*storgē*," "*stergeo*," "*philia*," "*phileo*," "*agapē*," "*agapao*," "*eros*," and "*erao*."

8. Quoted in Robert Burton, *Anatomy of Melancholy*, 3.1.1.2 (London: Bell, 1893), 3:14.

9. Plato, *Symposium* 180d, 181d, trans. Michael Joyce, in Plato, *Collected Dialogues*, ed. Edith Hamilton and Huntington Cairns (Princeton, N.J.: Princeton University Press/Bollingen, 1961), pp. 534–35.

10. Gurdjieff, *All and Everything*, p. 361.

11. *A Course in Miracles*, text, pp. 290–94 et passim.

12. See, for example, the *Gospel of Philip*, 63–64, in *The Nag Hammadi Library*, p. 138.

13. Nicoll, *The New Man*, p. 79; cf. John 21:15–17.

14. Plato, *Symposium* 190a–191e, in *Collected Dialogues*, pp. 542–44.

15. Mouravieff, *Gnosis* 2:254.

16. Ibid. 2:257.

CHAPTER 10

SYMBOLS AND SACRAMENTS

1. Plato, *Republic* 477b ff.

2. René Guénon, *Introduction to the Study of the Hindu Doctrines* (1945; reprint, New Delhi: Munshiram Manoharlal, 1993), p. 117. Guénon points out that this faculty was also known to Aristotle and to the medieval Scholastics. See also Guénon, *Man and His Becoming According to the Vedanta*, trans. Richard C. Nicholson (New Delhi: Oriental Books, 1981), pp. 65–69.

3. Robert Lawlor, *Sacred Geometry: Philosophy and Practice* (London: Thames & Hudson, 1982), p. 31.

4. Tomberg, *Meditations on the Tarot*, p. 13.

5. Louis Charbonneau-Lassay, *The Bestiary of Christ*, ed. and trans. D. M. Dooling, (New York: Parabola/Arkana, 1992).

6. Gurdjieff, *Beelzebub's Tales to His Grandson*, pp. 308–10.

7. My discussion of this symbol differs from Mouravieff's in certain details, though the general import is the same. For his version, see Mouravieff, *Gnosis* 2:163–64.

8. Plato, *Phaedrus* 246b, in Plato, *Phaedrus and Letters VII and VIII*, trans. Walter Hamilton (London: Penguin, 1973), pp. 50–51.

9. Fulcanelli, *The Dwellings of the Philosophers*, trans. Brigitte Donvez and Lionel Perrin (Boulder, Colo.: Archive Press, 1999), pp. 36–38.

10. Mouravieff, *Gnosis* 1:91. A similar system appears in Ouspensky, *In Search of the Miraculous*, p. 94.

11. For many of the ideas in my discussion of the imagery of icons, I am indebted to Richard Temple, *Icons and the Mystical Origins of Christianity*.

12. Stephen Muratore, "Windows into Heaven," *Gnosis* 27 (spring 1993): 50–57.

13. For a discussion of this issue, see my article "How Ritual Works," *Gnosis* 11 (spring 1989): 14–18.

14. Edward Yarnold, *The Awe-Inspiring Rites of Initiation: The Origins of the R.C.I.A. [Rite of Christian Initiation for Adults]*, 2d ed. (Collegeville, Minn.: Liturgical Press, 1994), p. 1.

15. Ibid., pp. 19–20.

16. For a fascinating perspective on this subject, see Olof Alexandersson, *Living Water: Viktor Schauberger and the Secrets of Natural Energy*, trans. Kit and Charles Zweibergk (Bath, U.K.: Gateway, 1990).

17. Yarnold, *The Awe-Inspiring Rites of Initiation*, p. 21.

18. C. W. Leadbeater, *The Science of the Sacraments*, 2d ed. (Adyar, India: Theosophical Publishing House, 1929), pp. 297–98.

19. Ibid., p. 294.

20. In the Orthodox Church, where the mass, or "divine liturgy," as it is called, is generally more elaborate, the Mass of the Catechumens is preceded by a portion called the "Office of Oblation," in which the bread and wine are prepared for the divine sacrifice.

21. Guénon, *Man and His Becoming*, pp. 19–20.

22. Frithjof Schuon, in *The Transcendent Unity of Religions* (Wheaton, Ill.: Quest Books, 1984), p. 134n., notes that Paul himself draws this distinction in 1 Cor. 7.

23. *Oxford English Dictionary*, s.v. "symbol"; Liddell and Scott, s.v. "*symbolon.*"

24. For much of the following, I am indebted to Nicoll, *The New Man*, pp. 1–16, 28–37.

25. Hayim Nahman Bialik and Yehoshua Hana Ravnitzky, *The Book of Legends: Sefer ha-Aggadah: Legends from the Torah and Midrash*, trans. William G. Braude (New York: Schocken Books, 1992), p. 235.

26. Stephan A. Hoeller, *The Mystery and Magic of the Eucharist* (Hollywood, Calif.: Gnostic Press, 1990). See also Hoeller's article "Wandering Bishops: Not All Roads Lead to Rome," *Gnosis* 12 (summer 1989): 20–25, for a brief but engaging history of this movement.

27. See Draper, "A New Order of Priests"; also Hindes, *Renewing Christianity*.

28. James F. Billington, *The Icon and the Axe: An Interpretive History of Russian Culture* (New York: Knopf, 1967), pp. 135–44.

29. Quoted in Mary Strong, ed., *Letters of the Scattered Brotherhood* (New York: Harper & Row, 1948), p. 3.

CHAPTER 11

THE SECRET CHURCH

1. Tomberg, p. 6.

2. Lévi, *History of Magic*, pp. 149, 211.

3. Guénon, *Fundamental Symbols*, pp. 168–71.

4. A. E. Waite, introduction to I. V. Lopukhin, *Some Characteristics of the Interior Church*, trans. D. H. S. Nicholson (London: Theosophical Publishing Society, 1912), p. 51.

5. Karl von Eckhartshausen, *The Cloud upon the Sanctuary*, trans. Isabel de Steiger (Edmonds, Wash.: Holmes, 1991), pp. 16–17.

6. Watts, *Myth and Ritual in Christianity* (Boston: Beacon, 1968), p. 194. See pp. 193–99 for a more detailed description of the symbolism of the church.

7. Lopukhin, *Some Characteristics of the Interior Church*, pp. 65–66.

8. Ibid., pp. 64.

9. Ibid., p. 63.

10. Watts, *Myth and Ritual in Christianity*, p. 196.

11. See, for example, Gershom Scholem, *Kabbalah* (New York: Dorset, 1987), p. 21.

12. Lopukhin, *Some Characteristics of the Interior Church*, p. 61.

13. Emanuel Swedenborg, *Heaven and Hell*, trans. George F. Dole (West Chester, Pa.: Swedenborg Foundation, 2000), §94, p. 135.

14. Ibid., §96, p. 137.

15. *A Course in Miracles*, text, pp. 493, 495.

16. Mouravieff, *Gnosis* 1:241.

17. Quoted in Frances A. Yates, *The Rosicrucian Enlightenment*, p. 243.

18. Ouspensky, *In Search of the Miraculous*, p. 312.

19. Ibid., p. 313.

20. Ibid., p. 302.

21. Ibid., p. 313.

22. Ibid., p. 232.

23. Mouravieff, *Gnosis* 1:188–89.

24. Charles R. Tetworth, *Wielding Power: The Essence of Ritual Practice* (Great Barrington, Mass.: Lindisfarne, 2002), p. 172.

25. Andreev, *The Rose of the World*, pp. 20, 67.

AFTERWORD

CONTINUING THE JOURNEY

1. *Philokalia* 1:232.

2. Mouravieff, *Gnosis* 1:148.

3. *A Course in Miracles*, workbook, p. 227.

4. Rudolf Steiner, *How to Know Higher Worlds*, trans. Christopher Bamford (Hudson, N.Y.: Anthroposophic Press, 1994), pp. 74–75.

5. Ouspensky, *In Search of the Miraculous*, pp. 200–204; Mouravieff, *Gnosis* 1:50–53.

SELECTED BIBLIOGRAPHY

Alighieri, Dante. *The Divine Comedy*. Edited and translated by Charles S. Singleton. 6 vols. Princeton, N.J.: Princeton University Press, 1970.

———. *La Vita Nuova*. Translated by Barbara Reynolds. Harmondsworth, Middlesex, U.K.: Penguin, 1969.

———. *On World-Government*. Translated by Herbert W. Schneider. Indianapolis, Ind.: Bobbs Merrill, 1949.

Alter, Robert, and Frank Kermode, eds. *The Literary Guide to the Bible*. Cambridge, Mass.: Harvard University Press, 1987.

Amis, Robin. *A Different Christianity*. Albany: State University of New York Press, 1995.

Andreev, Daniel. *The Rose of the World*. Translated by Jordan Roberts. Hudson, N.Y.: Lindisfarne Books, 1996.

Anonymous. *The Impersonal Life*. Akron, Ohio: Sun, 1914.

———. *The Way of a Pilgrim and The Pilgrim Continues His Way*. Translated by Helen Bacovcin. New York: Doubleday/Image, 1978.

The Ante-Nicene Fathers. Edited by Alexander Roberts and James Donaldson. Reprint. Grand Rapids, Mich.: Eerdmans, 1994.

The Apocryphal New Testament. Translated by M. R. James. Oxford: Clarendon Press, 1924.

The Apostolic Fathers. Translated by J. B. Lightfoot and J. R. Harmer. Edited by Michael W. Holmes. Grand Rapids, Mich.: Baker, 1989.

Atteshlis, Stylianos. *The Esoteric Practice: Christian Meditations and Exercises*. Strovolos, Cyprus: Stoa Series, 1994.

Bamford, Christopher. *The Voice of the Eagle: John Scotus Eriugena's Prologue to the Gospel of St. John*. Great Barrington, Mass.: Lindisfarne, 2000.

Begg, Ean. *The Cult of the Black Virgin*. London: Arkana, 1985.

Berdyaev, Nicolas. *Freedom and the Spirit*. Translated by Oliver Fielding Clarke. London: Geoffrey Bles, 1935.

Besant, Annie. *Esoteric Christianity, or the Lesser Mysteries.* London: Theosophical Publishing House, 1918.

Bialik, Hayim Nahman, and Yehoshua Hana Ravnitzky. *The Book of Legends: Sefer ha-Aggadah: Legends from the Torah and Midrash.* Translated by William G. Braude. New York: Schocken Books, 1992.

Biblia Hebraica. Edited by Rudolf Kittel et al. 13th ed. Stuttgart: Württembergische Bibelanstalt, 1962.

Biblia Sacra iuxta Vulgatam versionem. Edited by Robert Weber et al. 2 vols. Stuttgart: Württembergische Bibelanstalt, 1969.

Blakney, Raymond B., ed. and trans. *Meister Eckhart.* New York: Harper & Row, 1941.

Blavatsky, Helena Petrovna. *The Secret Doctrine.* 2 vols. 3d Point Loma ed. Point Loma, Calif.: Aryan Theosophical Press, 1925.

Bolendas, Joa. *Alive in God's World: The Visions of Joa Bolendas.* Great Barrington, Mass.: Lindisfarne, 2001.

———. *So That You May Be One.* Translated by John Hill. Hudson, N.Y.: Lindisfarne Books, 1997.

Bonaventure. Edited by Ewert Cousins. Mahwah, N.J.: Paulist Press, 1978.

Book of Creation: Sepher Yetzirah. Translated by Irving Friedman. New York: Weiser, 1977.

Borg, Marcus J., and N. T. Wright. *The Meaning of Jesus: Two Visions.* San Francisco: HarperSanFrancisco, 1998.

Bourgeault, Cynthia. "Boehme for Beginners." *Gnosis* 45 (fall 1997): 29ff.

———. *Chanting the Psalms: How to Chant in the Christian Contemplative Tradition.* 3 cassettes. Boulder, Colo.: Sounds True, 1997.

———. "From Woundedness to Union." *Gnosis* 34 (winter 1995): 41–45.

———. "The Hidden Wisdom of Psalmody." *Gnosis* 37 (fall 1995): 27ff.

———. *The Holy Trinity and the Law of Three.* Unpublished ms.

———. *Love Is Stronger Than Death.* New York: Bell Tower, 1999.

———. "Reclaiming the Path of Erotic Love." *Gnosis* 51 (spring 1999): 42–48.

Brianchaninov, Ignatius. *On the Prayer of Jesus.* Translated by Father Lazarus. London: Watkins, 1965.

Brock, Sebastian, ed. *The Syriac Fathers on Prayer and the Spiritual Life.* Kalamazoo, Mich.: Cistercian Publications, 1987.

Brown, Peter. *Religion and Society in the Age of St. Augustine.* New York: Harper & Row, 1972.

Buber, Martin. *I and Thou.* Translated by Ronald Gregor Smith. 2d ed. Edinburgh: Clark, 1958.

Bulgakov. Sergei. *Sophia: The Wisdom of God.* Translated by Patrick Thompson et al. Hudson, N.Y.: Lindisfarne, 1993.

Bunyan, John. *The Pilgrim's Progress*. 1678. New York: Washington Square Press, 1957.

Burton, Robert. *The Anatomy of Melancholy*. 1630. London: Bell, 1893.

Caddy, Peter, et al. *In Perfect Timing: Memoirs of a Man for the New Millennium*. Findhorn, Scotland: Findhorn Press, 1996.

Cameron, Ron, ed. *The Other Gospels: Non-Canonical Gospel Texts*. Philadelphia: Westminster Press, 1982.

Carey, John.. *King of Mysteries: Early Irish Religious Writings*. Dublin: Four Courts Press, 1998.

———. *A Single Ray of the Sun: Religious Speculation in Early Ireland*. Andover, Mass.: Celtic Studies, 1999.

Cassian, John. *Conferences*. Translated by Colm Luibheid. Mahwah, N.J.: Paulist Press, 1985.

Charbonneau-Lassay, Louis. *The Bestiary of Christ*. Edited and translated by D. M. Dooling. New York: Parabola/Arkana, 1992.

Charles, R. H., ed. *The Apocrypha and Pseudepigrapha of the Old Testament*. Vol. 2. *Pseudepigrapha*. Oxford: Clarendon Press, 1913.

Clement of Alexandria. *The Exhortation to the Greeks and Other Works*. Translated by G. W. Butterworth. Loeb Classical Library. Cambridge, Mass.: Harvard University Press, 1919.

The Cloud of Unknowing and Other Works. Translated by Clifton Wolters. Harmondsworth, Middlesex, U.K.: Penguin, 1978.

Copenhaver, Brian P., ed. and trans. *Hermetica: The Greek Corpus Hermeticum and the Latin Asclepius in a New English Translation, with Notes and an Introduction*. Cambridge, U.K.: Cambridge University Press, 1992.

Coton-Alvart, Henri. *Les Deux lumières: La Science de la nature vivante dans ses mutations*. Paris: Éditions Dervy, 1996.

Couliano, Ioan P. *The Tree of Gnosis: Gnostic Mythology from Early Christianity to Modern Nihilism*. New York: HarperCollins, 1992.

Coulombe, Charles A. "The Secret Church of John." *Gnosis* 45 (fall 1997): 47–53.

Cross, Frank Moore. *Canaanite Myth and Hebrew Epic*. Cambridge, Mass.: Harvard University Press, 1973.

David-Neel, Alexandra. *Magic and Mystery in Tibet*. 1932. Reprint. New York: Dover, 1971.

Davies, W. G. *The Phoenician Letters*. Manchester, U.K.: Mowat, 1979.

Déchanet, J.-M. *Christian Yoga*. Translated by Roland Hindmarsh. New York: Harper & Row, 1960.

Decker, Ronald, Thierry Depaulis, and Michael Dummett. *A Wicked Pack of Cards: The Origins of the Occult Tarot*. New York: St. Martin's Press, 1996.

Draper, Sara. "A New Order of Priests." *Gnosis* 45 (fall 1997): 55–59.

Early Christian Writings. Translated by Maxwell Staniforth. London: Penguin, 1968.

Eckhartshausen, Karl von. *The Cloud upon the Sanctuary.* Translated by Isabel de Steiger. Edmonds, Wash.: Holmes, 1991.

Eusebius. *The History of the Church.* Translated by G. A. Williamson. London: Penguin, 1965.

Evola, Julius. *The Mystery of the Grail.* Translated by Guido Stucco. Rochester, Vt.: Inner Traditions, 1997.

Faivre, Antoine, and Jacob Needleman, eds. *Modern Esoteric Spirituality.* New York: Crossroad, 1995.

Fideler, David. *Jesus Christ, Sun of God: Ancient Cosmology and Early Christian Symbolism.* Wheaton, Ill.: Quest Books, 1993.

Fortune, Dion. *The Mystical Qabalah.* London: Benn, 1935.

Fox, George. *The Journal of George Fox.* New York: Capricorn Books, 1968.

Fox, Matthew, and Rupert Sheldrake. *The Physics of Angels.* San Francisco: HarperSanFrancisco, 1996.

Frazer, Sir James George. *The Golden Bough.* New York: Macmillan, 1922.

Fulcanelli. *The Dwellings of the Philosophers.* Translated by Brigitte Donvez and Lionel Perrin. Boulder, Colo.: Archive Press, 1999.

Fuller, Ross. *The Brotherhood of the Common Life and Its Influence.* Albany: State University of New York Press, 1995.

Funk, Robert W., et al. *The Acts of Jesus: The Search for the Authentic Deeds of Jesus.* San Francisco: HarperSanFrancisco, 1998.

Funk, Robert W., Roy W. Hoover, et al. *The Five Gospels.* San Francisco: HarperSanFrancisco, 1997.

Gaer, Joseph. *The Lore of the New Testament.* 1952. Reprint. New York: Grosset & Dunlap, 1966.

———. *The Lore of the Old Testament.* 1951. Reprint. New York: Grosset & Dunlap, 1966.

Garrigou-Lagrange, Reginald. *The Three Ages of the Interior Life.* Translated by M. Timothea Doyle. 2 vols. Rockford, Ill.: Tan Books, 1989.

The Gospel of Peace of Jesus Christ by the Disciple John. Translated by Edmond Székely and Purcell Weaver. Saffron Walden, Essex, U.K.: Daniel, 1937.

Graf, Susan Johnston. *W. B. Yeats: Twentieth-Century Magus.* York Beach, Maine: Weiser, 2000.

The Greek New Testament. Edited by Kurt Aland et al. New York: United Bible Societies, 1966.

Guénon, René. *Aperçus sur l'ésotérisme chrétien.* Paris: Éditions Traditionelles, n.d.

———. *Aperçus sur l'ésotérisme islamique et le taoïsme.* Paris: Gallimard, 1973.

————. *The Esoterism of Dante*. Translated by C. B. Bethell. Ghent, N.Y.: Sophia Perennis et Universalis, 1996.

————. *Fundamental Symbols: The Universal Language of Sacred Science*. Translated by Alvin Moore Jr. Bartlow, Cambridge, U.K.: Quinta Essentia, 1995.

————. *Introduction to the Study of the Hindu Doctrines*. Translated by Marco Pallis. 1945. Reprint. New Delhi: Munshiram Manoharlal, 1993.

————. *The Symbolism of the Cross*. Translated by Angus McNabb. London: Luzac, 1958.

Gurdjieff, G. I. *All and Everything*. 1st ser. *Beelzebub's Tales to His Grandson*. New York: Dutton, 1950.

————. *Meetings with Remarkable Men*. New York: Dutton, 1963.

————. *Views from the Real World: Early Talks of G. I. Gurdjieff*. New York: Dutton, 1973.

Halevi, Z'ev ben Shimon. *Kabbalah and Exodus*. London: Rider, 1980.

————. *A Kabbalistic Universe*. London: Rider, 1977.

Hall, Manly P. *Man: Grand Symbol of the Mysteries*. 6th ed. Los Angeles: Philosophical Research Society, 1972.

Harris, Paul T., ed. *The Heart of Silence: Contemplative Prayer by Those Who Practise It*. Ottawa, Canada: Novalis, 1999.

Hartmann, Franz. *The Life and Doctrines of Jacob Boehme*. London: Kegan Paul, Trench, and Trübner, 1891.

The Heart of Salvation: The Life and Teachings of Russia's Saint Theophan the Recluse. Translated by Esther Williams. Edited by Robin Amis. Newbury, Mass.: Praxis Institute Press, 1992.

Heidegger, Martin. *Early Greek Thinking*. Translated by David Farrell Krell and Frank A. Capuzzi. New York: Harper & Row, 1975.

Heindel, Max. *The Rosicrucian Cosmo-Conception*. Oceanside, Calif.: Rosicrucian Fellowship, 1909.

————. *The Rosicrucian Philosophy in Questions and Answers*. Oceanside, Calif.: Rosicrucian Fellowship, 1922.

Hilton, Walter. *The Scale of Perfection*. Edited by Evelyn Underhill. London: Watkins, 1948.

Hindes, James H. *Renewing Christianity*. Hudson, N.Y.: Anthroposophic Press, 1996.

Hoeller, Stephan A. *The Mystery and Magic of the Eucharist*. Hollywood, Calif.: Gnostic Press, 1990.

————. "Vladimir Soloviev: Russian Orthodox Apostle of Gnosis and Sophia." *Gnosis* 16 (summer 1990): 29–33.

————. "Wandering Bishops: Not All Roads Lead to Rome." *Gnosis* 12 (summer 1989): 20–25.

Houston, Siobhán. "Spiritual Directors: An Alternative to Gurus." *Gnosis* 51 (spring 1999): 7–10.

———. "Turning to Orthodoxy." *Gnosis* 31 (spring 1994): 39–42.

James, William. *The Varieties of Religious Experience.* New York: Longmans, Green, 1902.

John of Kronstadt. *Spiritual Counsels: Select Passages from My Life in Christ.* Edited by W. Jardine Grisbrooke. Crestwood, N.Y.: St. Vladimir's Seminary Press, 1989.

Johnson, Luke Timothy. *The Real Jesus.* San Francisco: HarperSanFrancisco, 1996.

Jonas, Hans. *The Gnostic Religion.* Boston: Beacon Press, 1958.

Josephus, Flavius. *The Jewish War.* Translated by G. A. Williamson. Harmondsworth, Middlesex, U.K.: Penguin, 1959.

Jung, C. G. *Aion: Researches into the Phenomenology of the Self.* Translated by R. F. C. Hull. Princeton, N.J.: Princeton University Press/Bollingen, 1959.

———. *Answer to Job.* Translated by R. F. C. Hull. 2d ed. Princeton, N.J.: Princeton University Press/Bollingen, 1969.

———. *Memories, Dreams, Reflections.* Translated by Richard and Clara Winston. New York: Random House, 1961.

———. *Mysterium Coniunctionis.* Translated by R. F. C. Hull, 2d ed. Princeton, N.J.: Princeton University Press/Bollingen, 1970.

Kadloubovsky, E., and G. E. H. Palmer, eds. and trans. *Writings from the Philokalia on Prayer of the Heart.* London: Faber & Faber, 1951.

Kelly, J. N. D. *Early Christian Doctrines.* Rev. ed. New York: Harper & Row, 1976.

Kempis, Thomas à. *De Imitatione Christi.* London: Methuen, 1919.

Kierkegaard, Søren. *Training in Christianity.* Translated by Walter Lowrie. Princeton, N.J.: Princeton University Press, 1967.

King, Ursula. *Christian Mystics: The Spiritual Heart of the Christian Tradition.* New York: Simon & Schuster, 1998.

Kingsley, Peter. "Poimandres: The Etymology of the Name and the Origins of the *Hermetica.*" *Journal of the Warburg and Courtauld Institutes* 56 (1993): 1?24.

Kovalevsky, Eugraph. *A Method of Prayer for Modern Times.* Translated by Esther Williams. Newburyport, Mass.: Praxis Institute Press, 1993.

Lamm, Martin. *Emanuel Swedenborg: The Development of His Thought.* Translated by Tomas Spiers and Anders Hallengren. West Chester, Pa.: Swedenborg Foundation, 2000.

Lawlor, Robert. *Sacred Geometry: Philosophy and Practice.* London: Thames & Hudson, 1982.

Leadbeater, C. W. *The Science of the Sacraments.* 2d ed. Adyar, India: Theosophical Publishing House, 1929.

Lévi, Éliphas. *Letters to a Disciple.* Wellingborough, Northamptonshire, England: Aquarian Press, 1980,

——. *Transcendental Magic.* Translated by A. E. Waite. 1896. Reprint. London: Bracken Books, 1997.

Lévi-Strauss, Claude. *Tristes Tropiques.* Translated by John and Doreen Weightman. New York: Atheneum, 1974.

Lewis, C. S. *The Great Divorce.* New York: Macmillan, 1946.

——. *Mere Christianity.* New York: Macmillan, 1960.

Little Russian Philokalia. Vol. 1. *St. Seraphim of Sarov.* Translated by Seraphim Rose. Platina, Calif.: St. Herman of Alaska Brotherhood, 1996.

Lopukhin, Ivan Vladimirovich. *Some Characteristics of the Interior Church.* Translated by D. H. S. Nicholson. London: Theosophical Publishing Society, 1912.

Loyola, Ignatius. *The Spiritual Exercises of St. Ignatius.* Translated by Anthony Mottola. New York: Doubleday/Anchor, 1964.

MacDermot, Violet. *The Fall of Sophia: A Gnostic Text on the Redemption of Universal Consciousness.* Great Barrington, Mass.: Lindisfarne, 2001.

Martinez de Pasqually, Jacques. *Traité de la réintégration des êtres.* Paris: Éditions Traditionelles, 1977.

Mathewes-Green, Frederica. *At the Corner of East and Now: A Modern Life in Ancient Christian Orthodoxy.* New York: Tarcher/Putnam, 1999.

Maxwell-Stuart, P. G. *The Occult in Early Modern Europe: A Documentary History.* New York: St. Martin's Press, 1999.

McGinn, Bernard, John Meyendorff, and Jean Leclerq, eds. *Christian Spirituality: Origins to the Twelfth Century.* New York: Crossroad, 1997.

Mead, G. R. S. *Pistis Sophia: A Gnostic Miscellany.* 1921. Reprint. Kila, Mont.: Kessinger, n.d.

——. *Thrice Greatest Hermes: Studies in Hermetic Theosophy and Gnosis.* 1906. Reprint. York Beach, Maine: Weiser, 1992.

Metford, J. C. F. *Dictionary of Christian Lore and Legend.* London: Thames & Hudson, 1983.

Meyer, Marvin W., ed. *The Ancient Mysteries: A Sourcebook.* San Francisco: Harper & Row, 1987.

Miller, D. Patrick. *The Complete Story of the Course.* Berkeley, Calif.: Fearless Books, 1997.

The Monks of New Skete. *In the Spirit of Happiness.* Boston: Little, Brown, 1999.

Monnastre, Cris, and David Griffin. "Israel Regardie, the Golden Dawn, and Psychotherapy." *Gnosis* 37 (fall 1995): 36–42.

Mouravieff, Boris. *Gnosis: Étude et commentaires sur la tradition ésotérique de l'Ortho-doxie orientale*. 3 vols. Neuchâtel, Switzerland: À la Baconnière, 1969–72.

———. *Gnosis: Study and Commentaries on the Esoteric Tradition of Eastern Ortho-doxy*. Translated by S. A. Wissa, Maneck d'Oncieu, and Robin Amis. 3 vols. Newburyport, Mass: Praxis Institute Press, 1989–93.

Muratore, Stephen. "Windows into Heaven." *Gnosis* 27 (spring 1993): 50–57.

Myer, Isaac. *Qabbalah: The Philosophical Writings of Avicebron*. 1888. Reprint. New York: Weiser, 1970.

Needleman, Jacob. *Lost Christianity*. 1980. Reprint. Boston: Element, 1993.

Nicolás, Antonio T. de, ed. and trans. *St. John of the Cross, Alchemist of the Soul: His Life, His Poetry (Bilingual), His Prose*. York Beach, Maine: Weiser, 1996.

Nicolescu, Basarab. *Science, Meaning, and Evolution: The Cosmology of Jacob Boehme*. Translated by Rob Baker. New York: Parabola, 1991.

Nicoll, Maurice. *The Mark*. Boston: Shambhala Publications, 1985.

———. *The New Man*. Boulder, Colo.: Shambhala Publications, 1981.

O'Connor, Kathleen M. *The Wisdom Literature*. Collegeville, Minn.: Liturgical Press, 1988.

Origen. *On First Principles*. Edited by G. W. Butterworth. New York: Harper & Row, 1966.

Otto, Rudolf. *The Idea of the Holy*. Translated by John Harvey. Oxford: Oxford University Press, 1928.

Ouspensky, Leonid. *Theology of the Icon*. Translated by Anthony Gittel and Eliza-beth Meyendorff. 2 vols. Crestwood, N.Y.: St. Vladimir's Seminary Press, 1992.

Ouspensky, P. D. *In Search of the Miraculous: Fragments of a Forgotten Teaching*. New York: Harcourt, Brace, 1949.

———. *A New Model of the Universe*. New York: Knopf. 1931.

———. *The Gnostic Paul*. Philadelphia: Trinity Press International, 1975.

Pagels, Elaine. *The Gnostic Gospels*. New York: Vintage Books, 1981.

———. *The Origins of Satan*. New York: Random House, 1995.

Papini, Giovanni. *The Devil*. Translated by Adrienne Foulke. New York: Dutton, 1954.

Paracelsus. *Selected Writings*. Translated by Norbert Guterman. Edited by Jolande Jacobi. Princeton, N.J.: Princeton/Bollingen, 1951.

Peck, M. Scott. *People of the Lie: The Hope for Healing Human Evil*. New York: Simon & Schuster, 1983.

Pennington, M. Basil. *Lectio Divina: Renewing the Ancient Practice of Praying the Scriptures*. New York: Crossroad, 1998.

———. *True Self, False Self: Unmasking the Spirit Within*. New York: Crossroad, 2000.

Philo. *The Works of Philo.* Translated by C. D. Yonge. Peabody, Mass.: Hendrickson, 1993.

The Philokalia: The Complete Text. Translated by G. E. H. Palmer et al. 5 vols. London: Faber & Faber, 1979–.

Pico della Mirandola, Giovanni. *Heptaplus, or Discourse on the Seven Days of Creation.* Translated by Jessie Brewer McGaw. New York: Philosophical Library, 1977.

Pseudo-Dionysius. *The Complete Works.* Translated by Colm Luibheid and Paul Rorem. Mahwah, N.J.: Paulist Press, 1987.

Quispel, Gilles. *The Secret Book of Revelation.* Translated by Peter Staples. New York: McGraw-Hill, 1979.

Raitt, Jill, et al., eds. *Christian Spirituality: High Middle Ages and Reformation.* New York: Crossroad, 1987.

Reich, Wilhelm. *The Murder of Christ.* New York: Noonday Press, 1953.

Richardson, Robert. "The Priory of Sion Hoax." *Gnosis* 51 (spring 1999): 49–55.

Riggs, Brian. "The Pope and the Pornographer: The Long Quarrel between Freemasonry and Catholicism." *Gnosis* 44 (summer 1997): 46–50.

Rihbany, Abraham Mitrie. *The Syrian Christ.* Boston: Houghton Mifflin, 1916.

Riley, Gregory J. *One Jesus, Many Christs.* San Francisco: HarperSanFrancisco, 1997.

Robinson, James M., ed. *The Nag Hammadi Library in English.* San Francisco: Harper & Row, 1977.

Rose, Seraphim. *The Soul after Death.* Platina, Calif.: St. Herman of Alaska Brotherhood, 1980.

Ross, J. P. *A Recapitulation of the Lord's Prayer.* N.p.: self-published, 1985.

Rudolph, Kurt. *Gnosis: The Nature and History of Gnosticism.* Translated by Robert MacLachlan Wilson. San Francisco: Harper & Row, 1987.

The Rule of St. Benedict. Collegeville, Minn.: Liturgical Press, 1980.

Russell, Jeffrey Burton. *Satan: The Early Christian Tradition.* Ithaca, N.Y.: Cornell University Press, 1981.

Saint-Martin, Louis Claude de. *Theosophic Correspondence, 1792–97.* Translated by Edward Burton Penny. 1863. Reprint. Pasadena, Calif.: Theosophical University Press, 1991.

Sales, Francis de. *Introduction to the Devout Life.* Translated by John K. Ryan. New York: Image Books, 1972.

Salomone, Gaetano. "The Forgotten Father of the Twelve Steps." *Gnosis* 34 (winter 1995): 9–10.

Scaligero, Massimo. *La Luce (The Light).* Translated by Eric L. Bisbocci. Great Barrington, Mass.: Lindisfarne, 2001.

Schmithals, Walter. *The Theology of the First Christians.* Translated by O. C. Dean. Louisville, Ky.: Westminster/John Knox, 1998.

Schneemelcher, Wilhelm, ed. *New Testament Apocrypha.* Translated by R. McL. Wilson et al. 2 vols. Cambridge, U.K.: Clarke, 1991.

Schneider, Michael S. *A Beginner's Guide to Constructing the Universe: The Mathematical Archetypes of Nature, Art, and Science.* New York: Harper Perennial, 1995.

Scholem, Gershom G. *Kabbalah.* Jerusalem: Keter, 1974.

———. *On the Kabbalah and Its Symbolism.* Translated by Ralph Manheim. New York: Schocken Books, 1965.

———, ed. *Zohar: The Book of Splendor.* New York: Schocken Books, 1949.

Schuon, Frithjof. *The Transcendent Unity of Religions.* Wheaton, Ill.: Quest Books, 1984.

Schürmann, Reiner. *Wandering Joy: Meister Eckhart's Mystical Philosophy.* Great Barrington, Mass.: Lindisfarne, 2001.

Schweitzer, Albert. *The Quest of the Historical Jesus.* Translated by W. Montgomery. 1910. Reprint. New York: Macmillan, 1968.

Scott, Walter, ed. and trans. *Hermetica: The Ancient Greek and Latin Writings Which Contain Religious or Philosophic Teachings Ascribed to Hermes Trismegistus.* 4 vols. 1924. Reprint. Boston: Shambhala Publications, 1985.

Sefer Yetzirah: The Book of Creation in Theory and Practice. Translated and edited by Aryeh Kaplan. York Beach, Maine: Weiser, 1990.

Septuaginta, id est Vetus Testamentum secundum LXX interpretes. Edited by Alfred Rahlfs. Stuttgart: Deutsche Bibelstiftung, 1935.

Service Book of the Holy Orthodox-Catholic Apostolic Church. Edited by Isabel Florence Hapgood. New York: Association Press, 1922.

Shumaker, Wayne. *The Occult Sciences in the Renaissance.* Berkeley and Los Angeles: University of California Press, 1972.

Smith, Huston. *Forgotten Truth: The Common Vision of the World's Religions.* San Francisco: HarperSanFrancisco, 1976.

Smith, Morton. *Jesus the Magician.* 1978. Reprint. Berkeley, Calif.: Seastone, 1998.

———. *The Secret Gospel: The Discovery and Interpretation of the Secret Gospel according to Mark.* New York: Harper & Row, 1973.

Smoley, Richard. "Heroic Virtue: The *Gnosis* Interview with Brother David Steindl-Rast." *Gnosis* 24 (summer 1992): 36–42.

———. "The Illumined Heart." *Gnosis* 51 (spring 1999): 12–15.

———. "Man As God and Creator." *Gnosis* 28 (summer 1993): 56–60.

———. "The Mystery of Regeneration: The *Gnosis* Interview with R. J. Stewart." *Gnosis* 51 (spring 1999): 24–29.

———. "The Old Religion." *Gnosis* 48 (summer 1998): 12–14.

Smoley, Richard, and Jay Kinney. *Hidden Wisdom: A Guide to the Western Inner Traditions.* New York: Penguin Arkana, 1999.

Solovyov, Vladimir. *Lectures on Divine Humanity.* Translated by Boris Jakim. Hudson, N.Y.: Lindisfarne, 1995.

———. *The Meaning of Love.* Edited and translated by Thomas R. Beyer Jr. Hudson, N.Y.: Lindisfarne, 1985.

The Song of Prayer: Prayer, Forgiveness, and Healing. Tiburon, Calif.: Foundation for Inner Peace, 1978.

Souzenelle, Annick de. *Le Symbolisme du corps human: De L'Arbre de vie au schéma corporel.* St.-Jean-de-Braye, France: Éditions Dangles, 1984.

Spong, John Shelby. *A New Christianity for a New World.* San Francisco: HarperSanFrancisco, 2001.

Starkie, Enid. *Baudelaire.* Norfolk, Conn.: New Directions, 1958.

Steinberg, Leo. *The Sexuality of Christ in Renaissance Art and in Modern Oblivion.* Chicago: University of Chicago Press, 1983.

Steiner, Rudolf. *The Christian Mysteries.* Translated by James H. Hindes et al. Hudson, N.Y.: Anthroposophic Press, 1998.

———. *Christianity As Mystical Fact.* Translated by James H. Hindes. Hudson, N.Y.: Anthroposophic Press, 1997.

———. *How to Know Higher Worlds.* Translated by Christopher Bamford. Hudson, N.Y.: Anthroposophic Press, 1994.

———. *The Mysteries of the East and of Christianity.* Blauvelt, N.Y.: Spiritual Science Library, 1989.

———. *An Outline of Esoteric Science.* Translated by Catherine E. Creeger. Hudson, N.Y.: Anthroposophic Press, 1997.

———. *The Reappearance of the Christ in the Etheric.* Edited and translated by Gilbert Church and Alice Wulsin. Spring Valley, N.Y.: Anthroposophic Press, 1983.

———. *Supersensible Knowledge.* Hudson, N.Y.: Anthroposophic Press, 1987.

———. *Theosophy.* Translated by Catherine E. Creeger. Hudson, N.Y.: Anthroposophic Press, 1994.

———. *A Way of Self-Knowledge.* Translated by Christopher Bamford. Hudson, N.Y.: Anthroposophic Press, 1999.

Stoyanov, Yuri. *The Other God: Dualist Religions from Antiquity to the Cathar Heresy.* New Haven, Conn.: Yale University Press, 2000.

Strausbaugh, John. *E: Reflections on the Birth of the Elvis Faith.* New York: Blast Books, 1995.

Strong, Mary, ed. *Letters of the Scattered Brotherhood.* New York: Harper & Row, 1948.

Swedenborg, Emanuel. *Heaven and Hell*. Translated by George F. Dole. Rev. ed. West Chester, Pa.: Swedenborg Foundation, 2000.

———. *Marital Love*. Translated by William Frederic Wunsch. 1856. Reprint. New York: Swedenborg Publishing Association, 1975.

———. *True Christian Religion*. Translated by John C. Ager. West Chester, Pa.: Swedenborg Foundation, 1996.

Talbot, Margaret. "A Mighty Fortress." *New York Times Magazine*, 27 February 2000, 34ff.

Teilhard de Chardin, Pierre. *The Heart of Matter*. Translated by René Hague. New York: Harcourt Brace Jovanovich, 1978.

———. *The Phenomenon of Man*. Translated by Bernard Wall. New York: Harper & Row, 1959.

Temple, Richard. *Icons and the Mystical Origins of Christianity*. Shaftesbury, Dorset, England: Element, 1990.

Teresa of Avila, Saint. *Interior Castle*. Translated by E. Allison Peers. New York: Doubleday/Image, 1961.

Tetworth, Charles R. *Wielding Power: The Essence of Ritual Practice*. Great Barrington, Mass.: Lindisfarne, 2002.

Theissen, Gerd, and Annette Merz. *The Historical Jesus: A Comprehensive Guide*. Translated by John Bowden. Minneapolis, Minn.: Fortress Press, 1996.

The Theologia Germanica of Martin Luther. Edited and translated by Bengt Hoffman. Mahwah, N.J.: Paulist Press, 1980.

Tomberg, Valentin. *Covenant of the Heart: Meditations of a Christian Hermeticist on the Mysteries of Tradition*. Translated by Robert A. Powell and James Morgante. Longmead, Shaftesbury, Dorset, England: Element, 1992.

———. *Meditations on the Tarot: A Journey into Christian Hermeticism*. Translated by Robert A. Powell. Warwick, N.Y.: Amity Press, 1985.

Unseen Warfare: Being the Spiritual Combat and Path to Paradise of Lorenzo Scupoli as Edited by Nicodemus of the Holy Mountain and Revised by Theophan the Recluse. Translated by E. Kadloubovsky and G. E. H. Palmer. London: Faber & Faber, 1952.

Van Engen, John, ed. *Devotio Moderna: Basic Writings*. Mahwah, N.J.: Paulist Press, 1988.

Versluis, Arthur. *Theosophia: Hidden Dimensions of Christianity*. Hudson, N.Y.: Lindisfarne, 1994.

———. *Wisdom's Children: A Christian Esoteric Tradition*. Albany: State University of New York Press, 2000.

Waddell, Helen. *The Desert Fathers*. 1936. Reprint. Ann Arbor: University of Michigan Press, 1957.

Waite, A. E. *The Hidden Church of the Holy Graal.* London: Rebman, 1909. Reprint. Des Plaines, Ill.: Yogi Publication Society, n.d.

———. *The Unknown Philosopher: Louis Claude de St. Martin.* Reprint. Blauvelt, N.Y.: Steinerbooks, 1987.

Walton, Christopher. *An Introduction to Theosophy, or The Science of the Mystery of Christ.* London: John Kendrick, n.d.

Wapnick, Kenneth, et al., eds. *Concordance of "A Course in Miracles."* New York: Viking Press, 1997.

Watts, Alan W. *Myth and Ritual in Christianity.* Boston: Beacon, 1968.

West, Jessamyn. *The Quaker Reader.* New York: Viking Press, 1962.

White, Ralph, ed. *The Rosicrucian Enlightenment Revisited.* Hudson, N.Y.: Lindisfarne, 1999.

Whitehead, Nicholas. *Patterns in Magical Christianity.* Albuquerque, N.M.: Sun Chalice, 1996.

Wirszubski, Chaim. *Pico della Mirandola's Encounter with Jewish Mysticism.* Cambridge, Mass: Harvard University Press, 1989.

Witt, R. E. *Isis in the Greco-Roman World.* Ithaca, N.Y.: Cornell University Press, 1971.

Yarnold, Edward. *The Awe-Inspiring Rites of Initiation: The Origins of the R.C.I.A. [Rite of Christian Initiation for Adults].* 2d ed. Collegeville, Minn.: Liturgical Press, 1994.

Yates, Frances A. *The Rosicrucian Enlightenment.* 1972. Reprint. London: Ark, 1986.

Zocatelli, Pier Luigi. *Le Lièvre qui rumine: Autour de René Guénon, Louis Charbonneau-Lassay et la fraternité du Paraclet.* Milan: Archè, 1999.

INDEX

central mystery of, 96
changes after establishment as
    official religion of Roman
    Empire, 149–50
early faith communities, 15–16
immutable truths of, 225
incorporating aspects of paganism,
    150
initiatic faith, 14, 15
interest in devotional tradition, 8
passions, 62
providing escape from karma,
    180–81
punishment for the Fall, 65
reincarnation, reticence about,
    73–74
as religion of the individual, 212
teachings on soul's immortality,
    70–71
warnings about spiritual
    experiences, 98
Christian Meditation, 167–68
Christian message, weakening of, 4
Christian mysteries, Tarot as key to, 37
Christian mysticism, 36
Christian origins, interest in, 2
Christian Science, 174
Christian symbolism, 38–39, 40, 228
Christian tradition, mystical and
    esoteric paths in, 3
Christian Trinity, 105. *See also* Trinity
Christos, 69
Christ the Saviour Brotherhood, 45
Christ within, 42
church, corporate structure of, 230
church architecture, 23, 199, 203,
    228–30
circles, 5–6, 201–2, 239
clairvoyance, 114
Clavelle, Marcel, 35
Clement of Alexandria, 13–14, 15,
    18, 72
Clement V, 25
Clement XII, 34
Cloud upon the Sanctuary, The, (von
    Eckhartshausen), 227–28, 245
Cloud of Unknowing, The, 3, 45, 168, 205
cognition, 139–40
collation, 29
colors, used in mental healing images,
    160–61
Comforter, 103
commandments, two great, 75–77
Communion, 219. *See also* Eucharist
communion of the saints, 77

complacency, danger of, 79
conditional love, 187
Conferences (Cassian), 21
Confessio fraternitatis ("The Confession
    of the Brotherhood"), 33
conscience, examination of, 159
consciousness, 68
    blank spot in, 165
    freeing from content of psyche, 90
    journey in, 97
    lifeblood of universe, 99–100,
        101, 103
    need for rescuing, 144
    rising of in creation account, 146
    as side or primary effect, 112
    two poles of, 78
    unencumbered, 130
Consecration, 219
Consolamentum, 25
Constant, Alphonse Louis. *See* Lévi,
    Éliphas
contemplatio, 169–70
Cornelius Agrippa, 32, 231
Corpus Hermeticum, 29–30
correspondences, 112–13
"Correspondences" (Baudelaire), 112
cosmic consciousness, 75
cosmic descent, 56
cosmic forces, found internally, 115–16
cosmic octave, 114–15, 172, 206–7, 208
cosmic spiral, 69–70, 78, 177
cosmology, mirroring composition of
    individual human, 109
cosmos, human irrelevance in, 99
Couliano, Ioan P., 134
Council of Nicea, 218
A Course in Miracles, 43–44, 59, 91, 92,
    96, 135–36, 174, 181, 188, 232,
    242, 245
courtly love, 193–94
creative visualization, 160
creeds, function of, 218–19
crescent, 198
Crime and Punishment, 180
Critchlow, Keith, 199
cross
    symbol of, 198, 202–3
    three-dimensional, 39, 67–70, 202
Crowley, Aleister, 198
crucifixion, evoking mystery of, 161
cube, as symbol, 203
Cult of the Black Virgin, The, (Begg), 147
curriculum, individual nature of, 244–45
Cyrenius (Publius Sulpicius Quirinius),
    126

Movement for Religious Renewal, 39–40, 224
mysteries, 214
Mystery of Golgotha, 39
Mystery and Magic of the Eucharis, The (Hoeller), 224
Mystical Body of Christ, 222
mystical realization, 97–98
mysticism, 3
myth, 64
Myth and Ritual in Christianity (Watts), 229, 246
mythical beasts, as symbols, 204–5

Nag Hammadi, 2, 14, 144, 145
Nag Hammadi Library in English, The 246
narthex, 229
natal astrology, 110
nativity accounts, 126–28
natural level, mastery of, 89–90
nature, humanity's responsibility toward, 113
nave, 229
Needleman, Jacob, 41, 156
Neilos the Ascetic, 241
nemesis, 180
New Age, 1–2, 42–44
New Man, The (Nicoll), 42, 246
Nicene Creed, 218
Nicholas II, 36
Nicoll, Maurice, 42, 129, 190–91, 246
nous, 51
numbers, as intelligences and archetypes, 198

Offertory, 219
"Office of Oblation," 263 n.20
Old Believers, 224
Old Catholics, 223

Oneness, dynamic of three proceeding from, 104
one-on-one transmission, 234
ora et labora, 156
oratio, 169
Origen, 4, 18–20, 31
  on the Fall, 54
  on Genesis, 126
  teaching redemption of the Devil, 179
  understanding possibility of reincarnation, 73
  view of nether realms, 72
original sin, 216

Orthodox Church, 205, 210, 211, 224
Osiris, 131
Our Father, 163
Our Town (Wilder), 83
ouroboros, 60, 61
Ouspensky, P. D., 40–42, 194
outer Christianity, 5, 26
outer rite, 216

Pachomius, 21
pagan Celtic traditions, 38
paganism, incorporated into Christianity, 150
Palamas, Gregory, 27
Papus, 36, 58, 104
parable of the Prodigal Son, 56
parable of the two servants, 63, 89, 90
parable of the unjust steward, 184–85
parable of the wicked servant, 182
Paracelsus, 32
Paradiso (Dante), 24
paranormal occurrences, 137
particular judgment, 70
Pasqually, Martinez de, 35
passions, 62, 63, 87, 91, 92–93
path, double process of, 156
pathos, 90
Paul (apostle), 15–16, 19, 64, 86, 97, 108, 149
Paul (Desert Father), death of, 95
Peck, M. Scott, 174
Pensatia, 43
pentagram, 198
People of the Lie, The (Peck), 174
perception, higher centers of, 214–15
Perceval (de Troyes), 161–62
personal evolution, 42
personality, 78
Peter, 122, 128, 227, 237
Phaedrus, 205
phenomenology, 40
philein, 190
philia, 186, 191
Philo of Alexandria, 31, 140
Philokalia, The 27, 42, 246–47
physical level, related to Communion, 220
physical senses, good and evil known through, 59–60
physical world, 19, 112
Pico della Mirandola, Giovanni, 31–32, 231
Pilgrim's Progress (Bunyan), 49
Pistis Sophia, 144
Pius XII, 151

Index